STUDIES

NEW AND OLD

OF

ETHICAL AND SOCIAL SUBJECTS.

BY

FRANCES POWER COBBE.

BOSTON:
WILLIAM V. SPENCER.
1866.

PREFACE.

The Essays in the present volume have been composed at intervals during the last three years. Though of a somewhat miscellaneous character, they are all, strictly speaking, *ethical studies*, developments in various directions of the views of morals advocated in the author's earlier works.

F. P. C.

London, May, 1865.

CONTENTS.

PAGE

CHRISTIAN ETHICS AND THE ETHICS OF CHRIST 3
(Reprinted from the Theological Review.)

SELF-DEVELOPMENT AND SELF-ABNEGATION .. 49
(Now first published.)

THE SACRED BOOKS OF THE ZOROASTRIANS .. 89
(Now first published.)

THE PHILOSOPHY OF THE POOR-LAWS 147
(Reprinted from Fraser's Magazine.)

THE RIGHTS OF MAN AND THE CLAIMS OF BRUTES 211
(Reprinted from Fraser's Magazine.)

THE MORALS OF LITERATURE 261
(Reprinted from Fraser's Magazine.)

THE HIERARCHY OF ART 289
(Reprinted from Fraser's Magazine.)

DECEMNOVENARIANISM 359
(Reprinted from Fraser's Magazine.)

HADES 397
(Reprinted from Fraser's Magazine.)

CHRISTIAN ETHICS

AND

THE ETHICS OF CHRIST.

Reprinted from the Theological Review, Sept. 1864.

The fundamental truths of morality and religion can never be traced to individual original teachers. Intuitions of them dawn faintly in the mind of the savage, and become gradually brighter as civilization advances, till at last they shine out clearly in the words of power spoken by the foremost men of each successive age. Even in physical science we all know there is rarely any absolutely new and original discovery. Each truth has been for some time vaguely apprehended or suspected before the hour arrive when some investigator, more fortunate or more gifted than his fellows, actually digs out the precious ore from the mountain-side, and calls aloud, "Behold, here is gold!"—and then thousands rush to share the treasure. But in each case of a new truth, moral or physical, it is to him that has so discovered, so uttered it, that all mankind may profit thereby, that our gratitude is due. It is not to Plato who dreamed the Atlantis, nor to the wild Vikings who first reached the western shore, but to Columbus who added a new world to the old, that we owe America.

And in like manner it is to the moral teachers who have given to the light of day and the common consciousness of mankind the principles vaguely believed or half remembered before, that we justly attribute their revelation; even though we may be able to trace out each of their precepts in the lessons of earlier prophets whose words have lain in the earth as seeds never germinating.

Among the truths which a great moral teacher brings to light, it is not impossible to distinguish two classes. The first class consists of such as are already current in his age and country, of which he has merely made a selection, guided by his own moral taste. The second consists of such as are different from those of his age, and which he has either caught from the sheen of some far-off traditions in the past, or else worked out altogether from his own inner life and experience. The truths of this second class are in a peculiar sense his own. They are the intuitions of his deepest consciousness, his "original revelation." And when the teacher's moral lessons are so pure and divine that we rightly attribute them to the inspiration of God, it is peculiarly these intuitive truths to which we turn as the manifestations of such inspiration. What was common to his age and country we conclude him to have learned by the external teaching of his parents or masters. What was peculiar to himself, what he was enabled to see was true in spite of contending prejudices, that we conclude him to have learned from the Spirit of God enlightening his soul.

Thus if we could separate the precepts of any moral teacher into the two classes, and eliminating all which was common to his time and country, reserve only what was peculiar to himself, we should arrive at conclusions interesting in a double point of view. We should have on the human side a transcript of the man himself, a portrait of his spiritual physiognomy—not indeed as he may have been in deed and word while "wrapped in this muddy vesture of decay" and obeying falteringly the law within, but as he ought to have been, as his own soul required him to be. We should have before us the photograph, not of the outer, but of the "inner man." And on the divine side we should have the nearest approach attainable to a record of the inspiration granted to him. We should see brought together the sum of his share of the great lessons of the Divine Master whereby the human race has been training since creation. His rank in the hierarchy of prophets would be determined by the fulness and importance of such inspiration. Such a task as this is manifestly beyond our power in the case of most of the great moral teachers of antiquity. We can rarely obtain their genuine precepts with any completeness, and still less often can we form a just estimate of the current morals of their countrymen, so as to discriminate what in their teaching was common to their contemporaries, from what was peculiar to themselves. Half-shadowy prophets like Menu and Thoth and Zoroaster and Buddha, and even historical philosophers like Pythagoras and Confucius and Socrates and Zeno, are mostly too far beyond our reach to enable us to treat their recorded precepts by any such process as we have imagined; and in later times, when the teacher's own doctrines might be better ascertained, the share of them truly to be called original would be still more impossible to discriminate. Ancient moralists were properly Prophets of Morals; but modern ones have had little else to do than to frame intellectual systems in which their precepts should be properly fitted in scientific order.

There is, however, one instance in which it would seem that we actually possess materials for forming a tolerably trustworthy estimate of the current morals of the age and country in which the greatest of moral teachers lived, and consequently of eliminating them from his recorded precepts, retaining a residue which shall truly represent his peculiar and proper morality. The Old Testament prophets, the treatise of Philo on the Essenes, the histories of Josephus, and the Jerusalem and Babylonish Talmuds (certainly preserving the precepts of ante-christian schools of rabbins), afford us a very large insight into the state of thought on moral subjects in Palestine in the first century. The careful study and collation of these books with the Gospel parables and precepts, as partially accomplished by German scholars, at once reveals the identity between a large share of Christian doctrines and those which were taught habitually (although with many puerile additions) in the Rabbinical schools of the same period.*

* For example, as quoted by Hennell:—Targum, Hierosol., Genes. xxxviii. 26: Judah speaks thus, "It is better for me that I should be burned in this world with a little fire, than that I should be burned in the world to come with a devouring flame." Debarim Rabba, sect. 7: Rabbi Simeon ben Chelpatha said, "He who hath learned the words of the law and doeth them not, is more guilty than he who has learned nothing. A certain king sent two gardeners into his garden. The one planted trees, but afterwards cut them down. The other planted nothing, and cut down nothing. With which of these was the king wrath?" Mechilta, fol. 32, 1: "He who created the day, created also the food thereof. Whosoever hath whereof to eat to-day, and saith, But shall I eat to-morrow? he is of little faith." Schabbath (tract of the Mishna), fol. 131: "Whosoever hath mercy on men, on him will God have mercy; but he who showeth no mercy to men, neither to him will God show mercy." Schabbath, fol. 883: Our rabbins deliver to us, "They who receive scorn but scorn no man, who bear reproaches and return them not, who show love to men and rejoice in tribulations, of them the Scripture saith, They shall love Him and be as the sun going forth in his might." Aboth R. Nathan, c. 23: "He is a hero who maketh his enemy his friend." Sanhedrin, fol. 48: "Suffer thyself to be cursed, but do not thou curse others." Synopsis, Sohar: "A man ought every night to forgive the fault of him that offendeth him." Sohar, fol. 4: "Whosoever lendeth to any one in public, with him God dealeth according to justice; but he who does it secretly, with him rests the blessing." Sanhedrin (Mishna), fol. 43: Rabbi Jehuda ben Levi said, "Whilst the temple stood, if any man offered a holocaust, he obtained the reward of a holocaust; if an oblation, the reward of an oblation. But if a man be of an humble spirit, the Scriptures consider him as having offered all sacrifices."

But beyond these precepts common in his age —precepts which the Founder of Christianity no more despised because they were common than he despised the lilies which carpeted the hills of Galilee, and served to illustrate his lessons of truth and love —beyond these Jewish-Christian precepts, there is another series of moral doctrines to be found in the Gospels of a character quite *sui generis* and peculiar. These latter precepts we may justly consider to be essentially and in a special sense Christ's own lessons, the moral ideas which he gave to the world.

It would be superfluous to point out how valuable would be the work which should adequately perform the task of thus collating the ethics of Christ with those of his contemporaries, and throwing into full relief for our study the residue of doctrines which belong peculiarly to himself. We should obtain by such a process a view of the character, or (as we may say) of the moral physiognomy and individuality of the great Teacher, hardly to be gained by any other method. And we should at the same time arrive at a system of morals differing, it is to be believed, very essentially in many particulars from such as are habitually foisted upon us by modern moralists under the name of "Christian," but which are in truth far more nearly related to the schools of Pharisees, Sadducees, or Essenes, Stoics, Epicureans, or Cyrenaics, than to that of the great Prophet of Nazareth. Hoping that some man of learning adequate to such a task, and of moral taste high and pure enough to treat it worthily, may at some future time undertake the work and carry it to full completion, I have thought it might be of interest to sketch (necessarily very briefly and imperfectly) some of the results which it appears that such a research might obtain. Whatever view our special theology may lead us to take of the degree of authority pertaining to the dicta of Christ—whether we consider him as laying down the law of the universe as a God, or revealing it as the most inspired of men, or even simply as uttering the fallible opinion of a Galilean peasant whom Christendom has adored for eighteen centuries—in any and every case, a transcendent interest must attach to the question, "What was the verdict of this great Teacher regarding the moral controversies which had divided the instructors of mankind?" Perhaps also in the answer to this question may be found the best defence of those who (like the writer) reject the claim of his Divinity, yet hold Christ to have been the "man who best fulfilled the conditions under which God grants His inspiration." A merely popular acquaintance with contemporary morals (to which alone I can lay claim) may suffice to indicate generally whether in these controversies Christ agreed with the teachers of his age or diverged from them altogether. In the latter case, having constated the peculiar doctrines of Christ, it becomes a matter of vast practical interest to compare them with the teaching on moral subjects common in our own age, and especially with such as professes to be pre-eminently Christian,—the teaching of men who are understood and believe themselves to be in a special sense the disciples of Christ. If it should appear that in numerous instances the morals ordinarily accepted among us are not those which Christ taught,—nay, are even those which he diametrically contradicted and opposed,—it will surely be time to introduce a change in our method of treating these subjects. It will surely be time to rebuke the presumption wherewith the morals of Jews and Heathens are continually foisted upon us under the sanction of Christ's name. It will be time to distinguish once for all the so-called "Christian ethics" of modern teachers from the genuine and altogether different "ethics of Christ."

1. One of the broadest distinctions between different schools of moralists is that which concerns the positive or negative character they attribute to duty. In nearly all cases the earliest teachers confine themselves to negative precepts, "Do no murder," "Do not steal," and the like. Virtue in their eyes consists in abstaining from unlawful actions and passions. The affirmative duties, if any such there be, in their systems, are mostly of a ceremonial nature, such as offering sacrifices and performing ablutions. Quite a new and different aspect is given to ethics when some teacher arises to declare

that right is a positive thing, and wrong only its negation, *wrung from* the right. Virtue is then seen to consist in affirmative goodness, in love of God and service to man, not merely in abstaining from idolatry and injustice. It is the same advance in morals as it is in physical science to perceive that heat and light are positives, and cold and darkness merely their negations. We can no more attain to virtue by merely abstaining from offence, than we can construct a true theory of nature by treating caloric and light as the mere negations of cold and darkness.

But this step of progress is slowly reached. It is clear enough it was not attained by the Jews at the Christian era. The Decalogue (a series of negations*) and the Rabbinical law, so far as it is known to us, consisted in precepts all tending to forbid offence, but rarely enforcing positive duty except

* The Buddhists have a Decalogue (strangely resembling the Mosaic second table) given in the *Mahawanse:* "1. Do not kill. 2. Do not steal. 3. Do not commit adultery. 4. Do not lie. 5. Do not slander. 6. Do not call ill names. 7. Do not speak words which are to no purpose but harm. 8. Do not covet the property of others. 9. Do not envy. 10. Do not err in the faith or think it false." The Brahmins, on the contrary, seem at a very early age to have grasped the idea of positive law. In the Institutes of Menu (supposed to date about 1200 B. C.), chap. 6, v. 92, there is this singular arrangement of ten duties: Content, Returning good for evil, Resistance to sensual appetites, Abstinence from illicit gain, Purification, Chastity, Knowledge of Scripture, Knowledge of the Supreme Spirit, Veracity, and Freedom from wrath.

in matters of ceremony. The whole spirit of it was summed up (if we may believe a tradition in the Talmud) by the celebrated Rabbi Hillel, one of the princes of the Jews in Babylon. "A fellow went to the Rabbi and said, 'Can you teach me the whole law during the time I am able to stand on one foot?' 'Yes,' answered the Rabbi mildly; 'the whole law is contained in this one rule, Whatever you would not wish your neighbour to do to you, do it not to him. This is the law; the rest is only an exposition of it.'" *

One of the most prominent features in the morality taught by Christ is the introduction of the idea of the positive character of duty. He transposes the Golden Rule just quoted from the Rabbi's negative to the affirmative form (Matt. vi. 12): "Therefore whatsoever ye would that men should do unto you, do ye even so unto them, for this is the law and the prophets." He sums up the Decalogue's negatives in two positive commandments, expressed with every possible force of affirmation: "Thou shalt love the Lord thy God with all thine heart, and with all thy soul, and with all thy

* The same aphorism is used literally by Isocrates (in Nicoc.): "Do not do to others what you would not they should do to you;" and (what is most remarkable) in both its negative and positive form by Confucius: "Do to another what you would he should do to you, and do not unto another what you would not should be done unto you. Thou only needest this law alone; it is the foundation and principle of all the rest."—Confucius, Maxim 24, Yun Lu.

strength; and thou shalt love thy neighbour as thyself." And after laying down by precept and showing by example a life of active beneficence as the life of virtue, he proceeds to the length of representing men as condemned hereafter for *faults*, for the mere neglect of positive duties, without any infraction of negative commandments. Dives is sent to "torment" (for all that we can see) only for neglecting to aid Lazarus and his compeers. The man who hides his talent in a napkin is cast into outer darkness merely for burying it. Finally, in the descriptions of the last judgment, it is said that those who have not fed the hungry or clothed the naked or visited the prisoner, shall "depart into everlasting fire." Whatever sense may be given to these words, it is clear that Christ meant to convey the idea that the greatest of all condemnations might be incurred by men who are accused of no positive crime, murder or adultery or theft or lying,—men whose creed was correct, for they called him "Lord, Lord!" and did wonderful works in his name, but who simply did not benefit their fellow-creatures.

Of the infinite value and importance of this transformation of a negative into a positive law, it is needless here to speak; the whole spirit of morality is altered thereby. The standard of right is fixed, and we are henceforth able to perceive that all divergence from it is wrong. Virtue is given a spirit and life it could never possess while contemplated as a mere innocence of harm. "Being good and doing good" are aims to place before the soul worthy to stir the ambition of an archangel, while the warning not to commit offence can hardly touch one of the nobler chords of the human heart. We have passed from death to life when we believe that human virtue is a reality, not a negation; and that there reigns on the eternal throne the Impersonation of Goodness absolute, affirmative, Divine. "The universe has a Sun of light and warmth. It has no sun whose rays are darkness and frost."

But of this glorious reformation, introduced by Christ into the morals of Judaism, what traces are to be found in modern Christian ethics? Have we all quite clearly understood that it is not enough to refrain from evil, and lead harmless lives, and hold correct views about the office of Christ? Does the preaching of our churches tend altogether to set forth this truth, that a mere timorous conscience, carefulness of wrong-doing, and devotion in words and feelings without corresponding deeds, is of no sort of avail? Surely, on the contrary, we are perpetually led to understand that scrupulousness of conscience and a correct faith go together to make up the idea of a Christian, and that men and women may depart in "sure and certain hope" of immediate entrance into the kingdom of heaven, who have done no great offence, and who have said, "Lord, Lord," with unwavering confidence at the last.

2. All teachers of ethics necessarily reiterate the various canons of the immutable moral law. They differ, however, from one another in nothing more remarkably than in the relative value they assign to these principles of natural morality and to the precepts connected with the religious worship of their country. In the eyes of some moralists, *mala in se* and *mala prohibita* are almost of equal guilt. In those of others, they are altogether and utterly different. Herein will usually appear the result of the original distinction at the bottom of the minds of the two orders of teachers—those to whom morality is a part of religion, and those to whom religion is a part of morality. To the former class, as all moral laws appear simply as expressions of the will of God, it will frequently happen to confound together offences against the ceremonial and the natural law, both being believed by them to be equally divine commandments. Thus those moralists who are primarily religious instructors are continually led into a style of teaching which has its climax of absurdity in the Institutes of Menu, where reading the Vedas is alleged to purify alike "the crimes of him who has eaten with unwashed hands, and of him who has killed the inhabitants of the three worlds."* On the other hand, the teachers who are primarily moralists, and who regard the moral law as the ultimate principle of

* Institutes of Menu, Book xi. v. 264.

right, impersonated in that holiest Will whereby the universe is ruled, yet *not* (according to the heresy of Ockham) the mere arbitrary result of that divine Will,—by these teachers the gulf between *mala prohibita* and *mala in se* is felt to be wide as the poles. Their lessons will commonly be found to include depreciatory remarks and even invectives on ceremonial observances of all kinds, whereby they throw into higher relief the inherent sanctity of the eternal law. They say with all the prophets, "Of what avail the multitude of your sacrifices? Your new moons and sabbaths are an abomination. Cease to do evil. Learn to do well."

Again: There is not only this great difference between two schools of moralists which it behoves us to recognize when we seek to ascertain the characteristic doctrines of Christ. There are also two classes to be remarked among all religious minds,—the class to whom ceremonies are naturally valuable, and the class to whom they are rather stumbling-blocks than assistances.* It would be most desirable for us to recognize more than we have hitherto done this constitutional difference, and, giving to each order our share of respect, cease to strive by argument or force to change the instincts of the one for those of the other.† By

* This distinction the writer has endeavoured to delineate more fully in "Broken Lights," chaps. iii. and iv.

† We have heard of endless cases where this has been done, and always to the injury of those whose benefit was desired. A

ignoring this second class of minds, with its need of extempore prayers and entire simplicity of cultus, the great Church of England, with all its liberality of feeling and breadth of doctrine, has never been able to include in its fold thousands of pious souls whose theological divergencies from it are altogether trifling. Again, on the other hand, by neglecting the solemnities of worship and ignoring the benefit which the first class of minds naturally receives from the accessories of art, Protestant churches generally (up to very late years) have abnegated much of the power possessed by the Church of Rome in virtue of its impressive cultus. And those among us who as individuals have stood aloof and

"Counted reason ripe
In resting on the law within,"

who have striven, "forsaking the landmark, to march by the star," how often have they become experimentally aware how the neglect of stated periods and formal observances of worship entails with it dangers so formidable that, while rejecting external laws, they are driven "to be a law to themselves," no less stringent and rigorous?

clergyman of the English Church striving once to induce his semi-Methodist parishioners to attend evening service in church instead of at prayer-meetings, received the astounding replies, "Why, sir, we would go to church to please your reverence, but you see we go to the chapel to *pray!*" and, "Sir, if we were to go to church both times on Sundays, *what would become of our means of grace?*"

In a large way these two orders of minds may be designated as those of the Priests and their disciples and the Prophets and their disciples. In all ages the Priestly order has insisted on the value of ceremonial observances, and has looked with distrust and disfavour on all religious fervour displayed outside such regulations. And from the first of the Prophets and Apostles to the last, the same burden has been repeated. "Behold, to obey is better than sacrifice, and to hearken than the fat of rams. What doth God desire of thee, O man, but to do justice, and love mercy, and walk humbly with thy God? Pure religion and undefiled before God and the Father is this—to visit the fatherless and widows in their affliction, and to keep himself unspotted from the world."* In all creeds probably, could we reach their inner history, the same oppositions of orders of minds, and the same progress by the antagonism of the two, would be observed. The most formal and ceremonial religion in the world, the Hindoo, yet contains in its sacred writings such lessons as this: "A wise man should constantly

* See likewise 1 Sam. xv. 22; Ps. li. 16, and xl. 6—8; Hosea vi. 6; Amos v. 21—24; Micah vi. 6—8; Isa. l. 14—17; lviii. 6; Ezek. xviii. 5, 9, 20, 28. This is to the prophets "as constant a topic as the most peculiar and favourite doctrine of any eccentric sect or party is in the mouths of the preachers of such a sect at the present day, and it is rendered more forcible by the form which it takes of a constant protest against the sacrificial system of the Levitical ritual in comparison with the moral law."—*Stanley's Jewish Church.*

perform all the moral duties, though he perform not constantly the ceremonies of religion."* "He who purifies himself in the river of a subdued spirit, the waters of which are truth, its waves compassion, and its shores holy temper, will be liberated from this world; but liberation cannot be obtained by any outward observance."

In England, in our time, the two orders are of course mainly represented, the priestly mind by the Anglican party, and the prophetical by the Evangelical. But, in one singular instance, the Low-churchmen exceed their High-church brethren in regard for a ceremonial observance. The sabbath stands alone in this respect, doubtless from causes traceable to an historic origin.† The sabbath alone

* Inst. Menu, 4, 204.

† Beside the many passages commonly quoted from the Fathers to prove that the sabbath was altogether suffered to lapse into abeyance in the primitive ages (the Sunday being a day of prayer but not of rest, as the Moslem Friday is now), there are two which, so far as we are aware, have hitherto failed to attract the attention they deserve. The greatest Fathers of the Eastern and Western churches have recorded their opinions in these words:

"For what purpose, then, I ask, did he add a reason respecting the sabbath, and did not do so as regards murder? Because this commandment was not one of the leading ones (*τῶν προηγουμένων*). It was not one of those which are accurately defined of our consciences, but a kind of partial and temporary one. And for this reason it was ABOLISHED AFTERWARDS (*κατελύθη μετα ταῦτα*)." St Chrysostom, Homil. 12.

"Of all the ten commandments, only that of the sabbath is enjoined to be observed figuratively, which figure we have received of Church observances could be invested with Scriptural authority, and it was to Scriptural authority that the Reformers turned for anchorage when they had cast themselves adrift from the Church of Rome.

As the Reformation developed into Puritanism, the theocratic idea of Judaism served to supply the blank to which it was impossible for men at once to accustom themselves. Thus a ceremonial observance which could be enforced out of the Bible (however illogically dissevered from the rest of the abolished Mosaic law) became at once a rallying-point, magnified into importance by its very isolation. That terrible and almost unendurable sense of personal responsibility which weighs on all who let go the guiding hand which has directed and supported them and their fathers, was mitigated doubtless in no slight degree when it could be believed that, after leaving the Church of Rome or even the Anglican Church, men had still not only a divine infallible guide to all true doctrine in their Bibles, but also a grand ceremonial observance ordained by God himself for their practice. Once more the sabbath became the "token of a covenant" between Jehovah and a new chosen people.

These remarks have been offered for the purpose of clearing the way to an understanding of the relation between the peculiar morals of Christ and

to be understood, not to be still celebrated by the rest of the body."—St Augustine, Ep. 55, c. 22.

those commonly entertained by the stricter members of Christian churches.

Modern Christians of extreme views either belong to the priestly order and attach extreme importance to ceremonial observances, or else to the prophetic order, when they disdain ceremonialism generally, making an unique exception in favour of the sabbath. The mistake of the priestly order lies not in valuing observances as important "means of grace" for such minds as they are fitted to help, but in setting them up as things sacred in themselves, and obligatory on those to whom they are no "means of grace," but only hindrances. The mistake of the prophetical order lies in decrying absolutely what is of partial use, and, in their sole exception, attaching the guilt only due to such *mala in se* as theft or falsehood, to the *malum prohibitum* of sabbath-breaking. Let us observe the attitude which Christ's peculiar moral teaching bears to these two orders and their mistakes.

In the first place, if there be anything clear in the Gospels, it is that Christ did not attach any very great importance to the ceremonial observances of the Jewish Church. The lawyers and rabbins had laid down in the succession of ages a complete code, traceable more or less to the primitive Mosaic law; but whenever these observances are mentioned by Christ, it is invariably in a depreciatory and never in a laudatory manner. Washing the hands before meat, making clean the cup and platter, giving tithes of mint, anise, and cummin, making broad phylacteries, praying in the temple or on Gerizim,—all these matters he treated as of no importance or value whatever. Though he kept the great festivals of Judaism with the rest of his countrymen, there is never a word in his teaching to raise such observances to any high importance; and while he issued precepts for the uttermost religious devotion, for selling all and giving to the poor, and for leading a life of apostleship, it never once happens that he includes in his descriptions of such consecrated lives the slightest reference to sabbath-keeping or temple worship, or ceremonial observance of any kind. In his representations of future judgment, all such matters are utterly ignored. And, above all, in his lessons and examples of worship, there is not one word to make it appear he thought men could better pray in synagogues and temples, or with the pomp of a liturgy, than without it. He says, "Enter thy closet and shut thy door," or "say" (apparently at any time or place), "Our Father which art in heaven." When he prays himself, it is on the mountain or beneath the olive-trees of Gethsemane no less than in the Temple. Thus it would seem that, without actually setting them at naught, he could hardly have shown less reverence for the ordinances of the established church. If he had thought of them as things in themselves sacred, how often his lessons must have included precepts concerning attendance at the Passover and Feast of Weeks, purification, and going to the synagogue every sabbath, and uncovering the feet before prayer, and making the Levites (and the Levites only) offer due sacrifices of pigeons and lambs on all proper occasions! Had the Gospels been really designed to teach such ceremonialism, how different, how widely different, would those Gospels be! Or if we suppose that the approaching end of the Mosaic dispensation might have excluded the ratification of such observances, still the same principle (if entertained by Christ) must have shown itself in providing for the ceremonial of the future Christian church. There would have been chapters devoted to the spiritual powers of priests and bishops, to sacraments which should replace sacrifices, and to holy days of Christmas and Easter which should command the same reverence as Purim and the Passover. And finally, in the representations of the Last Judgment, the observance of ceremonial ordinances would never have been omitted, but we should hear the admission to heaven granted not only to those who had fed the hungry and clothed the naked and visited the sick and imprisoned, but to those also who had kept all the ordinances of the church blamelessly, and had never failed to worship in the right time and place and attitude, to partake of sacraments and reverently obey all priestly guidance.

Surely we have a right to conclude from these facts that Christ gave no sanction to any system whereby such observances are placed on a level with moral obligations? Here, as in so many other instances, we do not find him merely falling in with the morals of his age. He definitely opposed them. The current ethics of Judea in the first century were essentially ceremonial. As St Pacian describes them—"With Moses and the ancients, those guilty of even the least sin were immersed in the same æstuary of misery, as well those who had broken the sabbath as those who had touched what was unclean, who had taken forbidden food, or who murmured, or who had entered the temple of the Most High King when their wall was leprous or their garment defiled, or when under this defilement had touched the altar with their hand or with their garment come in contact with it. So that it were easier to ascend into heaven or better to die than to have to keep the whole of the commandments."* In finding Christ treat as trifles all such matters, we are discovering his own peculiar morality—the Christian doctrine as opposed to the Judaic. Doubtless, if we might paraphrase his view of the subject, it would amount to this: "The Levitical law was good in its place, and has had its use in building up the Jewish nationality. I am not come to destroy the law, but to fulfil, by bringing a higher and more spiritual law. But all this cumbrous ritual of Rabbinism, instead of a help to men's

* Paræenesis S. Pacian.

souls, has become a hindrance. They give tithes of mint and anise and cummin, and neglect justice and mercy and truth. This is grievous error. On love to God and love to man hang all the law and the prophets."*

And, on the other hand, how stands Christ's teaching as regards the sabbath? Did he also, like the prophetic party of our day, make a grand exception in favour of that most ancient and venerable of all ceremonial laws? The teachers of his time, and even many of the elder prophets, laid immense stress on its observance. Did his special and peculiar morality leave the matter where he found it? The case is far otherwise. The question of the sabbath came before him many times, according to the history, but invariably he treated it with the same slight regard. The Pharisees condemned him for healing on the sabbath on three distinct occasions—the man with the withered hand, the woman with an infirmity, and the man with the dropsy (Luke vi. 9, xiii. 15, xiv. 3); and on each occasion he justified himself, calling them hypocrites for their remonstrance. And again, when they upbraided

* Assuredly no teacher disposed to elevate the priestly office very highly would have given utterance to such a parable as the Good Samaritan, where a priest and Levite neglect the act of humanity which a heretic performs. Many teachers in our time would have described the philanthropist of the road to Jericho as running after the priest to obtain the "sanction of the church" before he poured oil and wine into the wounds of the poor victim who "fell among thieves."

him with allowing his disciples to pluck the ears of corn on the sabbath, he defended them by the example of David (Luke vi. 3), and gave utterance to the noble aphorism, which may be understood to sum up his view of the whole subject, "The sabbath was made for man, and not man for the sabbath" (Mark ii. 23). This and all other ceremonial laws are means, not ends, of sanctification.

If we could divest ourselves of preconceived notions and judge simply what result such treatment of a moral question by such a Teacher ought to have on the minds of his disciples, we should be startled to find, after all, how little weight his words have possessed. Let us imagine our late Japanese visitors struck with the phenomenon of an English Sunday. The roaring streets stilled into silence, and the crowds of well-dressed persons hurrying to the churches, would doubtless impress them reverently. But when they proceeded further to observe that the lower working classes, who had toiled through the week like cattle, and were on that day alone free to cultivate their human intellectual powers, to expand their minds and hearts by the sight of the beauties of flowers and trees, of painting and sculpture, were on that day only strictly debarred from entering the public gardens, museums, palaces, and galleries, wherein such culture might be obtained, it would be natural for the observant strangers to inquire by what precepts of the Christian religion were these people thus virtually excluded from such elevating influences. If we suppose the interpreter of the embassy to have sought to gratify their curiosity by reading to them the words of the Founder of Christianity, explaining to them at the same time that he was regarded by the whole nation as nothing less than a divine Buddha, whose authority was absolutely final, we must needs imagine the perplexity of the Japanese to be very considerable. Perhaps also this perplexity would not be removed by receiving the further information, that the real authority for the sabbatical observance lay in certain commands issued by much lesser teachers long before the time of Christ, to another nation than the English, to keep another day than Sunday as a peculiar covenant between that other nation and Jehovah.

Here again, as in the whole case of ceremonialism, the same mistake has been repeated. Ordinances good, wise and useful as means, have been transformed into ends, and upheld even when they not only ceased to be the means fit to produce their original end, but manifestly become hindrances thereto. The sabbath has not been enforced upon its real grounds,—because it is the most precious institution which has floated down to us upon the stream of time, the most suitable to the natural wants of humanity, the most venerable from the long sanctity of three thousand years. It is enforced as a law equal in authority to the eternal and immutable principles of morals, and which is to be blindly adhered to in all times and ages and under all states of society, whatever may be its results upon the condition of mankind. In a word, it is precisely taught that the Rabbins were right and Christ was wrong,—that "man was made for the sabbath, and not the sabbath for man."

3. A third great difference between moralists may be traced in their varied treatment of the two orders of human offences, or what we may call the fiend-like and the brute-like sins. The one order leads frequently to the other, and the most hideous of all conceivable horrors is that combination of the two in mingled cruelty and lust, of whose possibility many a page of history bears witness. But in their origin, and most commonly in their development, the two are widely apart. There are the sins which men commit under the influence of the animal passions—sins of unchastity, drunkenness, gluttony—and these rob them of their manhood's crown of moral self-control, and sink them for the time to the level of the brutes; and there are the sins which men commit under the influence of self-interest, hatred and all the anti-social passions—sins of cruelty, perfidy, malice—and these do more than sink men to the level of the unmoral brutes; they degrade them to the likeness of devils. As God is love, so is His antithesis hatred: and as man rises to the god-like through love, so he falls to the fiend-like by hatred. He is not merely

losing his higher life, dormant to the joy and glory of his birthright, as when he lies sunk in the slough of the passions which he shares with the dog and the swine; he is placing himself in antagonism to God and goodness; he is turning his back on Heaven, and going further from it every step he treads.

Dividing, then, these two orders of sins, the brutal and the fiendish, we find Christ's treatment of the first to be in this wise. A woman was brought to him taken in adultery, and after bringing her accusers to the judgment of their own consciences, he set her free, saying, "Neither do I condemn thee; go and sin no more" (John viii.). To another woman of sinful life whom he met by the well of Samaria, he entered into converse, spoke of her actions without scorn, and then went on to open to her simple mind the very highest doctrines of theology (John iv.). Again, another woman "who was a sinner," of the last, lowest order of woman's fallen state, came to him as he sat in the house of Simon and wept over his feet. How does he treat her? He excuses her strong display of devotion with a tender reference to his own death, and assures her that her sins are forgiven, "for she hath loved much" (Mark xiv. and Matt. xxvi.). So far from shrinking from such offenders, he sits down to meat with "many publicans and sinners," and formally justifies himself in doing so. And perhaps the most remarkable fact of all is, that he had gone so far in this direction that it became possible for his enemies to give currency to the calumny that he was "a gluttonous man and a wine-bibber, a friend of publicans and sinners." Assuredly no one ever dreamed of calling him a cruel man or a vindictive, the friend of the malicious or the deceitful! He deliberately contrasts on two occasions the spiritual condition of professed sinners with that of those who "devoured widows' houses and for a pretence made long prayers;" and on each occasion gives an unquestionable verdict for the avowed sinner against the cruel hypocrite. The publican's prayer in the temple is accepted rather than that of the Pharisee; and the publicans and harlots are said to "go into the kingdom of heaven" before the Pharisees, with all their ceremonial observances and (as we may presume) strictness of life. In a word, whenever sins of the brute-like order are in question, they are treated with almost startling leniency. Not one word implies any hopeless condemnation of them. They are grievous sins, needing forgiveness; nay, their guilt may be incurred by impure looks and wishes, and to escape them (as the passages are generally understood) a man should pluck out his right eye or cut off his right hand. But always, while recognizing their guilt, Christ treats them with a grave divine pity and compassion, which perhaps, more than all besides in his teaching, has invested him with the grateful love of the human heart. He always holds out the prospect of forgiveness. No offence of the whole class, is threatened with the final condemnation denounced so frequently and freely against the uncharitable and the cruel.

And on the other hand, in the treatment of the fiend-like order of sins, every case which comes up is judged with a severity quite inconsistent with the popular view of its relative guilt to that of the sins of the flesh. Whosoever is angry with his brother without a cause, is in danger of the judgment; and he who calls opprobrious names, of the council and of hell-fire. Reconciliation with an enemy is a duty having precedence of divine worship. All injuries are to be forgiven till seventy times seven, and no retaliation made for blows or robbery. Men who do not forgive their debtors as God has forgiven their greater debts will be cast into outer darkness. Those who neglect to feed the hungry and clothe the naked, or who see Lazarus in want and do not relieve him, will all be condemned to "everlasting fire." Whatever weight we may attach to such words, they can only bear the meaning that Christ considered such mere omissions of charity as more hopeless than the sins of the brute-like order, for which he always held out prospect of pardon. His whole teaching in the matter may be summed up in the two cases:—To the woman taken in adultery he says, "Neither will I condemn thee; go and sin no more." To the men who "devoured widows' houses," he says, "How shall ye escape the damnation of hell?"

The contrast is, to say the least of it, very remarkable, and it becomes all the more so when we observe that in this, as in so many other cases, Christ set himself in opposition to the current morality of his countrymen. The hard *lex talionis* has always been the favourite principle of Jewish ethics. "An eye for an eye, and a tooth for a tooth," was the old Mosaic rule; and the rabbins had added doctrines such as these: "But for men who commit injuries and never return with benefits, it is nowise forbidden to be avenged of them and to keep anger against them." * Rabbi Isaac said, "Show not benevolence nor mercy to Gentiles." † Rabbi Samuel ben Isaac says, from the mouth of Raf, that "it is allowed to hate him in whom one observes a base action." ‡ And, on the other hand, the brute-like order of sins was held in special condemnation. To the Jews, according to the best historians of ethics, the duty of chastity is indebted for the high place it holds in our modern conceptions of virtue, —a place quite unparalleled in the noblest ethical systems of Greece and Rome. The subject would lead us too far for present investigation, but a remarkable instance enables us to perceive how, in judging the character of their greatest hero, they recognized offences of this class as a sin, while ig-

* Rabbi Elijahu in addereth, quoted by Triglandius, p. 167.

† Midrasch Jehillim, fol. 26.

‡ Pesachim, tract of the Mishna (all quoted by Hennell, p. 459).

noring the guilt of actions against which Christ would assuredly have pronounced a far deeper condemnation. David's adultery with Bathsheba, and not his perfidy to Achish, his inhuman tortures of the Ammonites, or his implacable resentment at the last against Joab and Shimei, was supposed to have been his great and sole transgression. "He sinned not, save in the matter of Uriah the Hittite" (1 Kings xv.).

If, then, the summary of the peculiar morals of Christ must be admitted to place the fiend-like class of sins in the lowest category of condemnation, and the brute-like sins in another and far less hopeless one, what shall we say to the position these two classes take in the estimation of the stricter Christians of modern days? Do we find among them the utmost horror, as of the worst of sins, of vindictiveness, malice, and hatred—of calling our brother, "fool"—of slander—of a selfish, self-centred life? Do we find preachers condemning, as the most soul-destroying errors, evil words and unkind actions and bitter feelings, and pretences of being better and more strict than our neighbours? When they speak of the sins of the flesh and make appeals for Penitentiaries or give Temperance lectures, do they ever remind their hearers sitting complacently in their well-cushioned pews, that they may be in a much worse spiritual condition, for all their well-ordered lives, their correct creed, their sacramental privileges, and right views about "justification by faith," than the poor "lost souls" for whom their charity is implored; and that Christ has assured us that "harlots" "go into the kingdom of heaven" before Pharisees? Do they in their invectives against intoxication put always forward the truth, that the madness of hate and spite is devil-like, and the madness of wine only bestial; and that Christ used and blessed the "fruit of the vine," while he bade his disciples "beware of the leaven of malice and uncharitableness"? We should need to reconstruct half the ethics of the churches if we should harmonize them in this great matter with the morals of Jesus, and in our estimate of the sanctity of various classes of society, the "first" would henceforth be "last, and the last first." How deep and far such a change would go, it is startling to contemplate. Fraternities binding themselves to speak or write no bitter words, societies for the reconciliation of enemies, and *agapæ* for the preservation of friendship among discordant sects, might then spring up beside Temperance Leagues and Refuge Unions and meetings of clergy and bishops to denounce heretical books and throw stones at heretics. And each of us, in the solemn courts of conscience,—

> Each before the judgment throne
> Of his own awful soul,—

would look back with shame indeed and regret upon the scenes wherein he had

> Profaned his spirit, sunk his brow,
> And revelled in gross joys of earth,

resolving, with God's help, to "go and sin no more." But he would shed more bitter tears over the memory of cruelty—of the careless or vindictive infliction of moral or physical pain—of slanderous words—of implacable feelings—of hardness of judgment—of refusal of help implored—of those cutting words and unkind looks which make up often the sum of a miserable life to husband, wife, parent, or child, who is their object. The prudent, well-ordered life, with its sabbath-keepings and church-goings and prayers night and morning and avoidance of all "dissipation," would then be often stripped of its cloak of respectability and revealed to sight as a life of utter selfishness—mean, dull, morose, and envious—abominable to God and worse than useless to man. God will forgive us, in this life or the life to come, for repented sins of the flesh: shall we ever quite forgive ourselves through our immortality for the anguish we have caused to good and patient hearts, or for the neglect of means once in our power to produce the happiness of those around us, now passed away from our reach for ever?

We must pass more rapidly over some of the minor points of peculiarity in Christ's doctrine, and the strange fatality by which they have been neglected, while the lessons of Moses and Paul have been remembered.

4. Christ insists peculiarly on reserve and secrecy

in the matters of the soul. If we pray, we are to "enter into our closet and shut the door"—if we fast, to "anoint the head and wash the face, that we appear not unto men to fast"—if we give alms, to "take heed that the left hand should not know what the right hand doeth." A strange comment on this would be the immense importance attached in Christendom generally to public over private worship, and the pomp and clang of bells and pretentiousness of dress wherewith our public worship is heralded—the admiration in so many sects for a "mortified" aspect and solemn demeanour, in preference to a happy face and cheerful manner*—and, lastly, the principle, of which we have heard so much of late, that if women desire to devote themselves to works of charity, they ought to relinquish the usual costume of their class, and adopt a "modest garb and veil" of black or grey which shall announce,—not only to the left hand, but all down the street,—what their right hand is going to do!

5. Christ rebukes as heathenish making long prayers and thinking a man will be heard for his much speaking. Yet nearly all the churches stretch their prayers to the most inordinate length, and the very Prayer which Christ taught us for the purpose of avoiding "vain repetitions," is itself three times repeated in the English service, in consequence of

* The writer once heard a pious young woman remark that a certain clergyman "must have been such a good man—nobody could laugh in the room where his picture was hung!"

the lumping together of the three services in one, and the obstinate refusal of the "religious world" to allow them to be separated again.

6. Again, one of the most remarkable histories in the life of Christ is that beautiful one to which we have already alluded, his treatment of the woman taken in adultery. The sentence he passed was, "Let him that is without sin among you first cast a stone at her." What new principle of morality was this? Because a *man* has sinned in some way or other against the strict law of chastity, is he therefore to throw no stones at a *woman* taken in adultery? Who ever heard anything like this before—or since? *

Would to God that this Christ-like doctrine might ever become the received Christian doctrine—that the sin of the man does not differ from that of the woman—that all pretences of such differences vanish before the solemn appeal of conscience!

7. The last great characteristic of Christ's peculiar morality to which we shall draw attention was his conception of a perfect life. Among his contemporaries there were extant apparently three typical ideas on the subject. There were the Sadducees, who occupied themselves with practical affairs, guided by the noble principle of Antigonus of Socho (the disciple of their founder, Sadok), that "right must

* The internal evidence of this beautiful story may, I think, suffice for the present argument, albeit the external evidence be against its authenticity.

be done for its own sake and not for sake of reward," —a sect which seems to have lacked spiritual aspiration and future hope, and to have thought of no higher perfection than an honest worldly life. There were also the Pharisees, who aimed at what they esteemed perfection through minute observances, wearing phylacteries of texts and prayers on their garments and door-posts, washing their persons and cups and platters with scrupulous care, and giving tithes of even the smallest of their possessions. There were, lastly, the Essenes, who wholly devoted themselves to the attainment of a high degree of sanctity by living apart from the world in monastic seclusion and the practice of self-austerities.

To none of these types can we assimilate in any shape the ideal of perfection set forth by Christ. As for his example, it is needless to repeat what has been so often shown by Christian divines, that he was the reverse of an ascetic Essene, no less than of a Sadducean worldling or Pharisaic formalist. Had there been anything in his personal habits resembling those so common among religious teachers, of contempt and disregard of the body and its wants, we should inevitably have found his disciples recording tales like those of Romish saints, of garments worn unchanged for years,* of the unkempt beard

* One of the seven ways in which wisdom is manifested (according to the Eastern mind) is "the habit of wearing worn-out clothes"! (Solwan, by Ibn Zaffer.) It is remarkable that the histories both of Zoroaster and of Gautama Buddha represent

and hair of the Nazarite, and of penances and macerations without end. But, except the long wandering in the wilderness with which he commenced his prophet's life, we read of nothing of the kind. Such traditions as have reached us all point the other way, to dignity and beauty of person and demeanour, and we are bound to believe that he gave the example as well as the precept "to anoint the head and wash the face," to conceal any vestige of self-discipline.

Further, he was not only far removed from the Stylites or Dervish type of sanctity, he was eminently social in his habits of life. He seems to have accepted the hospitalities of every class of persons—Pharisees, rulers of synagogues, publicans, and private friends like the family of Bethany—in fact, so far as we know, of every one who invited him. To the house of Zaccheus he invited himself frankly. He objected nothing when "many publicans and sinners sat at meat with him." At the marriage feast of Cana he is asserted to have aided the conviviality of the banquet by fresh supplies of wine when men "had already well drunk," and at his own Last Supper may be said not only to have sanctioned, but to have consecrated, the use of the fruit of the vine. He excused Mary Magdalene for expending her

them as wandering and fasting in the desert and the forest before commencing their ministries. Ahrimanes appeared to Zoroaster to tempt him astray, and Gautama, after a night of prayer, suddenly "attained the wisdom by which he became Buddha."

"exceeding precious ointment of spikenard" on his feet, speaking with infinite tenderness of her demonstrations of grief and gratitude. He reproached his entertainer on the same occasion for neglecting to give him the kiss of welcome and the offer of water to wash his feet; and this latter gentle courtesy he himself afterwards practised towards all his own disciples. Such was his example; and his teaching is in full accordance therewith. He always assumed that social pleasures are right and fit. Throughout his parables there is perpetual reference to feasts and guests; nor does he hesitate to do what would amount to blasphemy were such things less than perfectly right and good in his estimation,—he continually represents God himself as the Giver of the feast. For the returning Prodigal He "slays the fatted calf;" and at another time "gives a great supper and bids many;" and again He gives a marriage feast, where wedding garments must be worn. Finally, Christ represents such pleasures as having their archetypes in heaven: "I shall no more drink of the fruit of the vine till I drink it new with you in my Father's kingdom." He tells his disciples, "when they are bidden to a feast" (not by any means to stay away, but) "to take the lowest room." And when they give a feast (which he assumes they are sure to do), to invite the poor, the halt, and the blind. There is never one word to the purpose that it is holier to dine alone on herbs and water, than in a large company on meat and wine.

Again, in his precepts concerning the perfection of virtue there is nothing resembling the inculcation of seclusion or a contemplative or ascetic life. Though the forms in which he described a life of beneficence were of an Eastern type, belonging to an era of convulsion, and different from those our modern political economy would point out as most suitable to the end in view, yet they were always forms of *social,* never of *ascetic,* self-sacrifice. He who prayed so often never told men that prayer was enough by itself, or that they might shut themselves up and fulfil all duty to their neighbours by imploring God to favour them. Those who said, "Be ye warmed and fed, and gave not those things that were needed," were simply hypocrites in his eyes. To the young man who asked what he lacked of perfection, he said, "Go and sell all thou hast, and give to the poor, and come and follow me." To his disciples he prescribed a life of self-abnegation, that they should journey perpetually preaching the "good tidings of the kingdom." And, lastly, in the most remarkable passage of all, he describes "being perfect as our Father in heaven," as being, like Him, kind to the evil and the unthankful. It is always the same, even in the picture of the final judgment. Nobody is represented as saved by any ascetic privations or religious practices. The prayers he had counselled as "means of grace" in this life, are "counted as righteousness" to nobody in the life to come. Fasting and watching are not taken into the account, and saying, Lord! Lord! is of no sort of avail. The accepted souls are those who have actually served the poor and miserable, and the condemned ones are those who have neglected to do so.* Everything is in keeping—examples, parables, precepts, and representations of the principles which shall determine future trial. Asceticism and solitary virtue has no merit, and is a delusion. Goodness consists in active love to God and man.

Having gained this insight into Christ's idea of perfection—Christ's peculiar idea, be it noted, differing from that of all his contemporaries—must we not pause and ask, how far the moral systems of modern Christians have embodied this idea? Are there no supposed disciples of Christ who are in fact aiming at Essene asceticism, or Sadducean worldly uprightness, or Pharisaïc formalism, as in each case their goal of perfection? It needs, alas! a very small acquaintance with either what is called the religious world or religious literature, to be aware that in this matter Christ's lessons and example are the rarest of all to be followed. How do "truly pious" people regard those who, like Christ,

* It is noticeable as another instance how Christian morals differ from the morals of Christ, that we continually hear, as if of a specially meritorious thing, of "seeing Christ" in the poor. But Christ himself represents the blessed as being extremely surprised when he identifies himself with the poor. "Lord, when saw we thee an hungred?" &c. These "blessed of the Father" had manifestly helped the poor for the poor's sake, not for any other's sake.

accept invitations to social pleasures freely, and "sit at meat" and drink wine with men of all characters, including "publicans and sinners"? How do other pious people of a different persuasion regard those who neglect such small ceremonies of the modern church as are equivalent to the washing of pots and tithing of herbs of the Pharisees of old? Place together the three elements of Christ's lesson —the acceptance of social pleasures, the disregard of ceremonies, and the devotion of life to purposes of true human love and beneficence—and how few do we find who even recognize that such was the perfection he would have enjoined!

And, last of all, it would seem that Christ conceived there was one point in which human virtue could rise above the level of mortal perfection, and actually imitate and share the infinite perfectness of God. It was, THE LOVE OF THE UNLOVELY. To love those who love us and who are pleasing to us, that is a small thing. To pass over all moral and physical deformities, and wrongs and insults against ourselves, and to see in every soul which God has made, what His eye also beholds, the germ of that immortal goodness which must bloom at last in His paradise, perchance millenniums hence—that is the great and beautiful thing—that is the culmination of human virtue, where it meets and blends with the infinite holiness of God. To see this germ of goodness under all the clay beneath which it may lie—to have faith in it—to love it—to bear all things, forgive all things, hope all things, for its sake—is the highest perfection of humanity. The one only thing in the universe which the creature can do even as the Creator, is, to "love his enemies, to bless them that curse him, and do good to those who hate him." Thus man becomes the child of Him who "makes His sun to rise on the evil and on the good, and sendeth rain on the just and unjust." Thus he becomes "perfect even as his Father who is in heaven is perfect."

How far the Rabbins or the Stoics of old ever grasped this idea, is a matter of speculative interest.* How far modern Christians who perpetually extol it in theory ever work it out practically to its logical conclusions, is a very different matter. Let us suppose for a moment what the world would be if

* The Rabbins had perceived how divine was this sending of rain on the just and unjust. "Rabbi Afhu said, 'The day on which rain is sent is greater than the resurrection of the dead, for this pertains to the just alone, but rain to the just and unjust.'"—*Jaanith.* fol. 71. *Mishna.*

"The highest of all characters, in my estimation, is his who is as ready to pardon the errors of mankind as if he were every day guilty of some himself, and at the same time as cautious of committing a fault as if he never forgave one." (Pliny, Ep. 22.) "It does not divert the Almighty from being still gracious, though we proceed daily in the abuse of his bounties. . . . . What then should we do but that very thing which is done by God himself—that is to say, give to the ignorant and persevere to the wicked." (Seneca, c. 14.) "Oh blessed Ormusd, pardon my offences against thee, even as I pardon those committed against myself." (*Vendidad Sadè*, *Zend Avesta.*) "By forgiveness of injuries the wise are purified." (*Institutes of Menu,* 107.)

in daily life as well as in the pulpit it was the received belief that we should despise no one, dislike no one, despair of no one, if meanness and depravity and (what is more to the purpose) vulgarity were to give us no excuses for reprobating anybody, if shrinking from contact with those below us, morally or socially, were recognized as being not a proof of higher taste and more exalted feeling, but of altogether a wrong and imperfect moral condition, if conquering fastidiousness and forgetting insults and overlooking slights were characteristics honoured, instead of despised, by the Christian world at large,—how different, how widely different, would be that Christian world from that which we behold it! Let us at least gather thus much from this brief glance at the peculiar morals of Christ. When men speak as if Christian virtue consisted in doing no harm and believing correctly—when men insist upon ceremonial observances and sabbath-keepings as things in themselves holy and imperative, whether useful or the reverse—when men treat sins of passion as unpardonable, and sins of malice and hatred as venial—when men proclaim the advantages of ostentatious example-setting in church-going and charity, and of conventual dress for philanthropic work—when men rank long and reiterated prayers and services as duties peculiarly pleasing to God—when men treat female unchastity as altogether a different offence from masculine profligacy—and, finally, when men set up as their model of perfection formalists, or worldlings, or ascetics, or persons whose virtue consists in care for their own souls, not in love and faith and tenderness for their fellow-creatures,—when men do this, let us at least take courage to reply: Your doctrines and views may be true or they may be false, but you have no right to claim for them the sanction of that Prophet who taught precisely the reverse,—your "Christian ethics" are not the "ethics of Christ."

SELF-DEVELOPMENT,

AND

SELF-ABNEGATION.

It happened last year to the writer to witness a scene of singular beauty from the terrace of an old villa on Bellosguardo, once the abode of Machiavelli. The atmosphere was in a condition unusual in Italy, being soft and hazy. The full moon had risen an hour or more above the snowy ridges of the Apennines over Vallombrosa, and was shining broad and bright, with the golden glow of southern moonlight, against the huge old Michelozzi Tower which crowned the olive slopes to the left and stood out with its machicolated roof clear and sharp against the sky, even as when the "starry Galileo" made it his home ere he "descried new worlds"

"At evening from the top of Fiesole."

Below, far down the vineyards and the cypresses, lay a soft dim sea of mist, filling the whole valley of the Arno, and reflecting the moonlight like a fleecy cloud. Of all the busy city of the day which slept beneath, no house or wall or even roof might be seen. Only out of the haze rose into the radiance of the upper air Giotto's Campanile, and San Lorenzo, and the tower of the Palazzo Vecchio, and the marble Duomo sublime and solemn over all, and Santa Croce,

> "In whose holy precincts lie
> The dust which makes them holier:"

Michael Angelo's grave, and Galileo's and Alfieri's and Machiavel's—and Dante's empty cenotaph. The City of a Dream it seemed, and not an earthly town. Or rather was it not the City of Memory, since here, as in human remembrance, all things poor and mean were blotted out, and only the beautiful and the grand remained, and were lifted up in a purer and more lovely light than that of common day?

Strange was it to look down and consider that in that hollow of the hills under the mist lay the cradle of such great and various genius, that our world would be other than it is had FLORENCE never existed. And strange too to reflect that, many as have been her gifted sons, far more by thousands have been they who, for centuries back, passed within those crumbling battlements, lives low and poor and ignoble, and sunk one after another under the shrouding mists of oblivion, leaving only to tower on high into the light of history the splendid memories of the mighty dead, while they slept, for ever forgotten, at their feet.

Is glory, then, and earthly immortality truly a thing worthy of human ambition? Was the old heathen hero right in its ardent pursuit, or the Christian saint in its contemptuous rejection? In the vast balance of eternity where all souls are measured, will genius still wear his starry crown after all earthly honours are over? Or will the value of each immortal spirit, in right alone of its divine sonship, place the philosopher and the savage, the poet and the boor, upon a level for ever? Like every other question which surges up concerning that unseen world, the same reply comes back—We know not, we cannot know.

> "Who telleth a tale of unspeaking death,
> Or lifteth the veil of what is to come,
> Or painteth the shadows which lie beneath
> The wide-winding caves of the peopled tomb?"

Yet some conclusion as to the actual value of mental greatness, viewed even in the reflected light of our faint idea of immortality, is not without its purpose. Transferred in thought to that higher sphere, the aspect of all things is changed. Earthly power and noble race, and wealth and beauty and renown,—all have vanished. Even Learning's treasures must have a somewhat altered value there; their chief preciousness the largeness of the soul they have built up and strengthened. Of human things Love must live ever, and Joy in the beauty and the wisdom of the Father's works. But will Genius survive also? Will the great painter, poet, sculptor, musician, philosopher, be great still among the blessed? On the answer which might come to this question would depend even somewhat of the practical purposes of life. If the development of such gifts as we may inherit will determine not only our career here, but the standing-point where we must be placed on our entry into the future world, then indeed to cultivate each germ of power to the uttermost, to devote life with unwavering purpose to whatever pursuit may seem the highest within our reach, *that* only can be the course worthy of reason. If, on the other hand, the most glorious gifts of the thinker or the artist will all be effaced in another life, and the only inequalities there be purely moral and religious, then indeed the cultivation of such gifts on earth must be a matter of altogether secondary importance, a thing to be considered as without bearing on the durable interests of existence.

It would seem as if this question, like many others, had been lying unrecognized under the habitual modes of thought of different classes of mankind. Such questions are not distinctly contemplated at all by one in a thousand, but an idea which would form an answer to them is adopted by each, and thenceforth the matter is settled, as if such an idea were an indisputable principle. Thus, it appears, that among the old Greeks and among most of those men and women who, in our time, inherit the Greek æsthetic nature, there is a conviction that Self-development is the grand purpose of life,—an idea, be it observed, which must either admit the result of such self-development to be eternal, or ignore the eternal aspects of life altogether. Again, among those who throughout the East and West, but more especially among the more ardent sects of Christians, have given religion a paramount place in all their interests, there is a latent idea that Self-abnegation is a far nobler and more meritorious thing than self-development; an idea obviously resting on the conception that the type of virtue produced by such abnegation is the type which shall hereafter "inherit eternal life." It appears to me that an inquiry into the full meaning and value of these apparently conflicting principles will not be without interest. At every turn of life they confront us, sometimes leading to great good, sometimes productive of immense evil. As a general rule *men* follow the principle of self-development; and often by so doing grievously neglect the claims which should have bound them to an opposite course; and *women* follow the principle of self-abnegation; and frequently by so doing narrow their natures and renounce the use of great powers committed to them by the Creator for the benefit of mankind. As Parker said, "Most men fail of their moral growth by the attempt to extend their own self too far, most women by attempting to contract it too much." Let us attempt to define the two courses as clearly as may be, with their good and ill results.

Self-development may be described as a principle whereby a man, contemplating life as a whole, resolves to make it his first care to use to the best and uttermost whatever powers the Creator may have bestowed on him. Such a man will naturally rank the social and domestic claims on his attention as secondary to the great purpose of his life. For example, a man adopting this principle and believing himself qualified to become a useful politician, a profound metaphysician, or a successful artist, would devote himself to seeking the proper training for such work; and would pursue his labours as a statesman, thinker, painter, or sculptor with a perseverance to which he would suffer the claims of his parents, wife, children, or other dependents to offer little interruption. If their imperative wants enforced his attention, he would, at all events, disregard their mere wishes and inclinations; even as he would deny himself his personal gratifications for the furtherance of his great purpose. Such a man, if religiously disposed, would attach to his pursuit the sanctity of a path of life designed for him by his Creator. He would consider his labours therein as the fulfilment of the task given him in this world, and he would naturally consider that by fulfilling it he had pleased his Maker and fitted himself for a still higher task in the world to come. He would practise much *self-denial* although no self-abnegation.

Self-abnegation, on the other hand, is a principle whereby a man resolves to give up all his faculties to meet the claims which are nearest to him. Whosoever comes first with such claims carries him in the direction of his requirements; and his own private pursuits and purposes are abandoned for such service, whether the sacrifice be, or be not, imperatively demanded by any pressing need of the claimant. He starts with the inquiry, "Who claims me first?" and not with the inquiry, "What can I best do?" For example; such a man may imagine he has gifts fitted to render him serviceable to science, literature, or general philanthropy. But the pursuit of any one of these things is constantly barred to him by some want, wish, or request of his parents, his wife, or his friends. His father desires him to undertake an uncongenial profession; his wife implores him to live where she can be near her family; his neighbours call for his services at so many public and private meetings, and come so constantly to consult him, that he has not an hour left for his study. In matters great and small his personal domain of freedom is invaded and his energies absorbed. He denies himself his own pleasures and also the pursuit he deems best fitted to make him useful in a large sphere; and in doing this on the principle of self-abnegation he conceives that he best obeys the will of God; that Will being (as he supposes) marked out in each case by the natural and proximate claims made upon him. Thus he deems that he fits himself by self-sacrifice for a purer world. He practises *both* Self-denial and Self-abnegation.

It is surely time that we should carefully weigh

the claims of these two principles. The first is commonly looked upon by religious persons as a somewhat heathen idea, and the other as a peculiarly Christian one. The first is often adopted by men against their theories of duty, simply because the force of their natures drives them to such assertion of their powers. The second is nearly always preached to women, and usually conscientiously adopted by them as if all other principles of action were immoral and irreligious. But, after all, the steady devotion of life to a high and worthy end is not a principle we can afford to scoff at as "heathen;" and to yield passively to the impulse of every wave of circumstance till we are stranded at last as useless wrecks upon the shore of life, is a very strange reading of the lessons of Christ. Heroism and heathenism, quietism and Christianity, are not, we presume, convertible terms. Let us strive to see light through this contradiction of principles, each good and each evil under different aspects. It appears that Self-development is right under certain conditions and Self-abnegation right under others. What may these conditions be?

It cannot be too often repeated that all that is noble in human nature springs from the centrifugal force of Love—disinterested feeling, whereby we are carried out of, and above, our own paltry individual aims in pure devotion to God or man—to the good, the beautiful, or the true. To love God because He is supremely love-worthy, *not* because He can send us to heaven or hell; to strive to make man happy and virtuous, because he is a creature capable of happiness and virtue, and *not* because he will serve us in return; to pursue the good, the beautiful, the true, because the good is good, and beauty is beautiful, and truth is true, and *not* because philanthropy will redound to our honour, or art bring us wealth and fame, or science forward our interests—this is right, this is noble and holy. And all that is poor and base in human nature springs from the centripetal force of Selfism, whereby we are chained down to our own interests and pleasures in pitiful care for *them*, even when we appear to devote ourselves to higher aims. To be religious for the rewards of heaven; moral, because "Honesty is the best policy;" benevolent, that we may be "seen of men;" to pursue art, science, literature, because through them we may obtain worldly aggrandizement—this is wrong, this is base and miserable.

But if these things be so, it is clear what must be the conditions under which either self-development or self-abnegation must be good or evil. Both must be good when they spring from Love. Both must be evil when they spring from Selfism. Self-development must be a noble thing when it is inspired by love, by the pure love of God leading a man to strive to lift up his soul to nearer communion with Him through virtuous effort and extended knowledge, or by the love of his fellows leading a man to endeavour to serve them by whatever task his powers best qualified him to fulfil. Self-development, on the contrary, must be a base thing when it is inspired by Selfism, by the personal ambition, vanity, covetousness, or thirst of private happiness, which makes a man seek his own welfare before all things, and build up his own "pyramid" for the dwelling-place, nay, rather, for the sepulchre of his own loveless soul.

And Self-abnegation may likewise be noble or likewise base. It is noble when its sacrifice is inspired by the conviction that thereby God's work may best be done and man's wants best supplied. It is base when it springs from cowardice; from indolence; from a readiness to make spiritual capital out of the selfishness of others whom it encourages in a soul-destroying vice, while it tries to build itself up in a celestial virtue; from an immoral acceptance of the principle of passive endurance, which relieves the mind from the agony of strife or the solemn weight of responsibility.

Theoretically, then, the solution of the problem is clear enough. Each man's duty is to develope or to abnegate himself, precisely as by doing one or the other he conscientiously believes he can best serve God and man. Does he think by the development and careful culture of the powers he possesses he can do good as a statesman, mechanician, author, artist; and that such good will outweigh the benefit he might render to those about him by keeping himself at their beck and call? Then assuredly it is his duty to devote himself to the development of those powers calculated so to benefit mankind. Does he, on the contrary, think that nothing he is likely to be able to do will be so serviceable as holding himself constantly at the disposition of his neighbours? then equally clearly it is his duty to postpone all larger personal schemes to the daily performance of the kindnesses in his reach. One great class of cases alone will be removed out of reach of these decisions. The imperative claims of the nearest domestic ties can leave no space for option regarding their fulfilment. Whatever a man may think of his own faculties for exalted utility, if his parent, wife, or child really require his aid, there can be no liberty left him to choose what *other* good he will achieve. The moral obligation is inevitable—to assist before all others those who have such claims of affinity or gratitude upon us. The discussions which have been sometimes raised (as, for instance, a very remarkable one detailed in Follen's "Life" between Follen and Channing) on the problem "Whether a man in case of shipwreck ought to save his own father or the greatest benefactor to mankind," all ignore the fundamental canons of morality. We are not left in the dark to guess whom we ought to aid in such cases, for *our* duty is plainly laid out for us—to aid those nearest to us, and to whom we owe the debt of gratitude. As well might a man turn from his creditor to give alms to a beggar, as refuse to save his own father that he might save another man.

Thus the *theory* of Self-development and Self-abnegation seems clear enough. Supposing no imperative claims to exist against us, we are called on to develope, or to abnegate ourselves, precisely as by doing one or the other it appears that we can best serve God and man.

Practically, however, the case presents some of the most difficult problems which beset the course of life. How is each individual to judge what he might do; or to decide whether he may fairly postpone, for any end however seemingly great, the little daily acts of kindness and service whose result is apparently certain, while the larger end is problematical? The more tender conscience a man has, the more difficulty he will find in deciding in favour of the larger future, over the smaller present, duty; and yet in a thousand cases, if that larger good is ever to be done by any man, it must be done by the steady resolution to place it before the daily calls which beset us all.

There is a story of a French tradesman, who early in life was struck with the want his native town suffered of a good hospital for the sick. For long years he laboured on, secretly purposing to accumulate a fortune which might suffice to endow such an institution. To effect this, he refused to give the smallest assistance either to his poorer relatives or to the mendicants who thronged the town, and he denied himself almost the necessaries of food and clothing. His neighbours, observing his trade to flourish, while he lived in the most penurious manner, and refused the smallest alms to solicitations alike of priest and beggar, soon gave him the character of a miser. He was first shunned by those whose social life he would not indulge himself by sharing, and by degrees more and more distrusted and disliked, till the children hooted him as the *Avare* in the streets. At last, when the years were over in which he might have enjoyed the pleasures of existence and the comforts of home and domestic affections, the old man in his threadbare coat, whom all the town knew as the selfish miser, suddenly realized his property, built a magnificent hospital, and endowed it with the whole of his fortune. The purpose of his life, for which he had toiled for half a century, was fulfilled, and every honour and reparation his fellow-citizens could offer surrounded his remaining years. Whether he was satisfied with his course, satisfied that he had been right for fifty years to pass by every appeal for mercy, that he might accomplish at last a work of vast and durable beneficence, the history sayeth not.

This story (which I have somewhere read as that of the true origin of one of the great charities of Southern France) is precisely a case in point. The philanthropist debarred himself from all the daily charities of life, that he might effect a great good otherwise unattainable. Assuming (as we have a right to do) that there were no natural claims of filial duty disregarded, we must admit the action was absolutely justifiable and laudable. No man may serve God or mankind by "saying to his father or his mother, Corban; it is a gift, by whatsoever thou mightest be profited by me," and leaving *them* to want what he gives elsewhere. But he is certainly at liberty to dispense with the claims of the ordinary poor, when he may far more effectually serve mankind otherwise.

But the adjustment of the duties of Self-development and Self-abnegation, if thus practicable upon paper, is, alas! in actual life a task of extremest difficulty. There are those among us to whom, let reason ever so loudly demand Self-development, are yet by their gentle and yielding natures continually driven to Self-abnegation; and there are those who are called to Self-abnegation by clearest conditions of life, to whom Self-development is, as it were, a primary instinct of the soul. Let us study these two classes a little; and the last first.

All human beings have a certain principle within them which we may call Self-Assertion. The rational free agent, be it man, woman, or even little child, recalcitrates from the very depths of its nature at any attempt to reduce it to a mere unit in a sum. It *demands* to be recognized as what it is—a human being, an *individual*. This being denied, its nature rises in disorder. Kindness, even rich indulgence, will not pacify it. It wants to be recognized as *human*, not indulged as a brute. The instinct of this truth has made judges, more severe than wise, attempt to obliterate the individuality of convicts by forcing them to bear a number instead of a human name, and the result is to create a new cause of rebellious spirit. In large schools the same thing in another way is done to children, and the mischief thence ensuing is only palliated by the boy or girl remembering that there is at *home* a fond mother to whom "James" or "Mary" is a most thoroughly recognized individual, and no mere unit in class three, or class five. Only in our workhouses where the poor young souls have no such blessed refuges of comfortable memory, is the evil pure and unmixed, and the result—what we behold.

Having at one time occasion to see much of a number of female criminal children in a Reformatory, I was struck by the observation of the benevolent lady to whose noble labours England chiefly owes these institutions, that she found her girls always struggling to be *individually* noticed. If at times, desiring to repress vanity, she failed to show that she recognized their efforts to do well, very soon they tried by conduct of another sort to force attention. Some showed the sentiment more strongly than others, but every one, even to the most stupid and wretched little ragged pickpocket of ten years old, displayed it sooner or later in some degree. If not noticed for good, they *would* be noticed for evil. Needless to say, that in the wealth of that good lady's heart they all found that recognition of their human souls for which they craved, and that by individual care and love their reformation was always sought, and often achieved.

We cannot descend, then, anywhere so low as to be beneath the natural sentiment of *self-assertion.* Nay, nor may we ever rise so high as to be above it. Can any of us endure that conception of the relation of creature to Creator which would represent us as a herd of human cattle, and He as the great Master, who could stoop to no individual recognition of one member or another,—who cared for the *race* alone, not the units thereof; and fed us in His wide pastures of earth with as little personal heed as a king might give to the deer of his park? Can we be satisfied with this idea—be it never so cleverly brought forward to explain the mysteries of the world? Will the most bounteous Providence suffice for us, if that Providence deign not to recognize us, each as we are, moral entities in the universe of souls? From the depths of our hearts comes the answer "No!" We ask for *individual* love,—and without it all the deepest part of religion is for ever closed to us. Blessed be God that we know and feel that such individual love is actually given, and that He, the Source of all love, cannot be defective in that which His poor creatures have displayed—the divinest thing in humanity.

But this ineradicable self-assertion of our nature,

though it might seem to do so, does not determine us either to develope our powers or abnegate them for the sake of others. It only affords a ground of unassailable individualism, which may in the one case serve for basis for the structure of self-development, and, in the other, cause the abnegation to be a real moral action, and not such a mere effacement as an animal undergoes in complete surrender to a man.

The spring of these opposite instincts seems to lie elsewhere,—in the propensity to make—in the one case an abstraction, in the other a person the centre of our interests. Putting morality aside, we have all a natural bias to make our chief object in life either an abstract aim of some sort (e. g. honour, wealth, pleasure, philanthropy, art, literature), or else personal (e. g. a certain relative or friend or succession of friends). As a general rule, the most masculine characters instinctively make an abstract aim their centre, the main purport of their existences; and though they may love at intervals, warmly and even passionately, they are not moved save temporarily from the grand purpose of their lives. The death of no human being altogether disturbs their equilibrium. Though they may grieve for it with bitterest tears, they still press on to their own goal, with heavier hearts, perhaps, but unrelaxing will. The most feminine characters, on the contrary, nearly always attach their souls to some human anchorage, some husband, parent, child, sister, brother, friend, and become utterly wrecked when that hold upon existence is lost. Though they may have seemingly pursued with ardour some aim of another sort, it becomes clear when the love is lost that it was only a secondary purpose, and that, uncheered by love, they have no energy to follow it more. Either life closes for them, or they in time find a new human being on whose affection to depend. In a word, the two classes were designated by the line of Byron—

> "Man's love is of his life a thing apart;
> 'Tis woman's whole existence."

That is to say, it is so of the typical man and woman. Practically, there are thousands of men whose love and life are not apart, and thousands of women whose existence is not wrapped up in love at all, but who centre their interests upon other aims, ambition, pleasure, art, philanthropy, quite as completely as any man. But the type of man who lives only in the object of his affections—wife, child, friend—is never a thoroughly masculine character, but one in many ways morbid. And the woman who lives for ambition or pleasure, for art, science, literature, or even purest philanthropy, and *not* for individual love, is always in a very singular way repellent to the other sex, as if she had transgressed her natural type and failed in her proper disposition.

Now it is clear that to the character which instinctively centres life on any abstract aim such as those we have been speaking of, self-development is the natural course, and self-abnegation a very hard and uncongenial one. On the other hand, to the character which centres life on personal affection, self-development is the difficulty, and self-abnegation is spontaneous. The two forms of duty are respectively attractive or distasteful, according to the idiosyncrasy of the individual who has to perform them.

Yet it is no less manifestly clear that the moral obligation of either course is not determined by any such circumstance as its congeniality or uncongeniality, but by the fact of it being the course by which the individual can best serve God and man. Of course the strength which urges self-development and the tenderness which urges self-abnegation are both in a certain measure indicative of the probable utility of one or other course. But this can at most form only one element of decision. Because we are strong it does not follow that no one has claims on our self-abnegation, nor because we are tender and yielding that no such claims exist to detain us from larger pursuits. An impartial consideration of the whole bearings of our own capacities and the demands of our neighbours can alone morally justify one course or the other. The evils attendant on a wrong line of action in these matters are very grievous both to the individual and to society, yet rarely, perhaps, are they traced to their proper source and set down as derived from the primary false principle. It cannot be useless briefly to indicate these results.

Let us suppose that a man or woman resolutely pursue the course of self-development when called on by duty rather to practise self-abnegation. The man says in effect, "I will become a writer, statesman, soldier;" the woman, "I will be an artist, a sister of charity, a student;" albeit in each case a blind father or poverty-stricken mother or helpless and untaught child call for the relinquishment of such schemes, and for a life of humble industry or home cares and nursing. The evil, so far as the immediate sufferers are concerned, is plain enough. In Victor Hugo's marvellous romance, when poor Valjean in his old age is gradually deserted and forgotten by the happy Cosette for whom he had toiled and suffered so much, we are admitted (for the first time perhaps in fiction) to a whole class of sorrows which the heart aches to think upon. Of the thousands of parents,—and men and women who have taken the place of parents,—who are left deserted in sad and lonely age, by children not wicked, not wholly thankless, but ambitious or selfishly engrossed in newer and more pleasurable affections, who shall tell? The sons who make homes and incur new charges on themselves when their parents' wants are beyond their means to supply,—the daughters who leave blind or helpless fathers or lonely mothers, to enter convents or to marry men who carry them to the ends of the earth, what bitter tears have they not brought from fading eyes? Or if it be not a parent but a child who is neglected, what has not that child, and often the world through him, to suffer, for the lack of the care and love to which each young soul is entitled from those who bring it into life? No achievement assuredly which the writer, artist, statesman, or philanthropist is likely to accomplish can outweigh the failure to do *that* good which he, and he alone, was bound to do to the parent and the child. And are men's own natures really ennobled by self-development practised under such circumstances? Do they advance thereby to heights otherwise unattainable, and which we may look upon as among the eternal glories of the soul to be perpetuated in the life to come? Surely it is not so. The highest achievement of the statesman's policy, the finest book, the grandest picture, the largest philanthropic institution in the world, are all tarnished and spoiled viewed in the white light of conscience, when the policy, the book, the picture, the institution have been wrought out at the cost of the most sacred duties,—when the man has achieved them with time and money he owed elsewhere,—has given the world an alms of that which belonged to his parents as a debt. In our moments of deepest insight we all feel the same, that under any conditions the triumphs of art, science, and even philanthropy, lack somewhat of the sanctity which overshadows the humbler tasks of natural duty,—the training of a young child's lips to pray, or the support of a mother's tottering steps. We feel that when such holy duties are over or are denied us, every other labour of life, however good and even sacred, is in comparison colder and less beautiful than those which we chose not for ourselves but which God appointed. How then, under the conditions which we have supposed of the natural duties being spurned and voluntarily neglected, shall we retain honour for the achievements of self-developed genius? How shall we grant to them any place in the glory of that world of realities of which our purest consciousness here is but the foregleam?

Again, let us suppose, on the contrary, that a man or woman choose the course of self-abnegation when in truth their duty lay in the exercise of the larger powers entrusted to them by Providence. What evil is here! what loss to the individual, to those for whom he makes his mistaken sacrifice, and to the race! Suppose a parent, husband, wife, brother, or sister absorb the time and care of a man or woman not really *needing* it, but only liking such attention, and therefore selfishly claiming it through their influence over the affections or their power over the destiny of their victim. Here is one of the very commonest tragedies of daily life, and I must be pardoned if I dwell on it somewhat lengthily, and appeal against the wrong it involves, especially as a woman,—not indeed one who has in any way suffered under it personally, but who has met it in almost every social circle, poisoning the lives which under a juster treatment would be both useful and full of happiness. Of course women are selfish as well as men, in some ways they are more selfish and *exigeantes;* and many is the kind, self-sacrificing father, husband, brother, who has a right to complain bitterly that his labours through days and years of toil for his family are met by no corresponding love and care for his happiness. But if this be so in many shameful cases, there is, on the other hand, a type of selfishness which is *not* common, save in men, a type which especially developes itself in the strength of that false self-abnegation which we are endeavouring to define, and which therefore may here be fitly marked out as one of the evils of our social system which it behoves us all to strive to check through the force of public opinion.

To describe this form of selfishness I shall take the commonest case of all, that of a father with his grown-up daughters. Probably every one of my readers will know of more than single instances such as the following to be found at this moment among their acquaintance. The father is not a bad man, not intentionally unkind or cruel, only selfish and systematically despotic. While his daughter is young he keeps her from following out studies which might have enlarged her mind and given her the noblest pleasures. And why? Simply because, forsooth, *he* has no interest in them and "dislikes a learned woman." He checks the warm friendships she would have formed with other women, because he "disapproves of female friendship." He debars her, in a measure, from those forms of social enjoyment in which she would have probably formed the natural ties of human existence, because he "has had enough of society long ago," and also, perhaps, though he does not *say* so, because he secretly deprecates her quitting her post beside him for any home of her own. He breaks up her whole time into small attentions to his comfort, giving her neither the leisure nor freedom of money to undertake any plans of usefulness or literary or artistic pursuits. Her life is narrowed into the smallest mill-round of little cares, not one of which is dignified by any real use. It is a *tread*-mill, not a mill to grind any bread of life. As her youth passes away and the woman ought to grow in breadth of thought and power of nature, and learn to perform her part in life to her own happiness and the good of others, she is cramped into the same bounds which fitted her as a school-girl, with no greater freedom to travel, to see friends, to obtain books, to help the poor; and the result is either torpid inanity or bitter restlessness. All this many a father brings on his daughters even when himself in full vigour of life and health, and having perhaps a wife and three or four of these unhappy ones all absorbed by his selfishness.

When he grows aged and falls into ill health the case becomes worse, the selfishness so long indulged becomes utterly tyrannical. Every consideration for his child's physical health is forgotten now as that for her mental health was neglected long ago; and close and heated rooms and incessant attendance (which he refuses shall be relieved by any friend or servant, because *he* likes best his daughter's service) leave her at his death with broken health and shattered nerves, to pass the rest of her life as best she may, having never been allowed to form either the ties of marriage or even of such strong friendships as might supply its place. Rarely does it happen that even in return for such self-abnegation as this has the father endeavoured to secure for the daughter's solitary age the full competence which might have supplied her at least with worldly comforts in default of home affections. The same father who has absorbed all her bright days will unconcernedly leave her dark ones to be supported by a mere pittance, which he has never denied himself a single gratification to enlarge.

I have drawn out this sketch to a length perhaps unwarranted, but the case is both a typical one of the evil of mistaken self-abnegation, and also a fair picture of a most common and grievous wrong which calls loudly for such public condemnation as may awaken the consciences of the offenders. For, be it noticed, this great and shameful injury (done often to most loving and innocent hearts only too ready to sacrifice themselves) is a thing not only unchecked, but actually *sanctioned* by the false morals constantly inculcated respecting the rights of parents and duties of children.

The very man who will have gone on for forty years in this course of unrelenting selfishness is often not only professedly, but in his own estimation, a good man and a devout Christian, and he will as deliberately with self-approval thus crush out the very life of his unfortunate daughter as he would take the services of his horse or his dog.* He has been taught to believe it is fit and right for a man and a parent thus to demand the whole existence of a woman. Nay, if argued with, he will, perhaps, have the effrontery to affirm that by such a life-long oblation of herself to him he has secured for her the highest moral and religious condition! As to her happiness—while the wrinkles gather on her once smiling face, and the lips become thin and hard, and the voice becomes shrill, and the laugh more and more rare,—the father will go on complacently assuring himself she is perfectly content, that all her nature is satisfied by being,—*not* a good man's daughter, friend, companion, aid,—but the poor drudge of an egotist who has no love

* An eminent physician, who has had unusual opportunities of witnessing the interior *politics* of innumerable families, once remarked to me, "I hear old people often talk of the selfishness of the young. All my experience goes to prove the inordinate selfishness of parents and the amazing self-sacrifice of their children."

to give or take, and might supply all she can do for him by the paid services of a menial. Surely, surely, it is high time that an offence like this, instead of being sheltered by public opinion, should meet the opprobrium it deserves, and that every friend and relative and neighbour of the selfish parent should endeavour to bring home to his dull conscience the truth that he is *not* exercising a "divine right," but committing a cruel and most odious wrong!

But to turn from the selfish father to the self-abnegating daughter. What shall we say to her duty in the matter? Is she (as many tell us) performing an act of saintly virtue in yielding unresistingly to all her father's invasions? Is she right to let him for his selfish indulgence take her whole life and devour it as he might a fruit from his garden, leaving only the dry husk when he has drank up all its juices? I can hardly think so. Only to describe such conduct is to condemn it, to point it out as a great and frightful sin: one of those slowly-wrought and long-extended sins which undoubtedly rust and ruin the soul as much or more than even the worst hot deeds of passion. How, then, is it the part of any one connected with the offender, to indulge him in his offence? How can the daughter herself be morally absolved for encouraging such a course of wrong? Suppose that it *were* a high discipline for her own soul (which is more than doubtful) to yield to such selfishness, how can she lawfully accept such spiritual gain for herself at such direful loss to another? True filial duty, as well as every other form of social duty, requires us to seek the *highest good* of its object, first, to conduce to his virtue, secondly, to produce his happiness. Hatred and malevolence themselves could do no more than to foster in another human soul the corroding vice of selfishness while we outwardly contributed to physical comfort and enjoyment. The debt of special benevolence due from a child to a parent must needs involve (as soon as the child is of an age to judge of it), at least, the care not to suffer a great visible moral defect to grow up in the parent's heart as the result of any conduct of the child. As one invasion after another of the daughter's natural sphere of liberty goes on establishing the precedent of parental selfishness, till at last it is erected into a sort of habitual principle, she is assuredly bound to pause and make a stand in behalf, not only of justice to her own soul and to the other claims upon her, but actually *for her father's own sake,* and in most imperative duty towards *him.*

The motives which blind women to these truths are of various kinds. Some are altogether evil. The chief of these is cowardice, and the next indolence. Girls are often cowed in early youth into hopeless moral pusillanimity. The strong will of a man overbears their feeble volitions, even as his loud voice drowns their puling remonstrances.

They simply *dare not* resist father or husband by any open opposition, albeit deception (the natural resource of cowardice) will often make them counteract his desires. Such poor, wretched women deserve our uttermost pity; but hard as it may seem, their moral salvation depends on their being able to rise above their hound-like fears, and assume the dignity of a human being in their relations to the tyrants who have thus beaten them down. Indolence, again, is a great besetting sin of all whose lives are narrowed and hopeless. A moral lethargy falls on the will, and the idea of contending for any point, however important, is dreaded just as an immense exertion of physical strength is feared by a weak and tired man. In the case of mothers, there commonly exists a care for their children's interests strong enough to bear down both indolence and cowardice, and, like timid animals made brave and resolute by love of their young, they speak and act with courage and decision. But a single woman has no such spur, and a tyrannical parent (unless her nature be unusually powerful) has an easy task to reduce her to most helpless subjection. But the source of false self-abnegation, which chiefly concerns us here to trace, is not the visible defects of cowardice and indolence, but the erroneous principle, conscientiously followed, that it is the duty of a child to yield implicitly to the demands of a parent be they never so obviously unjustifiable. *This* is the error which lies at the root of the whole evil, beneath which cowardice and indolence shelter themselves, and in whose shade offenders are blinded to the turpitude of their selfishness.

The subject is one of so great importance, and the principles involved cover so much larger a field than the special case of fathers and daughters which I have selected as the most obvious, that I hope I shall be pardoned for pursuing it yet a little further, and endeavouring to elucidate as far as possible the true morality of the whole matter. To do this we must ascend a little to the general principles of all social duty.

We owe benevolence to all our fellow-creatures, that is, we are bound to desire for all, and to seek for so many as we may, the highest good they can receive. For the merely *sentient* being we desire to bestow happiness; for the being who is both moral and sentient we desire, first, to conduce to his virtue, and, secondly, to produce his happiness. This is the great canon of social duty. Secondly, among those to whose virtue we may conduce or whose happiness we may produce, there is a precedence due to such as have *special claims* upon us, of either proximity of blood, gratitude, contract, or neighbourhood. Of these special claims those of parents over their children are manifestly the first, *always* resting on proximity and *generally* including gratitude also. Next to them come the reciprocal claims of husband and wife, resting on a contract or vow of special mutual benevolence. Now if, as we have said, an ordinary claim of benevolence requires us to seek the virtue and happiness of its object, the *special* claim calls on us to seek those ends primarily, i. e. before the virtue or happiness of any other claimant. We are not permitted to pass over the person holding them to aid any one else. It is the first and highest of all social duties to display to them this true benevolence. That is Filial Duty, neither more nor less. To what does it practically amount? The way in which we can best produce the happiness of those holding to us such a relation as a parent, will usually be by attending to their wants and wishes in the way they may themselves desire, their superior age making it a presumption that they can best judge for themselves what will make them happy. These desires of theirs they will naturally express in the form either of request, or (retaining the phrases which properly applied to childhood alone) of directions and commands. These requests, directions, or commands, in as far as they indicate the parent's wish in matters belonging to his own happiness, become morally imperative upon us, as expressing the precise form assumed at the moment by the parent's special claims on our benevolence. Filial duty consists mainly in attention to such parental desires, limited only in the case of the thing desired being either immoral, or visibly and unmistakeably qualified to injure instead of benefiting the parent who asks it.

But when these personal desires of the parent

are fulfilled by the child, has the parent a further right to dictate to the child in matters *not* concerning his (the parent's) welfare? Assuredly such a right, held provisionally during childhood, stops altogether when the son or daughter attains to full adult moral life. It *must* do so, for there is no ethical ground on which it can be further maintained, and its prolongation would nullify the primary postulate of all morality, which is the freedom of the individual will and its responsibility to God alone. If the parent were to decide for the son the questions of duty which arise in his life, the whole responsibility of the son's conscience would rest on the father, and the great purpose of human life be destroyed. As the son owes it *to God* in all cases to do as seems to his *own* conscience right, it is impossible he can also owe it to his father to do what *his* conscience may decide to be so.

Here then lies the grand distinction. Those commands of a parent which refer to *his own* happiness the child is bound to obey. Those commands (if he issue any) which refer to the child's own affairs he is *not* bound to obey, nay, he is bound to disobey whenever they clash with the decisions of his own conscience.

Of course all this reasoning regarding filial duty applies *à fortiori* to conjugal duty, which, resting upon a voluntary contract of special benevolence, can in no case attain to the same stringency of obligation as the filial duty which rests both on natural proximity and on a debt of gratitude incurred long prior to marriage. The two contracting parties in marriage mutually engage themselves to *special benevolence,* and the woman may further engage herself also to "obedience," i. e. to peculiar regard for her husband's desires respecting his own or the joint affairs of both. But more than this she cannot lawfully engage to do, and any vow implying it would be immoral. She is bound, as much as the daughter whose case we have supposed, to check her husband's selfishness and to *disobey* him whenever his injunctions clash with the mandates of her own conscience. Does this expression strike the reader as strange? Is the phrase "the duty of disobedience" somewhat startling? Assuredly we have all wandered far from a true and healthful morality if so it should be. The very fact that there is such a thing as a duty of Obedience implies that there must exist a duty of Disobedience also. Obedience to a rightful lord must involve disobedience to any one who usurps his authority. Loyalty to conscience can only exist by the repudiation of all interference with its sacred behests. To "obey God rather than man" is to obey God *against* man in all the thousand instances wherein human wills oppose the Divine. Strange would it be to trace how the errors of the ascetics of the early Christian church, and afterwards of dreamy mystics and Quietists, have perverted the ethics of Christ, teaching that servile obedience of son, daughter, wife, servant, subject, constitutes exalted virtue,—even while the whole Bible of humanity, Hebrew, Greek, Roman, and Teuton, is one great psalm of honour to the heroes and saints, the prophets and martyrs, who have defied the aggressions of the invaders of their personal or political freedom; who have chosen to obey Conscience rather than any mortal guide; and who have carried out even in blood and flames that same solemn "duty of disobedience."

If every son and daughter, every husband and wife, took solemnly to heart *as a duty* the obligation of checking, instead of encouraging, the selfishness of those most near and dear to them, there would assuredly be far fewer miserable, selfish men and women in the world. The omission of such a duty cannot be blameless. Shakespeare was right to say,

> "Self-love, my lord, is not so vile a sin
> As self-neglecting."

But how is selfishness to be checked? How is such a father or husband as we have described—or, alas! such a mother or wife as we might (though as a less common experience) describe also—to be arrested in his or her course of invasions? Assuredly not by the resisting party being themselves selfish, and reducing existence to the ugly and pitiful struggle between two contending wills! Rather must it be done by an unselfishness far *more* complete than that which pusillanimously yields to wrong,—an unselfishness which shall both abnegate and develope self, precisely when and how, after the gravest consideration, the interest of others seem to require. The line once drawn and plainly announced between the filial and conjugal services which are accepted obligations, and the obedience which will be refused to invasive commands, the task will not be so difficult. The time must surely come, if not in this life, then in the next, in which the parent, husband, or wife, prone to selfishness and love of dictation, will thank the child or wife or husband who steadily and tenderly places a limit on exactions and despotism, and saves him or her from the great sin and misery of a selfish old age.

It is needless to analyze other types of mistaken self-development or self-abnegation. Enough has been said, it is hoped, to indicate where the error in each case may lie, and on what high and solemn moral grounds the decision in one case or the other ought to be made. But turning from *false* choices and their deplorable results, how fair a sight is that of a true one, when man or woman rightfully pursues the course either of self-development or self-abnegation! How noble a thing it is to see a youth struggling bravely onward with one high aim before him, borne down perhaps often by the tide of circumstance, yet ever rising again undismayed, till he "grapples with his evil star," and the battle is gained,—the ignorant man has become learned, the soldier has won his laurels, the artist has created a great work, the writer has touched the heart of his nation, the statesman has achieved a wide and deep reform, the philosopher has discovered some grand eternal truth and "thought again the thoughts of God!" A glorious and ravishing sight truly; I know but one nobler. It is when the man who *might have been* the scholar, soldier, artist, statesman, author, or discoverer, who had it in his mind's grasp and his soul's resolute will to be so, has closed his eyes to the dazzling crown and turned aside, mournfully perhaps, but with unswerving resolve, to humbler tasks which could win no human glory, but which were DUTIES laid on him by his Maker. Such a life in its simplicity of allegiance to the holiest law, is the grandest sight which our eyes, were they truly illumined, could see in all the world. The man who leads it is as much greater than the successful scholar, statesman, philosopher, as the moral is higher than the intellectual, the æsthetic, or the animal nature. What he *might have been*, however great, is poor and small beside what he *is*. We may not be able to see this; we cannot fathom either the gifts that were latent in him, or the holy sense of duty (or of that love which is duty perfected and completed) which has made him abnegate their use. But in the world of Realities it must need be that we all shall perceive, what perhaps God alone sees now, the supreme transcendant glory of true self-sacrificing goodness. In that high world it may well be that Genius shall still wear his starry crown and joy in his divinely given powers. But it must needs be that a yet purer blessedness must belong to such Virtue as we have contemplated, and that in that "Kingdom of the Father" the Righteous shall "shine forth as the sun."

THE SACRED BOOKS

OF THE

ZOROASTRIANS.

A CRITICAL study of the various religions of the world is one of the many features which distinguish modern scholarship from that of earlier times. Three hundred years ago the foremost minds in England, who composed her noble liturgy, wrote the collect which intercedes for "Jews, *Turks*, Infidels, and Heretics,"—very obviously confounding "Turks" with Mahometans, and considering the six or seven hundred millions of Heathen in the world too inconsiderable to be included in any category. A century later, the Renaissance had done its work, and made men perfectly familiar with Greek and Roman Polytheism, yet leaving them still almost entirely ignorant of other creeds, insomuch that divines disported themselves at pleasure in comparisons between Mosaic doctrines and those of Roman paganism, as if no higher type of Gentile faith were to be found. Again another century arrived, and the dawning knowledge of the great religions of the East, obtained through travellers and students, suggested to the free-thinkers of France the brilliant idea of setting up Buddha, Menu, Confucius, Zoroaster, and Mahomet, as rivals to the prophets and apostles of Christianity. For that time "les Chinois et les Brachmanes" were credited with the possession of every exalted doctrine and every moral excellence—it must be confessed, on the slenderest evidence imaginable. The disenchantment of Voltaire, had he visited the court of Pekin, would probably have far exceeded even that which he experienced at Potsdam. Yet again a new era has come, and the religions of the East are subjected to a thoroughly searching inquiry, unwarped by any inclination to seek premises for either of the foregone conclusions of earlier times—that they are utterly base and bad, mere foils to Christianity; or that, on the other hand, they are equally pure and noble with the highest faith of Europe. The present state of Islam, Brahminism, Buddhism, and Parseeism; the popular doctrines believed by each great sect; its ecclesiastical arrangements, ceremonies, and forms of worship, are now all known to us tolerably well through personal experience, or the experience of thousands of our countrymen. The still more interesting problem of the original character of these creeds, when each was in its zenith of prosperity, is daily in process of solution, as one after another the sacred books of each are subjected to the microscope of modern criticism, examined, compared, commentated, and published in the original, and in translations in all the principal European tongues. As the geologist lays bare the long-buried archives of creation, so do the critics engaged in this great work open up the strata of human thought and faith, revealing, as they descend into the depths of the ages, simpler and ruder forms of religious life, but finding *life* always and everywhere. There are no *azoic* rocks in the geology of man's religion.

Of the five great creeds of Asia—Islam, Buddhism, Brahminism, the Confucian and Zoroastrian systems,—the last, albeit numbering in our time comparatively a mere handful of adherents, has perhaps the strongest of all claims on our interest. Mahometanism is, after all, only a great offset of Judaism; Confucius taught rather a morality than a Religion; and Buddhism and Brahminism deal with conceptions of Life and Deity and futurity so amazingly different from our own, that we feel, in studying them, as if we had passed into another planet, where the conditions of time and space, of the material and the spiritual, were altered. The Parsee or Zoroastrian faith, on the other hand, meets us, as if composed of ideas all familiar to us,—all open, if not to acceptance, yet at least to recognition as normal products of human speculation on the world such as we find it. Nay, so much is there in this old creed of Persia in harmony with our popular belief to-day, that we inevitably learn to regard it with a sort of hereditary interest, as a step in the pedigree of thought much more direct in our mental ancestry than the actual faith of our Odin-worshipping forefathers according to the flesh. Maimonides says that the Jews "derived all their knowledge of the angels from the Persians at the Captivity," and truly a perusal of the Zend Avesta affords the best explanation of that mass of ideas concerning good and evil spirits, current so long in Christendom, and yet supported by such slender authorization from the canonical writings of either Testament.

A brief and merely popular account of the results of recent investigations concerning the history of Zoroastrianism and the contents of the Zoroastrian sacred books will perhaps prove acceptable to readers whose knowledge of the subject stopped short at the point left by the discoveries of Anquetil du Perron in the last century, on which no important advance was made till very recently.

The first fact brought to light by modern Oriental scholars concerning the ancient faith of Persia is a startling one enough. It appears there was a time when Brahminism and Zoroastrianism were undivided, when the two great branches of the Aryan race which have since adopted those creeds dwelt together in unity and worshipped at the same altars. The schism which broke this primeval unity was the starting-point of the religious history of half the world.

At first sight it might appear that a fact like this, averred to have occurred before historic times, and not once clearly recorded or even alluded to in any ancient book, could never be satisfactorily established. Nevertheless, the evidence of its truth is quite incontestable. The subject is so curious that I shall be pardoned for condensing this evidence into a brief statement.

In the Brahmin religion *Deva* is the common title of all divine beings, and *Asura* of evil spirits. In the Zoroastrian religion and sacred books from first to last, *Deva* is the name of evil spirits, and *Ahura* (or Asura) of divine ones. Ahura-Mazda (Ormuzd) is Zoroaster's peculiar title for God. Thus we arrive at the presumption that at some period there was a revolution in which the gods of one party became the devils of the other.* But we advance a step further in the search when we find that the Zoroastrian Ahura or Asura was not always a demon to the Brahmin. The word is used in an evil sense only in the ages of the Puranas and later Vedas. In the Rig Veda Samhita in numberless places the word *Asura* is used in a good sense, and applied to the very highest gods—Indra, Varuna, Agni, Seeva, &c.,—the sense being "living" or "spiritual being." † Again, in the Yajur Veda there are certain parts in particular metres, distinguished by the epithet *Asurî*, and these metres (unique in the Vedas) are precisely those of the Zoroastrian *Gâthâs*, or most ancient sacred songs of the religion of Ahura-Mazda. Again, a number of

* This strange exchange was first noticed a few years ago by Lassen.

† Haug quotes in support of this, Rig Veda, 1. 54. 3; 1. 24. 14; 4. 2. 5; 723; 1. 35. 7; 5. 42. 11, &c.

the Vedic deities are found, some as good, some as evil, beings in the Zoroastrian books,—Indra, god of the sky, becomes the second of the devils; Seeva, under his name Sharva, is another devil. The Sanscrit Deva *Mitra* becomes the angel Mithra, and so on. A further evidence is found in the similarity of original rites, wherein the Zoroastrian religion seems to have copied (and purified of all sanguinary character) the Brahmin ceremonies and sacrifices. The sacramental Soma juice is but slightly changed for the Hôma; the investiture of the sacred thread whereby a man becomes either a Brahmin or Parsee belong to both religions alike. Thus an original unity and subsequent schism between the two creeds may be held to be established. But when did this schism take place? It must have taken place at the time when Indra was the chief god of the Brahmins and before the *Trimourti* was introduced into their religion—a trinity of which no traces can be found in Zoroastrianism. This is the period of the earlier Vedas, before the Brahmins had immigrated into Hindoostan, and when Asura was still a Brahmin name for a good god. At that remote period it is plausibly conjectured, the Aryan tribes having wandered from their northern home (described in the first Fargard of the Vendidad as a cold country, with ten months of winter), began to divide themselves into two great branches,—the Iranians who addicted themselves to agriculture in Bactria and its vicinity; and the Brahminic tribes who persisted in nomade habits for some centuries later, till they penetrated into India. The contest between the agriculturists and the nomades, and the forays of the latter on the lands of the former, would naturally engender the strife of creeds which followed.

This great schism, which M. Ernest de Bunsen ingeniously suggests may be the fact embodied in the myth of Cain and Abel, is assuredly a turning-point of immense importance in history. Asia then fell morally asunder. The eastern half of the Aryan race thenceforth diverged further and further from the simple creed of the earlier Vedas, and multiplied objects of worship, cosmical dreams, senseless ceremonies, and degrading and immoral superstitions without end, till Brahminism could boast of its three million gods for its three hundred millions of votaries.* The Western race, on the contrary,

* The depth of pollution to which Hindooism may descend has been fearfully revealed of late in an "Account of the Sect of Maharajahs of Western India" (Trübner, 1865). A religion whose rites are orgies and whose heaven is an eternal pollution, is a spectacle before which the mind stands aghast. We ask, out of what tree of evil can such a corrupt branch have grown? What could be that Vedic faith which after four millenniums has borne such poison-fruit? Yet perhaps even *this* perversion of the religious sentiment of humanity is not the worst the world has seen. A creed immeasurably holier than India has ever known has borne fruit even more unlike itself. He who would judge of the Gospel by the light of an *auto-da-fé* would surely form an idea of it no less wide of the mark! See the summary of Christian persecutions in Lecky's Rationalism. Vol. ii.

began in that remote primeval movement, a course wherein the *moral* part of religion, recognized from the first in its due ascendency, worked its way through millenniums, giving to the creed which embodied it a dignity and power unmatched elsewhere, till it leavened the thought of the mighty Hebrew race, and, through the Hebrews, of Christendom itself.

In one of the grandest stanzas in Childe Harold Byron says,

> "And if, as holiest men have deem'd, there be
> A land of souls beyond that sable shore
> To shame the doctrine of the Sadducee,
> And sophists madly vain of dubious lore,
> How sweet it were in concert to adore
> With those who made our mortal labours light;
> To hear each voice we fear'd to hear no more,
> Behold each mighty shade reveal'd to sight,
> The Bactrian, Samian sage, and all who taught the right."

Should we indeed in a future world be permitted to hold high converse with the great departed, it may chance that in that "Bactrian sage," who lived and taught almost before the dawn of history, we may find the spiritual patriarch to whose lessons we have owed such a portion of our intellectual inheritance, that we might hardly conceive what human belief would be now had Zoroaster never existed.

At the period when the breach took place between the Aryan tribes, it appears that the Iranians already possessed a priesthood, the Soshyantos, or Priests of Fire. They are spoken of with reverence in the earliest parts of the Zend Avesta, and to them a certain share in the work of forming the creed then in process of growth may be attributed. To Zoroaster himself, however, must be given the honour of being the true founder of the religion of Ahura Mazda; the prophet who raised a vague Nature-worship into a definite and noble Theism. The question is a profoundly interesting one, What can we know of this great teacher? What reliable record remains of his life and actions? The answer is very brief.

The name which the Romans called Zoroaster, the Greeks Zarastrades, and the modern Persians Zerdoscht, is, in the ancient Zend, *Zarathustra*, and signifies a Chief or Elder. The title was applied generally to the Magian high-priests, whence naturally arose the mistake of the Greek historians, who asserted that there had been several Zoroasters, prophets of different ages. The great Zoroaster is distinguished in the Zend Avesta as *Zarathustra Spitama*—the latter word being, perhaps, a title implying sanctity, or, possibly, a patronymic. His father's name (according to the Vendidad and Yasna) was Pouraschâspa, and his mother's (according to the Bundehesch), Dogdo. We also learn that he had sons, and a daughter;—proving him to have been no member of the order of celibate prophets. His home was doubtless in the locality where tradition has uniformly placed it, in Bactria, near the old cradle of the Aryan race; that "Aryana

Vaêjô," "the ancient home," so often spoken of in early Eastern books: Zoroaster indeed is especially entitled in the Zend Avesta "the celebrated in Aryana Vaêjô." His office was that of one of the Soshyantos; and as such he is represented as standing before the sacred fire and announcing the faith of Ahura-Mazda, in the *Gâṭhas*, or sacred songs of the *Yasna*. These Gâthas, which the researches of Haug have proved to have very high claims to be considered the actual compositions of Zoroaster and his immediate disciples, afford us the most reliable evidence which remains as to his real character and doctrine. In these he calls himself (or the composer speaking in his name calls him) a "Reciter of Mautras," a "Messenger of Ahura Mazda," a "Listener to the sacred words revealed by God."

As specimens of these original words of Zoroaster, showing somewhat of his theology and ethics, we may quote the following passages:

"I will believe in Thee, Mazda! the powerful holy God! With Thine helpful hand Thou givest to the pious man and to the impious, by means of the heat which strengtheneth all things. Thus I believe in Thee, Thou Wise and Living God, because I behold Thee to be the primal cause of life to Thy creation. To the evil Thou hast apportioned evil,—to the good the true good. I will believe in Thee, Thou glorious God, even to the last period of existence. At whatever time I have trusted in Thee,

Thou Wise and Living God! in that Thou camest unto me. . . To those who honour Thee, *Armaiti* (the Spirit of Piety) will teach Thy Laws which none may abolish . . . May the number of the worshippers of the Liar (Ahrimanes) diminish! . . . Thus prays Zarathustra." . . *Gâtha Ustavaiti* (II. Gâtha), *Yasna* 43, v. 4, *et seq.*

The following is styled the Inaugural Speech of Zoroaster, and is believed by Haug to have been used by the prophet at the opening of his mission, standing before the sacred fire in solemn assembly.

"I will now declare unto you who are gathered here the wise sayings of the Most Wise, the praises of the Living God. . . Every one, both man and woman, ought this day to choose his faith. . . In the beginning there were twins—the Good and the Base, in thought, word, and deed. Choose one of those two spirits! Be good, not base. Ye cannot belong to both of them. Ye must choose one, either the originator of the worst actions or the true holy spirit. Some may choose the hardest lot. Others adore Ahura-Mazda by means of faithful actions."* (*Gâtha Ahunavaiti, Yasna* 30.) These fragments, and the few more belonging to the same Gâthas, if really the words of Zoroaster,

* The four translations before me of these passages—two in English by Spiegel and Haug, one in Latin and one in German by Haug, all differ so considerably, and in those professedly English the grammar is so defective, that I have only ventured to give such phrases as in all bore somewhat of the same sense.

afford a very interesting glimpse of the character of his instructions. The clear moral note prominent through the whole cycle of Zoroastrian religion, has here been struck. The "Choice of Scipio" was offered to the old Iranians by their prophet 3000 years ago, even as it is offered to us all to-day. "Choose one of the two spirits. Be good, not base!"

Of the Life and actions of Zoroaster independently of his teachings, very little can be known with certainty. In the *Bundehesch* there is indeed his complete biography. We are told of his miraculous birth, his retirement into the wilderness, and his temptation by Ahrimanes, who offers him all power and prosperity on condition he will admit *him* to be God; whereto Zoroaster replies: "Evil Glory! It is for thee and thy race that Douzakh (hell) is prepared. As for me I will serve Ormuzd!" We are further told how he introduced himself by miracles to the notice of King Gushtasp; and becoming the monarch's friend and counsellor, established the true Mazdayasnan faith through his dominions. The age of the *Bundehesch*, however, though undoubtedly prior to the Christian era (a circumstance which renders some of its legends specially noticeable), is still so many centuries later than that of Zoroaster himself, that we can attach little or no value to its information. All that we can fairly rely upon amounts to this,—that he was, as already stated, a Soshyanto, or Priest of fire, at the period of the final schism between the Brachman and Iranian branches of the Aryan race; and that to him was mainly due the definite form which the religion of the latter then assumed. The invariable process by which the great prophets and heroes of humanity become wrapped in a halo of supernatural glory, and removed out of the sphere of the manhood they honoured, has not been wanting in the case of Zoroaster. In the later books of the Zend Avesta (the younger *Yasna* and *Vendidad*) we find him already raised to superhuman rank,—the Teacher of Monotheism has become a demi-god, elevated above the archangels. He is "the Abyss of all wisdom and truth, the Master and Head of the whole living creation." *

As to the date at which Zoroaster flourished, the utmost uncertainty prevails among critics. The belief of the modern Parsees (adopted by Anquetil du Perron) has been exploded, viz. that the Kava Vistaspa of the Zend Avesta is the Hystaspes, father of Darius of the Greeks, and that, consequently, his contemporary, Zoroaster, lived about 550 B.C. A much higher antiquity than this is required, if only to leave space for the growth of the whole cycle of Zend literature, which began with the prophet's songs and was complete in 400 B.C. The Greeks attributed to him various remote dates. Xanthus

* Haug's Essays, p. 252.

of Lydia (writing circ. 470 B.C.) says that he lived about 600 years before the Trojan war, or in 1800 B.C. Aristotle places him 6000 years before Plato, and Berosus makes him reign over Babylon, 2200 B.C. On reviewing all arguments, Haug determines his date as at the latest 1000 B.C., and probably three centuries higher.*

The religion which Zoroaster taught was undoubtedly a pure Monotheism. It degenerated in time into a partial Dualism combined with a remnant of the old Nature-worship,—or rather such degeneration took place in one sect called the Zendiks, adherents of the Zend (commentary on the Avesta), while another sect, the Magian, remained true to the purer ancient Theism. During the period of the greatness of the first Persian Empire, of which Cyrus is the central figure, the Zoroastrian religion was the universal faith of the nation, and the Jewish captives then learned from it their science of the angelic and demoniac spirits.†

* In his Introduction to the *Aitareya Brahmanam* (Bombay, 1863), Haug seems to have reached the conclusion that the date of Zoroaster is still higher than that which he assigned to it in 1862. He argues that the Brahmanas cannot be later than B.C. 1200, and that they describe the great schism of Iranians and Brahmans under legendary forms of Asuras and Devas in a manner proving an immense lapse of time since the actual event. Zoroaster certainly lived while the contest was carried on.

† "Dixit Rabbi Simeon Ben Lakis—nomina angelorum et mensium ascenderunt in domum Israelis ex Babylone." *Rosch Haschanah*, tract of the *Mischna*. Maimonides asserts the same fact.

The cuneiform inscriptions of Darius bear singular testimony to the importance attached by that monarch to his religion, every announcement of conquest and sovereignty being accompanied by the phrase "Ahura-Mazda helped me. By the grace of Ahura-Mazda I am king."* From the conquest of Alexander, B.C. 331, till A.D. 226, Persia submitted to the sway of Greeks and Parthians, who seem not to have persecuted the national religion, but rather to have superseded it by their own forms of worship. The accession of the Sassanian dynasty to the throne in A.D. 226 was the signal for a great revival of the Zoroastrian faith. At that period the whole of the vast region from the Red Sea to

* Journal of the Royal Asiatic Society, vol. 10. The phrase in the Latin translation reads curiously, like the inscriptions on our coins to this day, "Gratiâ Ahura Mazda ego rex sum." In Spiegel's German translation of the whole collection of cuneiform inscriptions, from Cyrus to Artaxerxes Ochus, found at Behistan, Persepolis, &c., the religious element almost seems to outweigh the historical, and we are reminded of the singular decree of Nebuchadnezzar in the Book of Daniel that "all nations should worship his god," rather than of any ordinary imperial ukase. The inscription of Alvend begins thus: "A great God is Auramazda, who created this earth and the heavens, who created mankind, and made them for blessedness, who made Darius the king." The inscription of Persepolis begins thus: "The great Aura Mazda, who is greater than all gods, has made Darius king. . . . O men! The will of Auramazda is this—think no evil; leave not the right way!" Xerxes begins his inscriptions in the same way: "A great God is Auramazda, who made earth and heaven, and made Xerxes king," &c.—Die Altpersischen Keilinschriften, von F. Spiegel. Leipzig, 1862, p. 45, *et seq.*

the Indus, and from the Phasis to the Mediterranean, formed the empire of kings who inscribed on their coins "Mazdiesn" as their highest title, placing on the obverse the fire-altar as the emblem of their creed. Ardeshir Babeghan, the founder of the dynasty, summoned the priests to collect the sacred writings of their religion, and thus formed the *Canon* of the Zend Avesta. The ancient Avestan language being even then completely obsolete, we may safely assume the works written in it to be real relics of remote antiquity, and not productions of contemporary priests.

In the 7th century the reign of the Sassanidæ ended, after a gallant struggle, with the fall of Yezdegird III., and the Moslem conquerors of Persia set themselves to extirpate the ancient religion. In a short time the Zoroastrians were reduced to a small and persecuted sect, whose traditions served only for a basis for the great epic poem—the *Shahnameh*—of the victorious race; and the adherents of the ancient faith who remained in Persia from that period continued to dwindle in numbers and condition, till at present they exist as a mere remnant equally poor and despised. When visited by Westergaard in 1843 at their chief seats, Kerman and Yezd, he found them utterly debased and ignorant. In a few years more the *Guebres* (as the members of the sect dwelling in Persia are called) will soon be lost among their Mahometan conquerors. By a singular fatality however the Zoroastrian faith has survived its extinction in its original country, and promises to enjoy some centuries more of life in another land. When the Moslem persecutions were at their height in the 9th century A.D. a band of Persians (called Parsees by the Indians) fled into Beloochistan, thence to the Isle of Ormuzd, and thence, after other migrations, finally to Surat. In this western corner of India they were hospitably received by the Hindoos, and here they have continued to dwell, and prosper notwithstanding both the Mahometan or English conquests of the country. At this moment they form a large community of wealthy and beneficent merchants, still retaining their ancient faith and peculiar rites; and to their munificence we are chiefly indebted for the most valuable recent editions and translations of their sacred books.

Very worthy of attentive study is assuredly the condition of a people possessing such a history. The Jewish race, existing in banishment for eighteen centuries, has been continually pointed at as a "standing miracle." But, not to speak of the Gipsies, the Parsees of India offer a still more singular spectacle, inasmuch as their numbers have always been a mere handful compared to the Jews; and during the ages of exile in which they have sustained their nationality they have exhibited a spirit of concession towards the customs of their neighbours, which has left the actual dogmas of their religion the sole bond of their national integrity.

They worshipped the One good God under the law of Zoroaster—three, four, perchance five—millenniums ago; and they worship Him still, although a mere remnant of a race, dwelling in the midst of idolaters, and having no distinctive rites, like circumcision; no haughty disdain of "Gentile" nations; no belief in a restoration to their own land on earth, or to exclusive salvation in the world to come. Their priests have been illiterate and despised; their sacred books have twice become obsolete in language and incomprehensible both to clergy and laity; their Prophet has faded away almost into an abstraction;—but the faith in Ahura-Mazda, the "Wise Creator," the "Rich in Love," remains as clear to-day as when it shone upon the Bactrian plains in the morning of the world. Nay more. The special moral virtues which are found inculcated in the earliest fragments of the Zend Avesta, and which Greek historians 2000 years ago remarked as especially characteristic of the Persians of the age of Cyrus, are even now markedly exhibited by the remnant of their descendants. These virtues, namely, truth, chastity, industry, and universal beneficence, are as notoriously deficient among the Hindoos with whom they have been mixed so long, as they are common among the Parsees. The adherence to truth and purity in the three forms to which their prayers and confessions always refer "of thought, of word, of deed," is really the practice of the race. Monogamy has been their law from the earliest times. "An unchaste woman is almost unknown among them;"* and it is a curious evidence of the confidence of their enemies in the virtue of the conquered race, that, in the gardens adjoining the harem of the Shah of Persia, Zoroastrians alone are permitted to labour, and are sought out among the poor remnant of Guebres for that employment. As to Industry, also, the lessons of Zoroaster have proved no less ineffaceable. "Centuries of contact with a weak and idle race have not exercised any perceptible influence upon the habits for which the ancestors of the Parsees were remarkable. The Zoroastrian is taught by his religion to earn his bread in the sweat of his brow, whereas the Moslem (and Hindoo) is taught to believe that he will be the favoured of God by becoming a fakir and living on alms." Even the physical result of such good training is stereotyped. "Centuries of oppression have not been able to destroy the strong, muscular, and hardy appearance of the Zoroastrian. He is greatly superior in strength to the modern effeminate and luxurious Persian."† Even as we write, the *Times* newspaper is recording the rich harvests of Parsee industry and commerce. Out of the 150,000 souls whom the community at the utmost can number (including the miserably oppressed Guebres of Persia), the *Times* avers there are five or six Parsees actual millionnaires, and many more possessed of enormous wealth. Such a thing as a

* *The Parsees*, by Dosabhoy Framjee. † Ibid.

Parsee pauper is unknown in Bombay. Finally as to Beneficence; the splendid charities of the Parsees probably outvie those of any people in the world. In the vast accession of wealth now flowing to their coffers through the cotton trade, we are told, immense sums are always set apart for charity. Even Mr Peabody's donation of £100,000 to the London poor (the largest, so far as we know, ever made in Christendom by a private person in his lifetime) looks small beside the £700,000 given away by Sir Jamsetjee Jeejeebhoy in charities of every kind, to men of every race and religion.*

The customs of the Parsees are singular, but not in any degree offensive or immoral like those of the Hindoos. The services of their fire temples are solemn and harmless, if they have become unmeaning. The ceremonies of purification, if extravagant, and, to our thinking, rather tending against cleanliness and delicacy than in their favour, are at least no worse than those of other Eastern nations, and are also rapidly falling into desuetude. Their practice of placing the dead in Towers of Silence apart from their cities, where the birds of prey devour the corpses in a few hours and remove all chance of noxious effluvia, may be defended on more grounds than one. Too early marriages and too close inter-

* The Committee of the Bombay District Benevolent Society in one of their Reports say, "Not one beggar of the Parsee caste has ever applied to his Society, for relief, nor is a Parsee pauper ever to be seen in our streets."

marriages seem to be the chief errors among their practices, and these are rapidly giving way before the influence of English ideas, to which the Parsees, more than any other people, show themselves accessible. On the whole, we may truly say that no nation deserve better that we should regard their religion with respect, and examine its sacred literature with interest, than the 120,000 Parsees of India,—the remnant of the once imperial race of Cyrus and Darius.

The manner in which our knowledge of the Parsee religion and of the books of the Zend Avesta has been obtained is not a little singular. A very brief sketch of the story must suffice.

In A.D. 1700 Hyde published his book "*Veterum Persarum et Magorum Religionis Historica.*" He drew his information from all available Classical resources, but though possessing Zend MSS. which had been brought some time previously to England, he was unable to decipher them. One such MS., however, falling, in 1754, into the hands of a young Frenchman, named Anquetil du Perron, he formed the heroic resolution of travelling to India to acquire both the language and the complete MSS. of the Zend Avesta. He actually enlisted as a private soldier in the Indian service on purpose to be conveyed to the scene of his intended labours, which he had no other means to reach. The French government, however, touched by his enthusiasm, set him free and gave him passage to India, with a pension of 500 francs. Du Perron returned to Paris in 1762, and deposited in the Royal Library a complete set of Zend MSS., with a multitude of notes and translations, still known there as "les brouillons d'Anquetil." In 1771 he published in French, in three quarto vols., a translation of the entire Zend Avesta and *Bundehesch*, together with a memoir of his discoveries.

This great work, so gallantly achieved, had its faults. Very imperfectly did the Parsee priests who taught Anquetil understand their own records; the more ancient and valuable they were the less they understood them. Neither Anquetil nor his instructors seem to have had any knowledge of the grammar of the language, and therefore at best translated very vaguely and by guess-work. Still, so far as in him lay, he accomplished his task with entire honesty of purpose. But that a Frenchman should have achieved such a task, and should have presumed also to sneer at Oxford scholars for possessing MSS. they could not decipher, was a matter not to be tolerated by English 18th-century feelings. Accordingly a chorus of abuse fell on du Perron,—Sir William Jones being the corypheus, and proving to his own satisfaction and that of his countrymen that the Zend Avesta of Anquetil was not the Zend Avesta at all, but an impudent forgery! German critics were not so short-sighted. Still they, and all European scholars, had made up their minds that in the writings of Zoroaster the deepest of all human wisdom would be found (they had not yet emerged from the superstition that the ages of light are behind us, and not before), and universal disappointment with the Zend Avesta was the result. Immanuel Kant settled its claims to attention by observing that there was not "the slightest trace of a philosophical idea in it from beginning to end!" The hope that the distinction between Reason and Understanding, the doctrine of intuitions *à priori*, "categoric imperatives," and the distinction of the "Homo noumenon," and the "Homo phenomenon," might have been found in a book dating 1000 B.C., was somewhat chimerical indeed. Perhaps had he gone to the study with different expectations he would have found ideas both moral and theological not unworthy of his respect.

Since the days of Anquetil a series of scholars have applied themselves to the study of Zend and its literature. Chief among them stands Eugène Burnouf, the real founder of Zend philology.* After him followed Olshausen, Bopp, Müller, Brockhaus, Westergaard, Spiegel, Lassen, and Haug, all of whom have contributed to bring our knowledge of the subject to a point very far in advance of that in which it was left by the brave but incomplete effort of Anquetil du Perron. We now possess,

* He laboured from 1829 to 1852. His "Commentaire sur le Yasna," 4to, Paris, 1833, is the foundation of all accurate Zend studies.

as the result of their labours, editions and translations of all parts of the Zend Avesta, with learned dissertations on the language, grammar, theology, and ceremonies of the Parsees. It is however greatly to be regretted that of these later translations, those professedly made in English are written by Germans whose acquaintance with our language is so imperfect that, between the original obscurity of the text, and the utter confusion of the construction of the English sentences, it is barely possible often to extract the sense of any passage for a page together. As to receiving any impression of sublimity from such writing it is wholly out of question.

The name *Zend Avesta* applied to the sacred writings of the Zoroastrians involves a little obscurity, arising partly from a popular misconception by which the word "Zend" has been commonly applied to the *language* in which they are composed. The AVESTA, in fact, signifies the most ancient and venerable texts, and to them and the original language in which they are still extant the word "Avestan" (as Prof. Whitney remarks) ought, if possible, to be confined. The term ZEND properly means a Commentary or Interpretation, and it appears that at a very early period this was added (doubtless in the original language) to the Avesta. Again, the priests, at the great revival of the Sassanian period, translated this Zend or Commentary into Pehlevi, a language which till lately was sup posed to have been at that period the vernacular of Persia, but which recent scholarship seems to prove a wholly fictitious tongue, curiously compounded from the Arabic and other sources, by the priests who used it as a secret medium for their instructions. This Pehlevi translation of the Zend or Commentary, we now possess. Lastly, portions of the Scriptures, still deemed canonical, are entitled Pa-zend, being the Interpretation *of* the Interpretation. These are in a more modern but still archaic language called the Parsî. A period of a thousand years, from B.C. 1300 to B.C. 300, is believed to have elapsed between the opening of the Zoroastrian canon and its close.

The original Zoroastrian books were very numerous, consisting of 21 Nosks, each containing text and commentary. Of these Nosks the names and subjects are all that is preserved, save the one entitled *Vendidad*, and possibly (though this is uncertain) some of the other books now recognized in the Canon under different names. Among these latter canonical writings are two books, the *Izeschné* or *Yasna*, and *Visparad*, the former being of higher antiquity and greater authority than any other of the sacred writings, and bearing to them about the same relation which the Vedas do to the Shastras and Puranas, and the Pentateuch, in the opinion of the Jews, to the later prophets and the Talmud.*

* See Haug's Essays, p. 128.

The existing Zoroastrian books are as follows: 1. The Yasna or Izeschné, divided into two main parts, and into 72 Hâs, or Sections. The second and elder part is the most ancient and venerable portion of the whole Zoroastrian canon, and contains the five Gâthas, or Songs in metre in the old Avestan language, plausibly attributed by Haug to Zoroaster himself and his immediate disciples. The name "Yasna" signifies "offering," and the character of the book generally, is that of a Ritual corresponding to the earliest Vedic hymns. Both the succeeding sacred books, the Visparad and Vendidad, speak of the Gâthas in the Yasna as the most venerable prayers; thus affording evidence that, at the still remote period of the latter compositions, the Gâthas possessed the rank of sacred antiquity.

2. The Visparad, containing 23 *Kardes,* or sections. The word Visparad is variously interpreted by Haug, Spiegel, and Whitney, as "all heads," "all Lords," or "Dispersed," the meaning being understood to be invocations, or a collection of prayers in chapters. The Visparad is a short book much resembling the latter part of the Yasna.

3. The Vendidad, consisting of 22 *Fargards,* or chapters. This book was the 20th among the 21 Nosks of the ancient Zend Avesta, and is the only one which has been preserved entire. It forms the religious and civil code of the ancient Zoroastrians, and evidently has been the growth of many centuries, beginning, perhaps, at the age of the prophet

himself, and descending to the Sassanian period. The regular series of Avesta, Zend, and Pa-zend (or text, interpretation, and interpretation of interpretation) may be traced throughout the work.

These three books, the Yasna, Visparad, and Vendidad, are joined together to form the VENDIDAD SÂDE, or Liturgy—the chapters of each of the three books being interlarded in a certain fixed manner, and the whole being a sort of breviary which the priests are supposed to repeat every 24 hours, and which they are especially required to use at all the sacred ceremonies of their religion.

4. The YASHTS, or 24 hymns in praise of as many beings, honoured in the Zoroastrian theology. "They are," says Haug, "to be traced to the songs of the Median bards mentioned by Greek historians, and are the primary sources of the legends of the Shahnameh. The word Yasht signifies "prayers" —worship. These, with the succeeding books, form what is called the Khordah Avesta, or Little Avesta, especially designed for the laity.

5. NYÂYISH, five prayers and praises to be repeated every day by each Parsee.

6. AFRIGANS, blessings to be recited by the priests over certain feasts in honour of the dead or the angels.

7. GÂHS or GÂTHAS. These are the five most ancient and sacred pieces already mentioned as embodied in the Yasna.

8. SIROZAH. A species of calendar enumerating

the 30 divine beings presiding over the 30 days of the month.

9. PATET. These are confessions of sin, written in Parsee, with occasional passages of Zend. They are probably more modern than the other books, but in a religious point of view are perhaps the most remarkable of all.

10. NIKAH. The marriage service of the Parsees.

11. AFERÎNS. Two invocations to Ormuzd and the Amshaspands.

12. Prayers on various occasions.

These books together form the whole Zend Avesta. There are, however, two other books belonging to the Parsee sacred literature, though not to the Canon. The first and most interesting is the BUNDEHESCH or Cosmogony of the Zoroastrians, a work to which Haug (Essays, p. 29) attributes an antiquity as high as the 4th century B.C. The resemblance of the legends in this book, as translated by Anquetil du Perron, to the earliest Hebrew histories of the Fall and the accounts of the Temptation in the wilderness, is most remarkable. Westergaard has published an edition of the work in the original Pehlevi for the advantage of scholars, and Haug has added an Essay, "Ueber die Pehlewi sprache, und der Bundehesch." The last book of all is the MINOKHIRED, a small theological treatise of no great account, in the Parsî language.

Regarding the MSS. of the Zoroastrian books from which modern scholars have derived their texts, the amplest information is supplied in the Preface to Westergaard's "Zend Avesta." He says in conclusion, "It will appear that I suppose, firstly, that the most essential part of the Zend Avesta dates from an age anterior to the Achæmenians; secondly, that at the time of the first Sassanians, the then extant remains were collected with fairness and honesty as they were found, and digested into the different writings which still exist, and perhaps in others now lost; thirdly, that though the existing copies are modern, yet their transcribers have sought faithfully to re-produce their original, and that all our copies come to us from Eastern Persia, and descend through different lines from the same archetype, a transcript of the Sassanian codex."*

The contents of these books, venerable at once from their antiquity and from the share they have had in perpetuating a religion of high moral excellence, is at first sight somewhat disappointing. If, as Whitney remarks,† we were to study the records of primeval thought and culture, to learn religion or philosophy, or to have our hearts touched and swayed by the power of poetic fancies, we should find little in the Zend Avesta to meet our purpose. Such however is not the point of view from which the value of the reco-

* Westergaard's Zend Avesta, vol. i., Preface, p. 22.

† Essay on the Avesta in Journal of the American Oriental Society.

very of these books can be estimated. We go to them to read the early history of the human race; to trace out the efforts of man to comprehend the universe; nay, we may rather say, to behold with reverence some of the first rays of the Light which lighteth every man that is born into the world, one of the dawning gleams of that eternal revelation "which shineth more and more unto the perfect day."

It would be vain in a brief article like the present to attempt to give any satisfactory summary of the contents of the Zend Avesta; I shall only cite as specimens a few passages which for moral or theological reasons may be considered most interesting. Beside these, and passages of the same class, there is an immense portion of the Canon occupied by repetitions of formulæ of praise, and by ceremonial legislation of a kind similar to that of Leviticus and Deuteronomy; the laws concerning women, purification, and clean and unclean food, being indeed nearly identical in the Jewish and Zoroastrian Scriptures. Many of these repetitions are wearisome and childish, and whole chapters would probably appear to the last degree tedious, even if we possessed them in the clearest and best language. Distorted as they actually are by Haug and by Spiegel's translator, Bleeck, into the most crabbed English imaginable, the reader is to be pardoned if he throw down the book in disgust and treat the existence of eloquence and wisdom in the Zend Avesta as an invention of enthusiastic students. Nevertheless, the few passages I shall now proceed to quote are fair specimens of no inconsiderable portion of the work. It will be understood that in selecting them I have been guided partly by their intrinsic merit, but chiefly by their use as forming together a general outline of Zoroastrian theology.

The Parsee "Confession of Faith" in its simple shape is to be found in the last chapter of the Khordah Avesta (lxvi.). It is almost as concise as the famous symbol of Islam.

"The good, true, and righteous religion which the Lord has sent to His creatures is that which Zarathustra has brought. That religion is the religion of Ahura-Mazda given to Zarathustra."

Ahura-Mazda (Ormuzd), the God of this faith, is thus described in the Ormuzd-yasht in the Khordah Avesta.

"Then spake Zarathustra. Tell me then the name, O pure Ahura-Mazda, which is Thy greatest, best, and fairest name?

"Then answered Ahura-Mazda: My name is He who may be questioned: the Gatherer of the people: the Most Pure: He who takes account of the actions of men. My name is God (Ahura), my name is the Great Wise One (Mazda). I am the All-beholding, the Desirer of Good for my creatures; He who cannot be deceived; the Protector, the

Tormentor of tormentors; He who smiteth once; the Creator of all."

In other passages God is described as "the Omniscient, the Lord over all lords, the Forgiving, the Rich in Love." (*Khordah Avesta,* vii.) I cannot discover any passage in which the noblest of all His titles, "Father," is attributed to God, but His character is conceived of as completely paternal, beneficent, and forgiving. No images of Him or of any of His ministering spirits have ever been used by Zoroastrians, who treat idolatry as a heinous crime. Nevertheless, the sun and fire (as is well known) are reckoned by them in a peculiar sense His emblems,—a sense defined in one remarkable passage of the Zend Avesta, where Ahura-Mazda is represented as saying, "My light is hidden under all that shines."

Beside Ahura-Mazda the Zoroastrian creed admits of no God, although it ordains a worship of *dulia,* very similar to Romish hagiolatry, towards a number of beings conceived of as the archangels and ministers of God presiding over various departments of creation. It is however a very interesting discovery, that in the early ages of the religion and under the teaching of Zoroaster himself, the subordinate ministers who occupy a place in the later theology were only described as various forms of action of Ahura-Mazda himself. In the Gâtha Spenta-Mainyus (*Yasna* 47) there is a passage which clearly proves this fact, and, by a happy coincidence, bears internal evidence at the same time to its own extreme antiquity. The passage can only have been composed at the period of the primeval Aryan schism when the agriculturist Zoroastrians were still vexed by the inroads of the nomad Brahmins, and when the use of the Brahminic intoxicating Soma was the object of Zoroaster's denunciations. The passages are very obscure, but may be thus read: (47, 1), "Ahura-Mazda gives by His holy spirit, through good thought, good word, and good deed,—health and immortality, prosperity and piety, to the world. From Ahura-Mazda's holiest spirit all good has sprung, from the words of Vohûmanô, and the works wrought by Armaiti. He who in His wisdom created both the Good and the Negative mind, rewards His obedient followers. Art thou not He, O Mazda, *in whom the last cause of both minds is hidden?*" (48, 4), "When will appear, thou wise God! the men of courage to pollute that intoxicating liquor which makes proud the priests of the idols? Such men as cause mischief to the farmers, and are devoid of all good works, *produce the devas* by the means of their pernicious thoughts."

In the first of these verses the words translated Health and Immortality, Prosperity and Piety, are respectively Haurvatât and Ameretât, Khshathra and Armaiti. They are all among the seven great Amshaspands or archangels, who became the Æons of the Gnostics; the "seven spirits" of the Apocalypse. The precise character of the two first seems to vary considerably, as sometimes they are represented as the presiding angels of the waters and the woods, and sometimes as "those two great powers" Health and Immortality. *Armaiti*, again, is sometimes the Spirit of the earth; sometimes Piety; sometimes Wisdom the daughter of God,—in a word, the *Sophia* of the Solomonic books and primitive Christians. *Vohûmanô*, the Good Mind, is a most singular metaphysical conception. In each rational being, from Ahura-Mazda down to men, there is, according to Zoroaster (and we may add, no less according to Emanuel Kant!), a good and holy Will, a *positive* will of righteousness. The shadow of this good mind is its negation, the *naught* (or negative) mind, as Haug quaintly translates it,—the *Homo phenomenon*, as Kant would have it, the Lower Nature blindly following its instincts and incapable of moral choice. In the earliest stage of Zoroastrianism, whose relics we are now considering in the Gâthas, these positive and negative poles of the moral world were both included in the idea of Deity, without apparently producing any difficulty in the conception of the absolute goodness of Ahura-Mazda. In later ages the Naught mind, Angro-Mainyus (Ahrimanes) became a positively evil being, introducing all pain and sin into the world in opposition to Ahura-Mazda, whose servants were called on to oppose the demon and destroy his works and creatures with all their strength, and thereby hasten the final consummation when Angro-Mainyus should be subdued and reconciled. When this idea of the personality of Ahriman and his independence, had been followed out to the utmost, the discrepancy of such a doctrine with pure Monotheism was perceived, and an effort was made, at the Sassanian Revival, by one party of Zoroastrians to repair the breach by introducing the doctrine of an eternal Being (Zeruane Akerene—Time-without-Bounds), as the First Cause of both Ormuzd and Ahrimanes. Modern Parsee Dustoors still explain some passages of the Zend Avesta as teaching the existence of Zeruane Akerene, but the European scholars, who have at last reduced the Zend grammar to some degree of clearness, have demonstrated that the whole idea is founded on a mistake in the case of the name, and is essentially foreign to the theology of the Zoroastrian Scriptures. Ahura-Mazda exists *in* boundless time. No eternal existence is imagined beside and above Ahura-Mazda.

A doctrine logically connected with the conception of evil as the negative power in all minds is that which may be traced in the last of the verses quoted above (*Yasna* 48, 4). The Brahminic marauders "devoid of all good works" are said to "*produce the devas by their pernicious thoughts.*" In later passages of the Zend Avesta evil-doers are continually described as "nourishing devas" and becoming themselves devas after death. Such a doctrine is obviously of a higher moral and philosophic character than that of the existence of beings "created evil, for evil only good," luring by their wiles innocent souls to perdition. Vohûmanô, the Good Mind, and Akômanô, the Negative Mind, indifferent to good, leading men through passion and interest down to one evil after another till they become apparently all evil, and Vohûmanô's higher influence seems lost—is a picture of the moral life hardly to be called mythical. It is, rather, as clear a description of the actual fact as language may permit. When the system of angels and demons became developed in Zoroastrianism, Akômanô was made the second of the seven Arch-demons (Angro-Mainyus, Ahrimanes, being the first), which corresponded with the seven Amshaspands or Archangels. But in Zoroaster's own theology, and even so far as may be traced down to the period of the cuneiform inscriptions of Darius, Evil was not thus definitely personified, but described as *Drukhs*, "destruction," "falsehood," against which Ormuzd and all good men contend.

The service of Ahura-Mazda consists essentially in good works, in the cheerful and industrious performance of duty; in purity, truth, beneficence,—in a word, in all possible contributions to the welfare and happiness of His creatures. The Zoroastrian is required to practise agriculture or some other useful art. He is to marry but one wife only,—if possible a near relation. The girl who at eighteen refuses to marry is threatened with an abode in Douzakh (hell) till the resurrection! Fasting is forbidden as a culpable weakening of "the powers entrusted to a man for the service of Ormuzd." He must be kind and merciful to all *good* animals, who are the creatures of Ormuzd; but noxious beasts and insects are creatures of Ahrimanes, and he performs a good act in destroying them; indeed, by such means can expiate some of his own sins.*

* The laws concerning dogs in the Vendidad are most curious, and, as Spiegel remarks, instead of deserving the scorn of Sir William Jones, serve to prove the extreme antiquity of the Zend Avesta and the care taken by the wise legislator to protect animals whose domestication was the indispensable prelude to agricultural civilization. In the 13th Fargard of the Vendidad, wounds to dogs of various degrees of value are ordered to be atoned for by lashes varying from 500 to 800, and giving bad food to such dogs by lashes from 50 to 200. The tenderness of the lawgiver is illustrated very quaintly by the following passage: v. 75. Ahura-Mazda says, "For in the corporeal world decay most swiftly approaches those creatures, the dogs, O holy Zarathustra, who find themselves along with those who eat without receiving anything to eat! Before the dogs who watch and nothing comes, shall they place milk and fat along with meat, as the proper nourishment for a dog. The dog have I made, O Zarathustra, with his own clothing and his own shoes, with keen scent and sharp teeth, faithful to men as a protection to folds,—for I have made the dog, I who am Ahura-Mazda." A dog has eight characters: one like an Athrava, one like a warrior, one like a husbandman, one like a villager, one like a thief, one like a wild beast, one like a courtesan, one like a child. "Creator (Zarathustra inquires), when a dog dies where does his spirit go? Then answered Ahura-Mazda, To the dwelling in the water goes he, O holy Zarathustra. There come together to him two water-dogs, which consist of a thousand male and a thousand female dogs." (This refers to an extraordinary idea that the Udra, translated "water-dog,"—perhaps the otter or beaver,—is the incarnation of a thousand dogs.) For killing an Udra the expiation appointed in the 14th Fargard is too enormous to be ever fulfilled, so the

The observation has been frequently made that the existence of a peculiarly rich vocabulary touching a particular subject in any language, is evidence of that subject having held a prominent place in the life of the nation using such language. Judging by this principle, the importance of morals among the Zoroastrians is very evident. In no other tongue (so far as we know) have all the different classes of human sins been similarly catalogued and named; nearly every shade of guilt having its peculiar title in the list of offences. We read, for instance, in the *Patet Aderbat* in the Khordah Avesta (written in Parsî), confessions for "the sins which burden the conscience, the sin Handrakhta, the sin Agereft, the sin Avoirist, the sin Yatu," and a dozen more which are explained to signify the sin of "seeing evil and not warning him who does it," the sin of teaching lying and doubts of the good, the sin of not giving alms, the sin of turning from repentance, the sin of afflicting a good man, the sin of saying there is no God, &c. Throughout these classifications also it is remarkable how large a place is taken by sins of omission, many of which are accounted as "the sin Margerzân," i. e. "worthy of death." The sins called "sins of the bridge," i. e. sins which hinder souls guilty of them from passing over the bridge Chinavat on the way to Paradise, are all sins of omis-

soul of the slayer is hopelessly consigned to Douzakh! It is curious that the name of an otter in Welsh is Y Dwfr-gi (Durgy, a water-dog).

sion. Again, there is in the same liturgical service an enumeration of sins described according to the persons against whom they have been committed. "Of the sins against father, mother, brother, sister, wife, child, against neighbours, fellow-townsmen, superiors, equals, servants,—of these sins I repent with thought, words, and works. Pardon them, O Lord, according to my repentance." In a further part of the same prayer there is an immense enumeration of possible transgressions, including "Pride, covetousness of goods, covetousness of another's wife, slandering the dead, anger, envy, discontent with the arrangements of God, sloth, scorn, false-witness," &c. &c.

It is impossible to read this remarkable Confession without being struck by its moral excellence. We find indeed occasional intrusions of the ceremonial spirit,—as when the omission to wear the sacred girdle, or the neglect of the midday prayer, is numbered along with the gravest transgressions. The share of these observances in Zoroastrian ethics is however probably inferior to that which they held in any other religion of antiquity. In the Hindoo law (Institutes of Menu), eating with unwashed hands and "slaying the inhabitants of the three worlds" are two sins of equal magnitude; and even Mosaism made the breach of the sabbath an offence legally punishable with death. But among the Zoroastrians, homicide seems to be too tremendous an offence to be expiated, and the omission of the great midday prayer and use of the distinctive girdle of religious membership (equivalent to Jewish sabbath-breaking and neglect of circumcision) are almost the only ceremonial faults among the hundred moral transgressions signalized.

It would be hard to imagine a more comprehensive form of confession than the following: "That which was the wish of Ahura-Mazda and I ought to have thought and have not thought, that which I ought to have spoken and have not spoken, that which I ought to have done and have not done,—of these sins I repent with thoughts, words, and works, corporeal as well as spiritual, earthly as well as heavenly. Pardon me, O Lord; I repent of my sins. That which was the wish of Ahrimanes and I ought not to have thought and yet have thought, that which I ought not to have spoken and yet have spoken, that which I ought not to have done and yet have done,—of these sins I repent with thoughts, words, and works, corporeal as well as spiritual, earthly as well as heavenly. Pardon me, O Lord; I repent of my sins." With these confessions are joined always resolutions of virtue of a singularly healthful sort: "I remain standing fast in the statutes of the law which Ormuzd gave to Zarathustra. As long as life endures I will stand fast in good thoughts in my soul, in good words in my speech, in good deeds in my actions. With all good am I in agreement, with all evil am I at variance. With the punishments (of the future life) am I contented and satisfied. I have taken hold of good thoughts, words, and works. I have renounced evil thoughts, words, and works. May the power of Ahriman be broken! may the reign of Ahura-Mazda increase!" (*Patet Aderbat*). Again in *Patet Erâni* (Khordah Avesta, xlvii.): "I am steadfast in this faith (in the pure Mazdayasnian law), and turn myself not away from it, for the sake of a happy life, or for the sake of a longer life, nor for power, nor for a kingdom. If I must give up my body for the sake of my soul I give it contentedly. I believe steadfastly in the good Mazdayasnian faith; in the Resurrection; in the bridge of souls; in the invariable reward of good deeds and punishment of bad deeds, in the everlasting continuance of paradise and the annihilation of hell; and I believe that at the last Ahura-Mazda will be victorious, and Ahrimanes will perish with the Devs and all the children of darkness." . . . "I am full of hope that I may attain to paradise and the shining Garathôman where all majesty dwelleth. I make this confession in the hope that I may hereafter become more zealous to accomplish good works and keep myself more from sin; and that my good deeds may serve for the lessening evil and the increase of good till the resurrection."

In this last passage, as in many others of the Zend Avesta, we find traces of the noble doctrine that individual virtue is not alone the gain of the soul which possesses it, but an addition to the whole power of good in the universe. In the Zoroastrian creed all beings are ranged on the side either of Ahura-Mazda or Ahrimanes; the good of one is the good of all, the sin of one the source of evil to all. There is a universal *solidaritary of souls.* Perhaps it would be hard to overrate the value of this doctrine in a moral point of view. The old Rabbins said, "Prayers which say nothing concerning the Kingdom do not deserve the name of prayers;"* and truly till a man rises to a general love and desire for the reign of Goodness transcending the limits of his own personal spiritual interests, he is as yet but on the threshold of religion. To desire, to strive, to pray that Right should be for ever victorious; that truth and justice and purity should prevail over the earth, and "love at length be Lord of all;" to contemplate God as the King of Righteousness, under whose banner we fight in all the inner and outer battles of the soul, and to care for victory in that dread warfare not merely for our own moral progress or happiness, but for the simple *good* itself, and that Right should be done rather than Wrong,—this and this alone is religion. The man who really feels the aspiration after such universal righteousness, and labours to further it in the world, is religious in the highest sense, even if he display far less direct devotion than another who acts and prays for his own salvation only. "Thy Kingdom come" is the prayer of every true Son of

* R. Jehuda and R. Scira. Sanhedrim, fol. 28. 2.

God. That the old Zoroastrian could daily say, "May Ahura-Mazda increase! Broken be the power of Ahrimanes!" is no small evidence how far on the right way his faith had led him.

Beside the personal and social duties inculcated as the service of Ahura-Mazda, the Zoroastrian creed also requires the performance of direct religious duties, of prayer and praise, forming a cultus of no small importance. The Dustoors and Mobeds (bishops and priests) are required to read the whole liturgy of the Vendidad Sadê in these services and to go through various rites of a sacramental character, in which the Barsom-branch and Homa-juice figure as well as the sacred Fire. The laity for whose use the Kkordah Avesta is assigned, repeat certain prayers at appointed seasons (including the confessions already quoted), wear a woven girdle called Kosti as a sign of religious membership, and are exhorted to address Ahura-Mazda with entreaties for help on all occasions, and to praise the angelic spirits and invoke speedy ruin on Ahrimanes and all his works. Phrases equivalent to "Thy kingdom come,"—or "May Ahura-Mazda increase! Broken be Ahrimanes,"—begin nearly every action of the pious Zoroastrian's life. Among the prayers so ordered are some frequently mentioned in the earliest books of the Zend Avesta, perpetually repeated in the ritual and assigned by tradition to the direct teaching of Ahura-Mazda to Zoroaster. The first of these (hardly to be called a prayer so much as a moral aphorism) is the Ashem-vohû or Asha Vahista. It is very obscure from its immense antiquity, but seems to mean somewhat as follows:

> "Purity is the highest good,
> Happiness is for him whose purity is most pure."

The second great prayer is the Yathâ ah Vairyo, or Ahuna Vairya:

> "The will of the Lord the pure Ruler:
> He who doeth the works of Ahura-Mazda shall receive the gift of Vohumano,
> And the kingdom we give to Ahura-Mazda when we offer succour to the poor."

If this latter prayer be truly rendered, the meaning is indeed sublime. Vohûmanô,—the *mens conscia recti*, the joy of a virtuous mind,—belongs to him who doeth the will of God, and this will is, that we succour the poor whereby His kingdom may more swiftly come.

Of other noble prayers of a later date we may quote the following:

(*Khordah Avesta* vii., *Qarset, Nyâyis* (Spiegel, p. 6.) "In the name of God I praise and exalt Thee, the Creator Ormuzd, the Brilliant, Majestic, Omniscient, the Perfecter of deeds, the Lord of lords, the Prince over all princes, the Protector, the Creator of all created beings, the Giver of daily food, the Powerful, the Good, the Strong, the Ancient, the Forgiving, the Rich in Love, Mighty and Wise, the Upholder of Purity. May Thy right rule be without ceasing, O Ormuzd, King! Of all my sins I repent with contrition. For all evil thoughts, words, and works, which I have thought, spoken, and done in the world, which I have committed, which cleave to my nature, for all sinful thoughts, words, and works, bodily or mental, I pray, O Lord, for forgiveness, and repent of them." (XI.): "Purify me, O God! Give me strength through Armaiti (the spirit of piety). Holiest, heavenly Mazda! give me in Thy goodness at my prayer, strong power and fulness of blessings, through Vohûmanô. Give me certainty that I may teach afar Thy joy, and the blessings of Thy kingdom." (XIV.): "In the name of God the Giver and Forgiver, Rich in Love, praise be to Ahura-Mazda, the God with the name: 'Who always was, always is, and always will be.' Ahura-Mazda the Wise, the Creator, the Over-seeing God, pure, good, and just! With all strength bring I thank-offerings and praise to the Lord, the completer of good works, who made men greater than all earthly beings, and through the gift of speech created them to rule over the creatures and to war against the evil spirits. Praise to the omniscience of God who hath sent through the holy Zarathustra, peace and knowledge of the law. All good do I accept at thy command, O God, and think, speak, and do it. I believe in the pure law, and by every good work I seek forgiveness for sins. I keep pure the six powers,—thought, speech, act, memory, reason, and understanding. According to Thy will am I able to fulfil (these resolutions),

O Accomplisher of good, to Thy honour, even good thoughts, good words, and good works. I enter on the shining way to paradise. May the fearful terror of hell not overcome me! May I pass the bridge Chinavat and attain to paradise, the bright and odoriferous, where are all joys. Praise to the Lord who rewards those who accomplish good deeds according to His will, who purifies the obedient, and at last purifies even the wicked in hell. All praise be to the Creator, Ahura-Mazda, the All-wise, the Mighty, the Rich in Love."

The idea of the value of prayer is beautifully set forth in a fragment of the *Khordah Avesta*, xxxvii. (Spiegel, p. 135). Zoroaster asks Ahura-Mazda in succession which is the prayer which in greatness outweighs a hundred, a thousand, ten thousand other prayers. Ahura-Mazda names the prayer "Ashem," used after eating the sacramental Hôm, the prayer "which a man stretched out for sleep speaks waking, praising the good thoughts, words, and works, removing evil thoughts, words, works; and the prayer which a man at the latter end of his life prays with purity." Finally, Zoroaster asks which is the prayer "which in greatness, goodness, and beauty is worth all that is between heaven and earth, and this world, and those lights, and all good things created?" Ahura-Mazda answered, "That prayer, O pure Zarathustra, when a man renounces all evil thoughts, words, and works."

This sublime conception of the highest prayer,

as the renunciation of all evil, the resolution of all good,—in a word, of perfect moral unity with the Holiest Will, is traceable through many portions of the Zend Avesta. Its most remarkable expression, perhaps, is that which occurs in the 56th Hâ of the Yasna, "To arrive at prayer is *to arrive at a perfect conscience*. The good seed of prayer is virtuous conscience, virtuous words, and virtuous deeds."*

A considerable portion of the Yasna is taken up by what may be termed "Psalms of Praise," bearing a strong analogy to the "Song of the Three Children"—all nature and angelic beings being called into the act of adoration. The difference between the Hebrew and Zoroastrian hymns is, that the Hebrew calls on all things to praise God, the Zoroastrian praises all things good and beautiful as the works of God. Poetical impersonation is higher in the Hebrew mind, since inanimate things are directly invoked to "magnify the Lord." The Zoroastrian attempts no such figure of rhetoric, but frequently addresses the Spirit or Angel of the thing praised,—these ideal spirits being sometimes singularly metaphysical conceptions, as the *Fravashis*, or archetypes of souls, *Armaiti*, the spirit of piety, and so on. As a specimen of a Zoroastrian Psalm, we may take the 17th Hâ of the Yasna, briefly compressed.

* Nothing resembling this passage is to be found in Spiegel's translation of the 56th Hâ; I quote it from "*The Parsee Religion*," by DADABHOI NAOROJI.

"Ahura-Mazda, the Lord of Purity, praise we.
Zarathustra the Pure, praise we.
The Zoroastrian Law, praise we.
The good Spenta-Armaiti, praise we.
Ahura-Mazda the Creator, praise we.
The Fire, son of Ahura-Mazda, praise we.
The pure Waters, created by Ahura-Mazda, praise we.
The Sun with swift horses, praise we.
The Moon, praise we.
The star Tistrya, the shining, the majestic, praise we.
Ahura-Mazda the Creator, praise we.
The Eternal Lights, praise we.
The brilliant deeds of purity, praise we:
At which the souls of the dead rejoice:
Milk and food, the running water and the growing trees, praise we.
We praise all good men, we praise all good women.
Ahura-Mazda, lord of purity, praise we," &c. &c.

This psalm, with its species of *refrain* alternating every five or six verses the praise of Ormuzd, may well be in the original a sublime composition not wholly unworthy of comparison with the 148th Psalm. In the Gâtha Ustavaiti, again (*Yasna* 43, 46), which Haug holds to be "the most important piece of the whole Zend Avesta," containing the words of Zoroaster himself—there are passages bearing a striking similitude to portions of Job. It is impossible, however, to gain an idea of poetical sublimity from any thoughts clothed in the grotesque phrases which Bleeck and Haug print as the English language. I shall endeavour to translate their signification into words less strangely distorted.*

(*Yasna* 44, 3). "That which I ask of Thee, tell me Thou aright, O living God! Who was in the beginning the Father and Creator of Truth? Who made the way of the sun and the stars? Who causeth the moon to wax and wane?

"4. That which I ask of Thee, tell me Thou aright, O living God! Who upholdeth the earth, and the unsupported heavens so that they fall not? Who made the waters and the trees of the forest?

* As an instance both of the absurdity of this pseudo-English and also of the variations of the two translations, the following parallel of the first verses of this Gâtha may be taken as a specimen:

Haug, p. 147.	Spiegel, translation by Bleeck, p. 100.
"1. Blessed is he, blessed are all men to whom the living wise God of his own command should grant those two everlasting powers — wholesomeness and immortality." (In another passage Haug translates "wholesomeness, *or integrity*"! evidently confounding moral "wholeness" with "wholesomeness.")	"1. Hail to him who suffices for happiness to each! May Ahura create, ruling after his own wish! May power and strength (the "wholesomeness" and "immortality" of Haug!) come to me according to Thy will.
"2. I believe Thee to be the best being of all, the source of light for the world; everybody shall choose as the source of light, Thee, holiest spirit Mazda."	"2. To the man full of brightness may brightness, which is the best of all, be given. Manifest thyself, oh holiest, heavenly Mazda."

Who driveth the winds and the storms that they so quickly run?

"5. That which I ask of Thee, tell me Thou aright, O living God! Who made the beneficent light and the darkness? Who made the blessedness of sleep and of awaking? Who made the dawn and the noon and the night, recalling man to his prayer?"*

A Parsee having diligently performed his natural duties and offered to Ahura-Mazda the prayers, praises, and confessions of the Zend Avesta, has nothing to fear in the future life. No religion, perhaps, has given an idea of that unseen world so calculated to meet the requirements alike of the moral sense, which demands that eternal justice shall there be done, and of the heart which longs for the final restoration and reconciliation of all God's creatures. For ordinary sins committed in this life, the Zend Avesta, as we have seen, appoints various forms of expiation and penance, and in one remarkable passage (*Vendidad, Fargard* viii.) holds out to the believer a promise of universal "justification by faith," even for sins not thus atoneable. "For the law will take away these sins from those who praise the Mazdayasnian law; if they, here-

* Haug reads, "reminding always the priest of his duties." In the next verse to this, among other excellent things of creation, Bleeck enumerates the "*going-cow*, Thy gracious gift!" "the locomotive-cow" would not have been more absurd!

after, do not again commit wicked deeds. For this Mazdayasnian law, O holy Zarathustra, takes away the bonds from the man who praises it. It takes away deceit. It takes away murder. It takes away the unatoneable sin. It takes away all sins that man commits. Similarly, O holy Zarathustra, does the Mazdayasnian law take away all evil thoughts, words, and works as the strong swift wind clears the sky." (*Spiegel*, 73.)

Entering the future life under such conditions, the soul of the faithful Mazdayasnian is believed to pass to paradise unfailingly. The description of the journey is told with curious Eastern simplicity in chap. xxxviii. of the *Khordah Avesta* (*Spiegel*, Part 2, p. 136). "Zarathustra asked Ahura-Mazda, Heavenly, Holiest Creator! when a pure man dies where does his soul dwell during the first night? Then answered Ahura-Mazda: Near his head it sits down, praying. On this night the soul sees as much joy as the whole living world possesses. On the second night, near his head, it sits down praying. On the third night, near his head, &c." (*Verse* 7): "When the lapse of the third night turns itself to light, then the soul of the pure man goes forward. A wind blows to meet it from the south, more sweet than other winds. In that wind there comes to meet him *his own law* in the figure of a maiden beautiful and shining, as fair as the fairest of the creatures. The soul of the pure man takes the first step and arrives in the paradise Humata; he takes the second, and arrives at the paradise Hûkhta; he takes the third, and arrives at the paradise Hvarsta. The soul of the pure man then takes the fourth step and arrives at the Eternal Lights. Then speaks a pure one deceased before, How art thou, oh pure deceased, come from the perishable world hither to the imperishable? Then speaks Ahura-Mazda, Ask him not, for he is come on the fearful trembling way, the separation of soul and body. Bring him hither of the food of the full fatness that is the food for a youth who thinks, speaks, and does good—that is, the food for the woman who thinks good, speaks good, does good—the pure after death."

Precisely the converse of all this is told of the wicked soul, who meets a hideous woman and the ill-smelling wind, and who Ahrimanes receives and supplies with poison.

This same doctrine of the resurrection after three days appears in the 19*th Fargard of Vendidad*, verses 27—32.

"Creator of the fenced estates (*quære* paradises?) with living beings, Thou True! what happens when a man gives up his soul in this world of existence? (Ver. 28): Then Ahura-Mazda replied, When a man is dead, then after the third night, at daybreak he reaches Mithra, rising above the mountains resplendent with their own spotless lustre."

On more than one account this description of the "Soul's Exodus" is worthy of attention. The notion of a progressive advance to the "eternal lights;" of the welcome received from the blessed, and from the gentle words of Ahura-Mazda Himself; the conducting Angel who represents the man's own earthly faith and life (like Bunyan's "*Mr Good Conscience*" meeting old *Honesty* beside the River of Death),—all these are beautiful thoughts. In the peculiar idea of the "three nights" during which the soul sits happily by the head of the corpse, arising at "day-break," or "when the lapse of the third night turns itself to light," may possibly be found the origin of an Essene doctrine concerning the Resurrection, whose results have taken the place of one of the great dogmas of Christianity.

While the future of the good Zarathustrians is thus laid out in a swift passage to the eternal lights of Garothôman, in the paradise of majesty and purity —the immediate presence of Ahura-Mazda,—the course of the wicked soul, as we have seen, is precisely in the converse direction, to Douzakh, the dark and noisome dwelling of Angro-Mainyus and all the evil Devs. There the sinner expiates his offences in torment proportioned to their enormity, till the general day of resurrection. Three nights, often referred to as of tremendous suffering, are then endured by all who have not fully atoned for their earthly transgressions; and it is a part of every confession taught the Parsee to contemplate this punishment as a just and righteous expiation. He says in each act of contrition, "If there be sins I have not atoned for before I die, I submit myself to the chastisement of the three nights." During this period, the Blessed, beholding the pains of the wicked, will feel grief and infinite pity, which will cause them to shed tears of compassion until the three terrible days are over. Then the heat shall melt the solid mountains of the world, and streams of liquid gold shall flow down wherein the righteous and the wicked shall alike receive a baptism of regeneration. "There shall be no more curse." Ahrimanes and his angels shall be converted; Hell shall be swallowed up. All created beings shall join in the worship of Ahura-Mazda, and the "universe shall remain pure for evermore." *

This brief and popular account of recent researches in Zoroastrian lore may, I hope, induce some readers to undertake the study of the original for themselves. It will be still more fortunate if it serve to arouse some scholar competent to the task of translating it into an English version sufficiently simple and grammatical to allow its merits to be perceived. The result of such studies of the Zend Avesta will assuredly *not* be that of placing the book, in the estimation of any, on the same level with the great classics of Greece, far less with that most precious heir-loom of humanity,—the sacred literature of

* *Zemyad Yasht.* According to some passages of the Zend Avesta it would appear that Ahrimanes is to be annihilated, not reclaimed. It would rather seem however, on the collation of all the passages referring to the resurrection, that it is only *evil* itself which is to be destroyed. The restoration of all *spirits* is frequently foretold.

Palestine. It may however serve another and a nobler purpose; it may afford fresh confirmation of the truth, that the moral sense and the religious sentiment of man are in all lands and ages essentially the same, and *therefore* are no mere results of local or temporary conditions or instructions, but prove themselves the uniform Voice of One who speaks in all the hearts He has made, and is the same yesterday, to-day, and for ever, the "Wise Creator," the "Rich in Love."

THE PHILOSOPHY

OF

THE POOR-LAWS.

Reprinted from Fraser's Magazine, Sept. 1864.

THE Poor-Laws constitute an apparent anomaly in our national legislation. Other laws concern themselves solely with the class of obligations distinguished by the old moralists as *Duties of Debt.* They forbid offence against person and property, and provide for the fulfilment of legal contracts. All taxes, also, which are imposed (exclusive of poor-rates), are matters of debt—the debt understood to be owed by the taxpayer to the State, for protection and other benefits.

In the Poor-Laws, on the contrary, we find *Duties of Merit* erected into civil obligations and enforced by legal penalties. The individual is not only bound to abstain from offence against his neighbour's person and property, and forced to fulfil his legal contracts; he is called upon also to provide for his neighbour's maintenance. The taxes imposed under the poor-laws are not understood to be paid for the taxpayer's protection or benefit of any kind. but exclusively for another man's advantage.

At a hasty glance it might seem that this anomaly was an invasion by the Civil Law of a province properly belonging to the Moral Law. The concern of civil and criminal law is to forbid offence; that of the moral law, to ordain beneficent action. The civil law cannot punish a man for not being virtuous: it can only punish him for committing a crime. It cannot punish him for withholding his hand to save a drowning man: it can only punish him for thrusting him into the water. The moral law alone covers the whole field of duty, by commanding the good action, and, by such command, leaving to condemnation both the *fault* of not performing it, and the *offence* of committing the opposite evil. Thus, then, to require of a man to give alms might appear to be a matter beyond the true sphere of the civil law, and rather to be a generous homage paid by a Christian country to sentiments of humanity, than a logically defensible principle of legislation. In this light the poor-laws are probably commonly regarded; and the popular idea of them might be interpreted to be, "We are very charitable in thus providing against the starvation of any man in our country." A deeper insight into the foundations of civil rights would, however, reveal a different state of the case. Grotius's *Justitia Attributrix* of such a "Duty of Merit" as we are discussing, is as much the province of the civil law as the *Justitia Expletrix* of the simplest "Duties of Debt." The grounds on which the rights of life are founded is one thing; the grounds on which the rights of property, another. When the right to life comes into collision with the right to property, there is found no basis of morals to support property against life. A civil law which should attempt to do so, would offend against the ultimate principles of justice. To hinder the starvation of one member of the State, the property of another may lawfully be mulcted, inasmuch as his whole claim to possess any property at all is subsidiary to the starving man's right to life. If no State existed, the starving man would have the natural right of self-preservation to seize his neighbour's food,—a right only limited by his neighbour's right to keep himself also from starvation. Where the State exists, it is its duty to intervene and secure that the starving man be fed by such taxation of his neighbour as shall invade as little as possible the right of the latter to his property.

Such is the fundamental principle on which the Poor-Laws rest, so far as they may be considered as a system of enforced taxation of the rich to supply the wants of the poor. Having admitted the right of such taxation, we next proceed to inquire into the application of the money thus procured. It will be seen, from the principle of the case as above stated, that poor-rates strictly are available to relieve the absolute wants of the pauper, and nothing more. To go beyond such wants, and supply him with superfluities of any kind, would be manifest injustice to the ratepayer, forced to supply such superfluities from his own property, to which he has the better right. The question, what are wants, and what are superfluities? is, of course, a difficult one. Practically, the justice of the case may be met by the rule that nothing which the poorer ratepayers may be commonly obliged from poverty to dispense with, can be fairly supplied to the pauper with their money. His condition ought to be distinctly inferior to theirs.

Another great principle of legislation here comes into view, and very happily harmonizes and completes the abstract view of rights we have been considering. Among the benefits for which the State lawfully taxes its citizens, is not only that of civil and military protection, but the general security and well-being of the community. A large share of its revenues is employed in the prevention of crime and reformation of criminals. In a similar manner it engages properly in the effort to correct an evil only second in mischief to crime itself—namely, Pauperism. The repression of pauperism is as clearly the duty of the State as the repression of crime, seeing that pauperism is the seed-bed of crime, and is itself one of the worst evils of the social body—a *plaie saignante*, as the French politicians have well named it, which must needs be healed before sound health can be established.

The two principles of the duty of the State to enforce the supply of the wants of the poor out of the property of the rich, and of the duty of the State to repress pauperism, fortunately coincide precisely. Pauperism can no doubt best be repressed by exactly supplying the wants of the pauper, while withholding all superfluities, and making his condition undesirable, by making it inferior to that of the humblest ratepayer.

The special practical applications, then, of these two harmonious principles, are our concern. Are the wants of the pauper really supplied—and is pauperism actually in process of repression—by our existing poor-laws and their local applications in the various Unions in the country? The question is a most grave one, and has for some time occupied a share of public attention. For three sessions of Parliament, Committees have sat to inquire into the working of the poor-laws, and their report has just been published in a Bluebook of unusual clearness and interest. Whether the results to which the Committee have therein given their voices were the legitimate ones to be drawn from the evidence placed before them, we shall not here venture to inquire. It is at least startling to find that they dismissed the testimony of three such witnessess as Miss Carpenter, Miss Louisa Twining, and the Hon. Mrs Way, with the observation that, "although they expressed opinions very strongly opposed to the system of educating children in workhouses, your Committee cannot report that these opinions were supported by facts, either authenticated, or, if they had been authenticated, sufficiently numerous to justify the conclusions founded upon them." (Report, p. 73.) The evidence of Mr Carleton

Tufnell, an inspector, is put aside as similarly unworthy of attention. The reader naturally asks if these persons—ladies of the highest judgment and ability, entirely devoted to the cause of the poor, and a gentleman appointed by Government to inspect pauper-schools,—if these are witnesses whose opinions are to be passed over, along with the Committee of Education, what grounds of reliance are left to us in the selection of persons who should be more competent to offer us their testimony? We shall at present, however, merely take a general review of the existing workhouse system in England, proceeding on facts known to all who have practically interested themselves in the matter, and then, in each department, quote the observations made in the Parliamentary Report, and leave it to the reader to draw his own conclusions as to whether the reforms recommended appear in any way sufficient to cope with the evil to be remedied. Our attention will be exclusively directed to the English and Irish poor-laws, and not to the Scotch. In Scotland the old poor-law had no existence, and the abuses attending it having never arisen, it has not been found necessary to have recourse to the same severity of test of destitution either, as in England, where these abuses were excessive, or, as in Ireland, where mendicancy was rife. In Scotland, we believe, able-bodied men have no claim on relief, and children are placed out first for nursing and then for schooling. Out-door relief is given in the agricultural districts much more freely than in England; and the arrangements of the hospitals are so far better, at all events, that the doctor's salary and his medicines are not lumped together.

To return to England. The modern system of division of labour is certainly nowhere so little exemplified in this country as in the workhouse. Elsewhere, health and disease, youth and age, virtue and vice, education and ignorance, manhood and womanhood, sanity and insanity, form classifications which are rarely practically transgressed. But poverty, as the old proverb avers, seems to "make acquainted" every form of human sorrow and sin. Every large workhouse combines the following institutions:

1. A workhouse proper, or place of labour for able-bodied paupers, males.
2. Ditto for females.
3. A temporary asylum, or casual ward, for pauper travellers, males.
4. Ditto for females.
5. A hospital for the sick, curable and incurable, males.
6. Ditto for females.
7. An asylum for aged and infirm males.
8. Ditto for females.
9. A blind asylum for males.
10. Ditto for females.
11. A deaf and dumb asylum for males.
12. Ditto for females.

13. A lunatic asylum, males.
14. Ditto for females.
15. An asylum for idiots and epileptics, males.
16. Ditto for females.
17. A boys' school.
18. A girls' school.
19. An infant school.
20. A nursery for infants.
21. A lying-in hospital.
22. A Penitentiary (Black ward).*

Twenty-two institutions amalgamated in one,

* The following is an analysis of the inmates of a London workhouse, not divided as above, but giving an idea of the proportions of some of the classes :—

Persons above 90 years of age	2
Ditto between 80 and 90	43
Ditto between 70 and 80	147
Ditto between 60 and 70	152
Idiotic	17
Infants under 16	33
Blind	10
Deaf and Dumb	3
Persons under 60, sick or maimed	56
Ditto under 60, subject to fits	32
Mothers nursing their children	11
Persons under 60 of such habits or character as to preclude permanent employment	32
Persons under 60 who might possibly earn their living	48
Total	586

The law requires all violent lunatics to be sent to the county asylum within a fortnight, but the harmless remain in the workhouses, where their cost is less by half than in the asylums.

and regulated by a single board! If such a thing were heard of for the first time, and only five or six of these heterogeneous charities were lumped together, what should we think of it?—say a Boys' school, a Hospital, a Lunatic Asylum, and a Penitentiary? How absurd it would seem! How we should ask why purposes all dissimilar should be carried on under one roof, when each one of them by such an arrangement was liable to be counteracted by the others? How we should marvel at the self-confidence of the Committee who felt themselves sufficiently instructed in each department to regulate at once the instruction of the young, the ordering of an hospital, the nursing of babies, and the management of the idle and vicious! Does the undertaking, which would be so obviously monstrous if it concerned the class of persons who frequent our other hospitals and asylums and schools, become immediately easy and practicable when it refers to paupers? or is a task which the most experienced philanthropist, entirely devoted to such work, would decline as utterly unmanageable, to be performed satisfactorily by busy shopkeepers and farmers, meeting for a few hours once a week, in the not very solemn conclave of the Board-room. Elsewhere it is admitted that it is dangerous for children, who are to be trained to virtue and industry, to be brought into proximity with vice and idleness; for the sane to behold constantly the spectacle of insanity; for the healthy to be brought near the diseased and fever-stricken; for innocent girls to hear and see continually the miserable servants of sin. But, because all these conditions of humanity are, in the workhouse, lost in the one great condition of pauperism, it is thought well to jumble them all together within the same walls, whose minor partitions of wards and departments permit a tainted atmosphere, both moral and physical, to pass from one to another. Each Board, therefore, has not only the stupendous task of regulating twenty-two different kinds of charitable institutions, it has the further work of obviating the complications and needless difficulties which, in each department, are produced by the neighbourhood of the others. As in the old fable, the man has not only to carry his property across the ford, but to provide that the fox, the fowl, and the corn are not left together. Endless rules, endless iron-barred windows and padlocked gates, endless assimilations to that which, above all, a workhouse should not resemble, i. e., a jail, are obliged to be used for the purpose of keeping asunder the classes who have been first senselessly brought together. And with what success are they kept asunder? Probably that the sick either watch the insane in their sad yards, or are distracted by the sounds of the labours of the able-bodied paupers; that any epidemic which breaks out in the hospital goes through the schools; that the decent and honest ruined tradesman or governess has to spend the last years of life beside the drunkard and the profligate; and, worst of all, that the young grow up with the visible memorials of sin constantly before their eyes, and the alternative presented to their imaginations of a life of vice outside the workhouse, and a life of interminable ennui and restriction within it.*

In the case of pauper children, this evil has be-

* All these "probabilities" have been realized in the writer's experience. There is a workhouse in London she has visited where the sick could not have their windows open all the summer because carpets were beaten by the paupers in the yard below, as their regular work; another, where a smith's forge just under them made speech nearly inaudible; another (in the country), where they could never look out without seeing the insane; another (in London), where a young woman occasionally, but rarely, afflicted by fits, was shut up for life with jabbering idiots; another (in Ireland), where 400 young girls were kept together, the mothers of many of them taking them out every summer to lives of profligacy, and then sending them back to associate freely with the rest. The following is a memorandum from the writer's notes taken in another workhouse:—

"Miss M. A. K. spent all her life in England and France as a teacher of languages, but had had the misfortune to be born in Dublin, of Irish parents, long since dead. In the decline of life her sight and health failed her. She struggled on in her little lodging, translating French books when she could obtain such employment, and selling her remaining property bit by bit, till every resource was exhausted. Finally she applied to H—— Union for relief, and before she well understood what was going to be done, she was sent to Ireland, according to the Law of Settlement. I saw her among a crowd of miserable paupers, and was struck at the piteous contrast of the delicate face and figure of the poor old lady, and the degrading dress she wore. I found she was not only obliged to live, but to share her bed, with the very lowest of the community."

come so manifest, that for some years the system of District Schools, apart from the workhouse, has been in action; and the evils, again, attendant on the massing together of the numbers sent to these schools, has occupied philanthropists to discover means of more effectively effacing the pauper brand, and cutting off the entail of pauper degradation. But, in various degrees, the same arguments apply to every department of the workhouse, except its original central one—of a place of shelter and labour for able-bodied poor unable to find employment elsewhere. As a hospital, as an infirmary, as a blind, deaf and dumb, insane, and idiot asylum, as a penitentiary and lying-in hospital, there are almost insuperable objections to institutions governed as workhouses are governed, and arranged as (in a degree) workhouses must be arranged. These are grave assertions. We shall endeavour to make them good by briefly reviewing, seriatim, the different departments of which we have spoken.

1st. The Hospital. It may be considered by some economists as a doubtful question, whether free hospitals are, in any case, institutions calculated to benefit the community; whether it be desirable to obviate for the working classes the necessity for making provision for the casualty of illness, and, at the same time, to separate families under the precise circumstances wherein family affections are most drawn forth and strengthened.

This may, we say, be considered by some as an open question, albeit the common judgment of mankind has decided that such evils are subordinate to the great benefits, sanitary and economic, obtained by such institutions. No question at all, however, can exist on the further proposition, that if free hospitals be desirable in the abstract, it is desirable that they be good hospitals, i. e., calculated to fulfil their proper objects—recovery from disease, and alleviation of suffering. It would be absurd to inquire whether we ought to encourage the poor to rely on an asylum open to them in sickness, and to accustom families to place their members in such asylums, while, at the same time, no counterbalancing benefits of recovery or relief were likely to be obtained thereby. Nevertheless, so strangely have we ordered these matters in England, that two-thirds of the free hospitals in the country are wholly defective in such appliances for recovery and relief, as have been admitted on all hands, and adopted by the remaining third, as absolutely needful for such purpose.

There are in all 245 hospitals and infirmaries supported by voluntary endowments and contributions in England and Wales.

There are 664 workhouses supported by enforced rates; each containing sick, surgical, and infirm wards, constituting hospitals where the poor are admitted free of cost.

In the 245 hospitals supported by voluntary aid,

there are nearly invariably surgeons and physicians of eminence attending and consulting; there are trained and paid nurses, except where there are Sisters of Charity; there is an ample supply of drugs; there are dietaries calculated for the use of the patients in various stages of sickness. The wards are usually built with all desirable arrangements for ventilation, light, and cleanliness. The beds and other furniture are provided with a direct reference to the requirements of the sick.

If these be the fitting preparations for a Hospital, let us ask how many of them are to be found in the Workhouses?

In the first place, workhouses have usually one surgeon, and no visiting physicians; the surgeon receiving so low a salary that only a man at the outset of his profession will accept the office. 2. They have very rarely any nurses for the sick except paupers; and pauper nurses must inevitably labour under either some grievous physical or moral defect (else they would be able to obtain remunerative employment elsewhere); consequently, such nurses are nearly always either women of bad character, drunkards, half-deaf or half-blind, or incurably stupid. They have never been trained to their task; their patients, as they know, cannot pay them for their services, while they can readily punish their patients for complaints; and their usual remuneration consists in rations of beer or gin, which serve to complete the measure of their unfitness for their task.* 3. The supply of drugs in workhouses, in all save a very few Unions, is included in the surgeon's scanty salary, thereby practically excluding the use of all costly tonics and anodynes, which are precisely the medicines needed by the half-starved younger patients, and the miserable sufferers from rheumatism and cancer. 4. The dietaries in workhouses, though variable at the surgeon's order, are usually all very ill-suited to the sick, infirm, and superannuated. The staple in all cases is boiled beef, which their stomachs cannot digest; and in many workhouse kitchens there is no possibility (even if the surgeon should desire it) of dressing meat in a more wholesome way. 5. The sick wards are commonly allotted with the smallest consideration for their suitability as to light, ventilation, and warmth; some being insufferably close, and others full of draughts, causing torture to the rheumatic and consumptive patients.† The workhouses themselves being usually built in the worst districts in the towns, and the lowest and most undesirable plots in the country, the diseased have, in any case, less chance of recovery in them than elsewhere. 6. The furniture of the sick wards is commonly altogether defective. The beds are mostly the same allotted to the able-bodied paupers, and

* In 1854, out of 570 nurses in the London Unions, only 70 were paid, and 500 paupers.

† The ward in St Giles's, where Gibson died, was by no means the worst the writer has seen.

are miserably small, hard, and cold for those who must lie in them for months and years together. Being usually formed of a bag of straw or flock,* the bolster (if such exists) only keeps the patient's head on a level with his chest; and he has no means of sitting in a less distressing position. Frequently the heads of the beds are drawn away from the wall, to prevent the hair of the patients from soiling the whitewash. Besides the beds there is rarely any other furniture suitable to the wants of the sick—often not a chair in which it is possible for them to sit. 7. Lastly, the one great curative agent in disease—mental cheerfulness—is most effectually debarred from the workhouse sick-ward by the gloom of the place, the absence of all books or prints, the stringent regulations against visitors, and, too frequently also, by the harshness and rudeness of the officials. Such are the conditions of the workhouse as a hospital, as regards the surgeon, the nurses, the drugs, the diet, the wards, the furniture, and the moral state of the patients.

Now, if this statement of the case be verified, the logic of our existing workhouse arrangements will appear somewhat questionable. We expend vast sums in our hospitals supported by voluntary

* Miss Nightingale tells us that straw should never be used as a bed for the sick. "In some cases," she says, "the abstraction of heat from the spine lowers the patient's vital energy to a degree which does not leave him a chance of recovery."—*Notes on Nursing.*

contributions, assuming that it is needful that the patients be treated in such and such ways, and, of course, limiting narrowly the number of such patients by the costliness of such arrangements. Then, when we come to determine the manner in which hospitals supported by enforced rates are to be administered, we at once assume that half the provisions of the other hospitals for cure and relief of suffering are altogether superfluous, and that the sick can be cured and relieved quite as well without them. There is no escape from this position, save by arguing that the pauper, when sick, ought not to be so rapidly cured or so much relieved from suffering as another patient—an argument, I presume, neither economy nor humanity can admit.

The sick in workhouses are of two classes :—

1st, the *curable* patients, who, if restored to health, will mostly leave the house, and support themselves for the future by their own labour. No doubt can exist of the saving to the rates which is effected by hastening and securing the recovery of these patients by all reasonable means. An unskilful surgeon, or one who yields to the temptation of withholding the costly drugs (whose price perhaps might employ half or all his scanty salary), is manifestly the cause of immense charge to the Union. Suppose that out of a couple of hundred patients, he keeps twenty or thirty in bed in the workhouse, when with proper treatment they might have left it to earn their living at home. The cost of those patients, amounting to some £300 or £400 a year, must be set against the *economy* of a surgeon with drugs included in his salary of £80, or £100, or £150 a year.* Of the humanity of thus keeping poor creatures in the pangs of disease and misery of helplessness, when we might restore them to the joys of health and strength, it is needless to speak.

2ndly, the *Incurables*. Public attention has at last begun to be turned towards this most piteous class of the community, but as yet the aid offered is but a drop in the ocean of their wants. Two hospitals in England are opened, which perhaps may hold two or three hundred incurables. There are also two small hospitals for them in Scotland, and one large and very old one in Dublin. The other 245 free hospitals in this country admit no incurable patient, and nearly always dismiss those whose cases become hopeless. Thus there is provision for about 500 in the United Kingdom at the utmost. There

* One case, precisely in point, came under the writer's knowledge very lately. She had visited a poor man, for years in B—— workhouse, believing him to be a hopeless sufferer from an internal disease. He frequently complained of the diet disagreeing with him, and that a "house pill," which did him more harm than good, was the only medicine the surgeon ever gave him. Another lady, having described the case to an eminent physician, determined to obtain his admittance into a regular hospital—of course a difficult task. Her trouble was well rewarded; three months afterwards the writer saw the poor man plying his trade (that of a tailor) in fully recovered health and independence.

are, however, 80,000 persons who die every year among us of three only out of the many forms of incurable disease, namely, consumption, dropsy, and cancer. Out of these 80,000 at least 30,000 belong to those poorer working classes to whom prolonged and hopeless illness is inevitably equivalent to ruin and destitution. Deduct the 500 who may find admittance into the hospitals—deduct some thousands who may have friends able and willing to endure the charge of supporting and nursing them, or who may be so happy as to die with unusual suddenness after first succumbing to disease—deduct, say, 10,000 of these, and there will remain some 20,000 who linger out a year, or two or three years, of pain and agony and hopelessness in the workhouse. It would be something worse than bad economy to question whether we should open an asylum to these piteous sufferers (often enduring the worst pangs to which our human nature is liable), and then leave them to want any mitigations which anodynes, or soothing drinks, or comfortable beds, might afford to their long agonies.*

* The plan suggested for the relief of these destitute incurables by Miss Elliot, daughter of the Dean of Bristol, has been tried in some unions with entire success, and it is much to be wished that it could be generally adopted. It is simply that these patients be (wherever practicable) placed in wards apart, and that private charity be freely admitted and invited to visit them, and supply them with such comforts as they may need, subject to the discretion of the surgeon. No irregularity could arise in the workhouse from this plan, the wards being separate, and professedly for a separate class; nor could any unfair advant-

Again, then, we say—both as regards curable patients and incurable—if it be proper to have such things as free hospitals at all, either supported by voluntary contributions or enforced rates, it is proper also to make them effective for their ostensible purposes—the cure of disease and the relief of suffering. With showy ornaments or handsome architecture, such as has been lavished on many workhouses, we have nothing to do. Such things are obnoxious and impertinent in an edifice whose cost is defrayed by taxes levied, like the poor-rates, partly on the poorer classes of the community. But with all that concerns the efficacy of the hospital as a hospital, all that facilitates recovery and relieves suffering, we have an interest. It is imperatively demanded by humanity, by economy, and by justice.

It may be alleged, in answer to this statement, that, even granting it to be desirable to introduce such improvements as would assimilate the workhouse with other hospitals, the thing is impossible. Such improvements would be beyond the resources of a vast number of Unions. To raise the rates sufficiently to meet such expense would be to pauperize the lower strata of rate-payers.

age be taken of it, as no one could feign the diseases which would warrant admission. (See for full accounts of the plan and its approval by 100 of the most eminent London physicians, *Remarks on Incurables in Workhouses*. Nisbet & Co., 1865. Price 2*d.*—and *Destitute Incurables*. Nisbet, 1865. Second Edition. Price 2*d.*)

To this we reply, that if the case be so, in truth, then, the equalization of the rates over large areas becomes imperative. The principle on which the whole poor-law system is grounded compels the State to secure that the wants of its citizens be supplied. If these wants cannot be supplied by other citizens a mile off, they must be supplied by those 100 or 500 miles off. The local arrangements of unions and parishes were matters of convenience. They must needs be revised if it be found that they militate against the fundamental principles of the law itself.

What (we now ask) are the suggestions made by the Parliamentary Committee with reference to this whole subject of the medical department of the workhouses? Passing by the observations in their Report concerning out-door medical relief—which does not here concern us—we find they arrive at these conclusions. (Report, p. 16):—"That there are no sufficient grounds for materially interfering with the present system of medical relief. . . Your Committee, however, recommend that in future cod-liver oil, quinine, and other expensive medicines, shall be provided at the expense of the Guardians." This solitary recommendation (due to the urgent representations of the excellent Dr Rogers, of the Strand Union) is actually the only reform proposed. Surely, taking into consideration the barest outline of the facts of workhouse hospital management, such as has been given above, and making every concession to the humanity with which such a system may be applied, it remains clear that, unless our Philosophy of the Poor-laws be utterly false, the case is one requiring to be treated in a very different manner from that of the gift of a little quinine and cod-liver oil! The reader is as competent to form a judgment on this matter for himself, after one visit to any large workhouse, as the committee man who may have listened to the pleasing testimony of twenty officials. Are the medical counsels, the nurses, the furniture, the drugs, the food of a workhouse hospital similar to those which have been deemed indispensable to procure recovery and relieve suffering in other hospitals? If they are not so, all the complacent calculations of increasing expenditure and accounts of "satisfactory evidence" are simply impertinent. We are either doing our best to cure and to relieve the sick poor, or we are not doing so—judged by the standard of medical science of our time. To do it, is our plain duty. To fail to do so, is equally bad economy and bad humanity.

2nd and 3rd. Workhouses are Blind asylums and institutions for the Deaf and Dumb. In nearly all the larger ones may be found three or four blind and two or three deaf and dumb—just too few to have any arrangements made for their benefit. Very rarely are they taught anything; for there is no one to teach the blind to read, nor any books for them if they could use them—nor any one able to instruct the deaf and dumb, who are treated by the other paupers as idiots, and grow up little better. Basket-making, mat-making, &c., would be opening a trade on a scale too small for the Board to admit on their accounts. The poor creatures, therefore, who might be employed, taught, and made moral and religious beings in the institutions devoted to relieve their infirmities, spend their dreary lives in the work-house in utter idleness and ignorance.

4th. Workhouses are Lunatic Asylums for all except violent cases. Many of them contain scores of insane patients. Here a totally different order of things comes in view. The Commissioners mercifully intervene in favour of these poor souls, and compel the guardians to treat them in a manner superior to those of the other inmates in many respects. The appearance of their wards, decently furnished, and often adorned with prints, and supplied with objects for their amusement, is at first a surprise to the workhouse visitor. Most right and fit is all this; but we must ask, further—are there any means taken not only to alleviate their condition, but to cure this saddest of human maladies? Every-day experience proves more and more the possibility of restoring mental disease; but it is with the utmost care, gentleness, and prudence, and with all appliances at command. Probably less than in any other disease does nature effect a cure here; certainly least of all under the conditions of confinement in one close ward and dreary yard, guarded by its frieze of iron spikes; among hapless fellow-sufferers. Yet, except the house surgeon, who visit them when ill, the insane in workhouses have no medical care whatever. All the chance of recovering from their grievous affliction, which they might have in asylums specially devoted to them, are altogether relinquished. They leave the insane pauper ward only for the pauper's grave. The cost of their maintenance in an asylum being double that in the workhouse, it is always with reluctance that the guardians now dismiss them when too violent to be kept in the Union.

5th. Workhouses are also Idiot asylums and Epileptic hospitals. Little is to be said respecting the treatment of the poor idiots in the workhouse, which is probably as good as may be deemed fitting. The evil is as regards the epileptic patients. These are, in a multitude of workhouses, classed with the imbecile, even when the recurrence of their seizures is still distant enough to allow long intervals of perfect sanity. The mental condition of these unhappy men and women—seeing constantly before them the spectacle of the condition to which they most dread to approximate, and debarred from intercourse with sounder minds—is deplorable indeed. Some of them (as we have known) suffer extreme misery from such a position. Yet the other sick in the workhouse would hardly be less injured by their presence than they are by that of the idiot. In workhouses where they are mixed with the sick or infirm, we have known great misery produced by the sight of their seizures.

6th. Workhouses are Boys' Schools. It is a profound truth that—on which Miss Carpenter has so often insisted—*there is no such thing as a Pauper Child;* and our classing children with paupers is a mistake fraught with evils. A pauper is one who has fallen through his own faults or misfortunes into a condition of unnatural dependence. Every child is naturally dependent—the king's son no less than the beggar's. Whatever faults or misfortunes of the parent may have left the child unprovided for, he cannot morally be made to bear the stigma of pauperism. Nay, our special duty is to secure him from receiving such a brand, and as completely as possible to cut off the entail of pauper degradation, and save him from adding another to the ranks who bear it. Ascending to the original principles of politics, each child born in the State is, as a future citizen of the State; entitled to certain privileges, and subject to certain claims. The old Spartans, who took him almost wholly from his parents, exaggerated these claims; the modern Prussians, who insist upon his receiving education, whether with or without their consent, probably enforce them with the nearest approach to justice.* In all civilized countries the existence of some State-rights over the children of citizens are admitted. Correspond-

* Enforced vaccination is a singular use of these rights of the State in England.

ing to these rights must be duties; and the most obvious of duties must be the support and education of such children as are left destitute either by the death or pauperism of their parents. So long as the parent lives, and is able to support his child, on him naturally falls the duty. But he has it only in the first place. Failing the parents there is the State, which represents the sum of all the responsibilities of the other members of the community. As we started by observing; the right to life is supreme over the right to property, and the office of the State is to secure that right of life (most of all the right of the weak and helpless) at the cost of the property of such as have it. Nor is it mere life the State must guarantee to the child. Another principle comes in—that of the public welfare. For the good not only of the child himself, but of the whole community of which he is to become a member, it must educate him for his future duties. Briefly, in fact, when the parent dies, or becomes a pauper, the duties of the parent devolve on the State. The question is; Ought the State to rear its children as paupers?

Of course we are here met by the bugbear of all enlightened policy towards the poor and the criminal: Would you make the condition of the children of paupers better than that which honest and industrious men are able to secure for their offspring? Will you hold out a bonus to idle and improvident parents? Will you tax the poor ratepayer A, who works day and night to educate his own children decently, that the children of B, who has never worked at all, may be educated as well or better than they? There are both truths and fallacies here. The fallacies are,—that idle and imprudent parents will consider it any bonus to have their children well educated, or be the less or more idle and improvident on that account;—and also that any expenditure of the State *can* equalize the condition of its adopted children with that of the children of honest and industrious parents trained in love and goodness at home. The truth of the argument is this—that it is not on the poor Ratepayer, *as such*, that the weight of the education of the children of the State ought to fall. That is a matter of the general expenditure of the nation, to be classed with the salaries of the officers of State, the army, navy, and public works of all kinds. The *support* of the child (as of the adult pauper) is all with which the poor-rates ought rightly to be charged. The property of the ratepayer is lawfully taxed for that only. He should pay for the child's education, as he pays for other matters of public welfare, by other taxes. We shall see presently how such an arrangement would not only be feasible, but would directly fall in with any true method of removing the workhouse taint—namely, the separation of the child from pauper associations.

The boys' schools attached to the workhouses are usually good, as regards instruction: the District schools (combining those of several Unions, and separated from the workhouses), better still. In nearly all cases, indeed, children boarded in these schools are in advance, as regards book-learning, of those who attend only by day, with the usual irregularity of the poor. In a few workhouse schools, also, the moral and physical training of the boys is excellent—in fact, there is little to be wished for, save that so much care and cost to effect the elevation of the pupils should be systematically rendered nugatory by the exclusive companionship of paupers, and the perpetual livery of pauperism. These are the best cases: very different ones are the Unions where the boys grow up under hard and tyrannical masters, with penurious guardians, and, from childhood to manhood, never know an hour of boyish sport or freedom, or one influence to soften their hearts to human sympathies or divine love. That a youth educated thus should grow up a cheerful, affectionate, self-respecting, and religious man, would be one of those moral miracles of which there are few examples.

The case of the Girls is far worse than the Boys, as all the conditions of workhouse management fall with peculiar evil on their natures. To mass boys together in large numbers, with no home influence or habits, and no attempt to draw out their affections, is dangerous. To do the same to girls, is fatal. Among all the endless paradoxes of female treatment, one of the worst and most absurd is that which, while eternally proclaiming "home" to be the only sphere of a woman, systematically educates all the female children of the State without attempting to give them even an idea of what a home might be. Girls want affection, want personal care, want household duties, want everything which can train them to honour the bodies, and keep pure the souls which God has given them. To effect this, we mass them by hundreds where they have no affection, no personal care, nay, hardly a personal existence at all, save as units in a herd, no household duties; and as much degradation as hideous uniform and cropped hair, and shoes which change the natural lightness of step of youth to the shuffle of age, can possibly achieve. The result is at last becoming so palpable that none may shut their eyes. The poor girls so trained, go out into the humbler class of service, where their ignorance of the simplest household duties, their want of self-control and hopeless stupidity, too often provoke the harshness of their employers. In their errands in the streets at all hours, the secret of another and all too easy livelihood is revealed to them. No mother or friendly teacher is there to save them; no house to which to go, when dismissed from service, save the weary workhouse again. Before they return thither, they try that dread alternative. Out of a single workhouse in London, inquiry was instituted two years ago concerning eighty girls who had left it and gone to service. It was found that every one of them was on the streets.

In a minor degree the evils of the boys' and girls' schools apply also to the Infant Schools, which likewise are contained in the workhouses.

What does our Parliamentary Committee (which has passed over the case of the blind, deaf and dumb, insane and idiotic) say to that of the children in the workhouse? The Report begins by admitting the importance of the matter, and traces a gradual improvement in the system, especially since 1847-8, when workhouse schools were placed under the inspection of the Committee of Council on Education, and a grant of £30,000 per annum placed at the disposal of the Poor-law Board for the payment of workhouse teachers. After this we are told that "the witnesses, Miss Carpenter, Miss Twining, and the Hon. Mrs Way, expressed opinions very strongly opposed to the education of children in workhouses, the inevitable result of which, they consider, is to demoralize the children and confirm them in habits of pauperism." The Committee, however, attach more importance to the Report of the Royal Commission on Education, which contains these "conclusions."

1. That pauperism is hereditary; and that children born and bred as members of that class, furnish the great mass of the pauper and criminal population.

2. That the best prospect of a permanent diminution of pauperism and crime, is to be found in the proper education of such children.

3. That district and separate schools give an education to the children contained in them, which effectually tends to emancipate them from pauperism.

4. That the workhouse schools are generally so managed, that the children contained in them learn from infancy to regard the workhouses as their homes, and associate with grown-up paupers, whose influence destroys their moral character, and prevents the growth of independence.

5. That the arrangements of workhouses are unavoidably such as to make it extremely difficult to procure or retain competent teachers.

The inference from these premises is, that the only means of improving the condition of pauper education, is to compel by law the general establishment of district and separate schools; and that this remedy is efficient, the experience of the district and separate schools already established, proves conclusively. (Report, p. 27.)

All these conclusions of the Commissioners of Education, however, the Committee of Inquiry into Poor Relief found of small value, on analyzing the method by which the late lamented Mr N. W. Senior, who drew up the document, had arrived at his convictions. Large examination of other witnesses proved to their satisfaction (what nobody ever questioned), that the intellectual education of workhouse children is good, and that a certain industrial training is also afforded to them. The case of the girls, and the total impossibility of affording them, in a workhouse, any preparation for domestic life, was, as usual, passed over; and their "occasional" intercourse with the prostitutes in the workhouse, treated as of no great consequence. Mr Tufnell, formerly Poor-law Commissioner, and, during the last fifteen years, Inspector of Poor-law Schools in the Metropolitan district, gave his opinion in favour of district schools for boys, and private industrial training-schools for girls, like the Brockham Home; and Mr Farnall, Poor-law Inspector of the London district, gave similar judgment. The whole conclusions, however, of the Parliamentary Committee were these :—

"That making reasonable allowance for the low condition, physical, moral, and mental, of a large proportion of the children when they first enter workhouses, and for the necessarily frequent changes in their admission and discharge, the state of workhouse education is upon the whole satisfactory in its character and result.

"The Committee think that it would be inexpedient, and in many cases impracticable, to enforce the general establishment of district or separate schools; but they are of opinion that schools entirely distinct from the workhouse should continue to be encouraged as being attended with beneficial results to the children, and affording the most effectual means of separating them from the other classes of paupers."

The idea of what constitutes a "satisfactory result," in the minds of the members of the Committee, must, apparently, be somewhat different from that which the "Philosopher of the Poor-laws" would lead us to predicate!

7. Workhouses are Nurseries for Infants. Two or three small wards, in most workhouses in England and Ireland, are devoted to the care of poor little babies, whose mothers (when they have any forthcoming), come in at stated times to feed them, and who, at other hours, or having no mothers, are in the hands of paupers unfit for other work, and commonly infirm and miserable enough on their own account, to have small patience to spare for the puling infants—heritors, in two cases out of three, of scrofulous disease.*

In Scotland these poor babies are sent out to be nursed by respectable peasant women, under proper inspection. How wise and benevolent such an arrangement is, may be judged from the simplest observation of the condition of those reared in the workhouses. Just as the moral entail of pauperism needs to be cut off by removing the boy or girl from all degrading influences before they are old enough to be susceptible of them, so the physical entail of poverty's diseases needs to be cut off by taking the infant, from the first attainable moment, into the healthiest conditions we can assign it.

* Hawthorne's terrible picture of the workhouse infant, in *Our Old Home*, will be fresh in many reader's minds.

That a baby should be in a workhouse, is presumption enough that its mother has been living in want or sin for months before its birth, and is in distress when she has given it its first nutriment. Often it has a double pedigree, on father's and mother's side, of profligacy, drunkenness, and want, whose consequences the hapless infant brings with it into the world. If this poor little creature is to be saved from a life of ill-health and helplessness—from a pauper life, in fact—it can only be by giving it the healthiest nurse, the freshest air, and, by-and-by, the wholesomest country food and exercise we can obtain. In the great hospital of San Spirito, in Rome, where more than 1000 foundlings are placed every year, and more than 503 of them die, we have thought the most piteous spectacle the civilized world could show was that of the pining little atoms of babies, two and three in a crib; and two, three, or *four* fed (or rather starved) by one single wet-nurse, unable to still their ceaseless wails for food. Such poor, weak cries as they were! such piteous little faces! It was too miserable to watch: and yet we have thought that to let them die thus, all save the strongest, by sheer want, was more merciful in the end than to give them, as we do, food enough, and let them grow up the inevitable heritors of disease.

Probably nothing we could do could make a class of workhouse orphans look like a class of thriving labourers' children. But all we could do ought surely to be tried,—and would be tried, but for this monstrous amalgamation of 22 institutions under one roof, and controlled by one Board. The simple idea of a committee of men undertaking the management of babies would be thought absurd enough elsewhere. Of course we are told they "rely on the matron,"—which is equivalent to saying that it is not a committee at all, much less a qualified committee of ladies, or a lady inspector, who regulates this department; but, singly and irresponsibly, the salaried matron. Do the gentlemen of the Board imagine they can superintend and check the proceedings of this supreme authority? We have heard the most experienced philanthropist of the age lay it down as a principle, "There never yet existed a gentleman, or a Board of gentlemen, whom the matron of an institution could not perfectly bamboozle respecting every department under her charge!"

8th. Again, workhouses are lying-in hospitals (another department for exclusive masculine surveillance!); and, lastly, they are penitentiaries. Both these portions of the institution are mainly defective in a moral point of view. A great, and often an only opportunity is offered for the reclaiming of women who have fallen into sin when they pass through the purifying ordeal of childbirth, or are compelled for a time to relinquish their evil courses from poverty or sickness. To seize such an opportunity has been the desire of many benevolent persons, and ought surely to be an aim of the heads of whatever institution they may make their temporary refuge. But we have never heard any but the same story of disappointment. The conditions of a workhouse—the evil company, the low nurses, the whole tone of the place—forbids almost always the entrance of moral or religious influences. Even if (as we have known) a death or other striking incident serve to touch them for a time, before any permament good can be effected the evil influences of the place are sure to prevail. The workhouse is no place for repentance. It would be a miracle if it were!

In somma, then, as the Italians say, what are the results of this huge agglomeration of charitable institutions in our workhouses—male and female Hospitals; male and female Infirmaries; male and female Blind, Deaf and Dumb, Insane, and Idiot asylums; Boys', Girls', and Infants' Schools; Nurseries; Lying-in Hospitals; and Penitentiaries? Simply what might have been expected—that every one is more or less a failure; that it is—not merely inferior to similar institutions under other management in point of splendour or luxury, for this would be only right and fit—but that it is inferior to them in fulfilling the purposes for which it exists; in some cases failing to fulfil these purposes altogether. These partial or complete failures are often accidental and remediable. The worst defects we have signalized are not known in the many Unions presided over by humane and intelligent guardians. But other evils are inherent in the principle itself of a huge *omnium gatherum* of human want, vice, folly, and disease. No sagacity can obviate them, or make the condition of the blind, or deaf mutes, or children, or fallen women, in such places what it is in institutions devoted to their sole use. Can these things be remedied?

If the public were once persuaded of the fact that one house cannot well be the receptacle for every misfortune, nor one Board of Guardians the fit regulators of 22 widely-varied institutions, the remedy might apparently be found readily enough; in fact, it is often found by Unions disposed to seek it.

Let us first suppose that the blind, the deaf and dumb, the insane, and the idiots be in every case sent by their Unions to the county asylums—the Unions paying for their support to the asylums. Where such asylums do not exist, or do not possess sufficient accommodation, they should be enlarged, or those of an adjoining county employed. If it were thought needful for the ratepayers' protection against overcharge, Committees of Guardians could annually inspect such asylums and their accounts. As they are all designed for the lowest working classes, there is (or ought to be) nothing in the arrangement of such county asylums other than is fitting for the pauper blind, deaf, dumb, insane, and idiotic—i. e., than that which is calculated to relieve or cure their afflictions in the most economical manner. The plan is so often exceptionally followed, from motives of convenience or humanity, that it is singular it should not yet be recognized as the only fit rule of treatment for the classes to which it applies. In particular, as regards the Insane, the law which compels the sending of the violent patients only into the asylums, and leaves the harmless in the workhouses, simply amounts to the consignment of the latter to hopeless aberration, without chance afforded of recovery. What should we think of similar treatment of the sufferers by any of the thousand other maladies far less terrible than that of the brain? Deaf and dumb children, again, growing up without the peculiar education suited to their defects, are almost consigned to idiotcy—certainly to the obfuscation of all that moral and religious element which elevates men above the brutes. The case of the Epileptics is a peculiarly difficult one. Oscillating between reason and a condition worse than imbecility, it seems alternately a cruelty to them and to their companions to class them either with the sound or unsound in intellect. Nor do there exist institutions outside the workhouse generally suitable for them. It would seem as if here, at all events, outdoor relief sufficient for their maintenance might be safely given wherever the sufferers have friends willing to keep them in their homes. Failing such friends, the infirm, not idiotic, wards seem their proper place.

For the Infants, the Scotch have demonstrated the excellence of the system of putting them out to nurse with respectable poor women, who bring them up with the nearest approach to family affection and healthful sanitary conditions attainable for them. No excuse remains for the English plan of close wards and indifferent (and commonly unhealthy) nurses, presided over by a board of gentlemen possessed of all the knowledge of their sex concerning babies' wants and ailments. For the lying-in wards, and wards for fallen women,—which ought to be Penitentiaries, and are rather *induratories*,—we are in grievous want of a revision of the whole system now in action, not only as regards workhouses, but the penitentiaries supported by private charity. It is not in a brief article like the present that this great subject can be discussed. Very valuable suggestions have been lately made regarding institutions which should combine lying-in hospitals for the class of women in question, and penitentiaries, and towards whose cost the fathers of children born in them should be compelled to contribute.* Could some scheme of this sort become legalized, and all the unfortunate women driven to seek for relief from the poor-rates be admitted

* See "A New Form of Magdalen Reformatory Home," by Miss Solly.

to them instead of to our present "Black wards," something might yet be done towards restoration, as well as towards the far more hopeful aim of prevention of sin.* In such institutions the payments of the guilty men, enforced by law, would fitly relieve the ratepayers, and form a most desirable check to vice. At the same time, regulations which such legally-established refuges might be qualified to make, requiring a notice of some weeks or months from the inmates before their departure, would vastly aid the feeble resolutions of the poor souls to persevere long enough in steady courses for reformation. The power of immediately procuring a discharge from the workhouse, at the first spur of weariness or temptation, has been, to the writer's experience, the ruin of many not unhopeful girls.

For the Schools of Boys and Girls, we have already pointed out how the principles of justice require that the support of a Pauper, and the education of a Child dependent on the State, should be separated as widely as possible. As a matter of right, no child ought to bear the stigma of pauperism; and, as a matter of public interest for the future of the community, every dependent child ought to be separated and removed as far as by any means may be possible from pauper moral in-

* The not very numerous cases of married women coming for confinement to the workhouse, would be met by one ward attached to the ordinary hospital.

fluences and pauper physical and social degradation. Instead of keeping our poor children in the workhouses, separating them from all other children, and clothing them in the hideous pauper uniform, our whole effort ought to be to take them miles away from any workhouse, to mix them completely with other children both in their schoolrooms and playgrounds, and obliterate in every possible way the difference between them. Practically, how can such a change be effected in the most radical manner? Two plans are open to us, either of which, it would seem, must attain the end in view.

The first plan would be to follow the Scotch system completely, both as regards boys and girls as well as infants; and to send the children out first to be nursed, and then boarded, by respectable poor families, under proper inspection. As they reach the age for going to school, the persons who have charge of the children being obliged to send them to the one in the neighbourhood chosen by the inspector, and to produce certificates from the teacher of the child's attendance, the desired end of education is fully attained, and with the immense advantage of it being an education in common with non-pauper children. The following account of the success of this scheme, given by the Clerk of the Edinburgh Parochial Board, is in the highest degree satisfactory:—

"In answer to your inquiries as to our mode of boarding out children here, I beg to state that the pauper children belonging to this parish were formerly maintained in an institution along with the children now in the Orphan Hospital, but so dissatisfied was this board with the results that, 18 years ago, they resolved to board the children with families in the country: and this plan has since been followed by almost all the large parishes in Scotland, the number sent out at present by the parishes of Edinburgh and Leith being upwards of 700; by Glasgow somewhat more; and by Dundee, Aberdeen, and other towns in proportion to their population.

"1st. The total cost of each child thus boarded out by the parish, for the last year, was £8 13*s*. 10*d*. The allowance of 2*s*. 6*d*. a week to the nurse pays for board, lodging, washing, and mending clothes. We supply the clothing in addition.

"2nd and 4th. I have an assistant, whose sole duty it is to superintend the children boarded out, both boys and girls, and to find good nurses for them. We board them with tradespeople and cottagers, and not with people who make the care of them their only task. We prefer people of good character, who have a steady income apart from the children, who will receive them, and treat them exactly as members of their own family; and we find, when the children are sent out young, they learn to call the parties to whom they are sent, father and mother. They acquire towards them the feelings of children, and the result generally is, that the nurses acquire for them a parental affection. When any one applies for children, my assistant, before granting the request, visits them, and inquires in the neighbourhood as to their character, inspects the house, as to its accommodation, dryness, ventilation; ascertains if there is a well-taught school in the neighbourhood; and, after being satisfied on all these points, children are sent out. He afterwards visits the nurse, as well as the school, at least eight times a year, satisfies himself that the children are healthy, sufficiently fed, cleanly kept, and their education attended to. We generally get superior people to take charge of the children; but, should we get inferior ones, our own close superintendence prevents them doing injustice. Should we in any case, however, find neglect, the children are at once removed; but, although we have had 300 boarded out, and some years ago had 400, I have only had occasion to remove children for neglect on three or four occasions during a period of five years. The localities we select are generally small villages, at a distance of 10, 15, or 20 miles from Edinburgh, and of convenient access by railway.

"3rd. We never send more than four children to one family.

"5th. In consequence of our requiring the regular attendance of the children at school, the teacher having to fill up a schedule showing each day's absence, our children generally are the best scholars, and carry off a large share of the school prizes; and when sent out to service prove as good servants as the children of the cottagers or workpeople not dependent on the rates usually do—certainly not inferior—and many of them rise to positions of trust.

"6th. It is a rare thing for a boy or girl who has been brought up in this way to become chargeable to the parish in after-life; and I may add that, where the children were brought up in the hospital or school here, which was apart from the poor-house, they very frequently became chargeable in after-life. We avoid crowding many in one locality, and have them not only in Edinburghshire, but in Fife, Haddington, and Lanarkshire.

"G. Grey,
"*Clerk to the Edinburgh Parochial Board.*"

If, for any local reasons, this plan be found impracticable, then there remains another, which, though less good, would yet surely be a great improvement upon the present system. 1st. To place the children in schools which should be also day-schools for other children—e. g., those of the national schools. 2nd. To charge the poor-rates only for their support, and defray their education from national grants for educational purposes. 3rd. To give Poor-law Guardians only such right of inspection as shall correspond with the payment of such rates for support of the children—i. e., as shall secure for the ratepayers that their rates actually supply the physical wants of the children, and no more. 4th. To place the management of the schools under the Board of Education, where, it may be hoped, the theory of *paideutics* will be better understood than by the farmers and small shopkeepers, who carry the votes at the Boards of Guardians. 5th. That the boys in these schools wear semi-military or naval dresses, and be trained to such exercises as may best suit them for those professions wherein they can effectually serve the country and efface all pauper associations. Under such circumstances, it is to be believed a vast majority of boys would joyfully enter the army, navy, or merchant service, and make families for themselves in their ships and regiments. 6th. That the girls in these schools be separated as much as possible in small schools and certified training-houses, where they can be taught household labours, and be fitted for domestic life.

Of course all these plans are beset with difficulties of a practical sort—especially those connected with girls. Yet we would fain hope that these difficulties cannot be insurmountable, while the cutting off by such means of the main source of hereditary pauperism in the country would hold out a promise worthy of every exertion.

Should such views as these ever be adopted, the result would be to remove from the workhouses boys, girls, infants, lying-in-women, fallen women, the blind, the deaf and dumb, the insane, and the idiotic. There would remain only two departments —that of the workhouse properly so called, for able-bodied paupers; and the sick-wards for all classes of disease and infirmity of age. Could these latter also be removed?

It does not appear that it would be practicable to open hospitals* which by any arrangement could contain all the sick in the workhouses, or even any important class of them. The incurables alone would cost (supposing house-room provided already) not less than £900,000 per annum, at the usual rate of hospital expense. It would need about treble our existing hospital accommodation in England to empty the workhouse sick-wards. Such schemes are not to be contemplated as either advantageous or otherwise. There remains only the practicable alterations in the present workhouse hospital arrangements, which shall as much as possible obviate the evils we have signalized. Keeping in mind the principle that the purpose of an hospital is to cure the sick who are yet curable as surely and as quickly as possible, and to relieve the sufferings of all patients, curable and incurable, we find that the task before us is to assimilate the workhouse hospitals to those free hospitals where these ends

* There are already, according to the census of 1861, 10,414 persons in hospitals in England, and 125,722 poor and sick in workhouses. How many of the latter are among the sick is not known.

are obtained at the smallest cost. There must, on the one hand, be no sacrifice of either end to the cost,—for this is at once inhuman and impolitic; and, on the other hand, no superfluous cost,—for this is injustice to the rate-payer. To ascertain precisely what are these arrangements best for the sick and cheapest for the ratepayer, what is it we require? Surely not the opinion of a couple of dozen laymen (none of whom perhaps ever entered a hospital in his life), and of one young surgeon, their nominee and dependent? We want the very largest experience and highest medical judgment we can obtain. We want surgeons and physicians who are acquainted with the last improvements in hospitals, the last discoveries respecting the results of temperature, diet, and medicine, and who are in a position to speak with authority as to what shall or shall not be done independently of the guardians' prejudices. Where does this point?

Surely to this—that special Medical Inspectors of Workhouse Hospitals are absolutely needed to make these hospitals properly effective. Already in the Inspectors for Lunatics and for Schools we have the plan in operation. A Commission given to three or four of the leading physicians and surgeons of the day to make a first general Inspection and Report of the workhouse hospitals in the kingdom would, we are convinced, produce very admirable results. Such a first inspection, under the highest authority, would result:—

1st, In the reform of bad sanitary arrangements of the wards and the introduction of proper furniture. 2nd, The revisal of the dietaries. 3rd, The appointment of proper nurses. 4th, The revisal of the medical books and accounts, whereby it would become manifest whether the surgeon was enabled to supply the patients with such drugs as science admits to be beneficial; and the guardians would be compelled to allot (not out of the surgeon's salary, but from a separate fund) the usual average cost of drugs for each patient in ordinary hospitals. All these most grievously needed reforms might be effected by a single visit of such a commission as we have supposed. The further regular rounds of ordinary inspectors of sufficient medical eminence would suffice to prevent a relapse into the present state of things. That the workhouse surgeon should also be encouraged and directed to call into consultation the leading physicians or surgeons of the neighbourhood for difficult cases, would also be needful to assimilate in any way the workhouse with the other hospitals.

The Aged and Infirm wards would share the benefits of these changes—so far as the inmates could be considered as *patients*. There are, however, in every workhouse, a large number of persons advanced in years far enough to be beyond work, and yet not requiring hospital treatment of any kind. The treatment of these, the healthy aged paupers, is one of the most difficult of all the problems presented by the poor-laws. On the one hand there is our natural tenderness and respect for age, urging us to indulgence and to the permission of such little luxuries as have become habitual, and such free intercourse between husbands and wives as can be easily arranged. On the other hand we have the fatal experience that the idea of ending life in the workhouse not only may become, but has become, all too familiar to the English labourer, to the great injury of his independence and the misapplication of the poor-rates. Even with the existing regulations, the separating of families, and the withholding of all luxuries, it has grown into a settled notion with the humblest class, in some districts, that they have a right to "come on the parish" in old age, and that to relinquish such a right would be an extravagance—much the same as for a lady or gentleman to refrain from drawing their dividends or using their box at the opera! Their own savings, if they had any; or their sons' and daughters' earnings, would be sadly thrown away in supporting them at home when there is this provision absolutely waiting for them at the workhouse. How mischievous this idea is, and how prevalent; how it degrades our peasantry, parents and children both; how it counteracts the whole principle of the poor-laws, need not now be told. In the face of such experience, can we propose to make the condition of the healthy aged paupers better than it is? We fear it is impossible. Rather is it some further deterrent that is wanted—such as charges to be paid by able-bodied sons who allow their parents to go to the workhouse. It would be impossible, without cruelty, to lower the actual condition of the paupers; but by such a tax on their relations who ought to support them, and by very arduously striving to bring public opinion to make it disgraceful for them to allow them to go to the workhouse, something might perhaps be done to check the evil. Only when it is checked, and the idea of "exercising a right" in going into the workhouse is changed among all classes, for that of submitting to a misfortune, will it be possible to extend greater indulgence to these poor old creatures.*

Casual wards appear in the country Unions to fulfil their purpose well enough. In London, however, it is otherwise. The average 12,000 "tramps" of the metropolis, swelled by the distress of the winters of 1860-61, when the whole pauperism rose from 96,752 to 135,389, became a source of universal distress, as accounts of their inability to find shelter in the workhouses were published day by day. Of the vast efforts made by private charity to come to

* Even the benevolent attempts to reunite husbands and wives seems to have proved a failure; not so much by encouraging them to go to the workhouse, but as failing to make them more happy therein. The chairman of a Union wherein it was tried, assured me the married couples were always more discontented than the others, and generally after a few months required to be separated.

their aid, we have no need here to tell. The Committee of Inquiry into the Poor-laws, which we are now considering, originated in the anxiety felt on all sides to remedy this great evil; and their labours seem in this particular respect to have arrived at a satisfactory—albeit somewhat illogical—result. They say (Report, p. 10)—

"That with respect to the extraordinary prevalence of distress in the metropolis in the winter of 1860-61, to which the attention of your Committee was particularly directed, they received strong evidence that such distress could have been relieved by the poor-law authorities, inasmuch as the legal machinery of administration was sufficient, and the guardians possessed the requisite powers for raising the necessary funds for the purpose; but the legal charge would have pressed very heavily on some parishes within the metropolis."

Nevertheless they finally decide (p. 41)—

"That in order to secure sufficient and convenient means for the relief of the casual and houseless poor within the metropolis, as defined by the Metropolitan Local Management Act, it is expedient that the charges incurred for the support of such poor should be paid out of a rate assessed on the annual rateable value of the whole of the said metropolis.

"That, in the opinion of this Committee, the machinery adopted under the Metropolitan Local Management Act might be made available for raising the amount of such charge, and your Committee recommend that authority be given to the Metropolitan Board of Works for such purpose.

"That the Poor-law Board be empowered to prescribe and enforce all necessary arrangements for providing the requisite accommodation in the several Unions and parishes, and otherwise carrying the foregoing resolutions into effect."

Finally, the Able-bodied paupers. What ought to be done with them?

Visiting one day the Lusk Intermediate Prison, in company with the late Sir Joshua Jebb, he remarked to us—"This is precisely what we want our workhouses to be. The difficulty is to draw the distinction between the treatment of criminals and of paupers, which shall punish the one and not the other, and be healthy morally and physically for both." On reflection, it did not seem as if the difficulty were so very great after all. The admirrable system of Sir Walter Crofton, whereby crime has been so wonderfully repressed in Ireland, begins with imprisonment of a penal kind, and then proceeds through regular steps towards the preparation of the convict for liberty and an honest future life. There is nothing in the nature of the case to make the latter steps of this progress inapplicable to the condition of the able-bodied pauper—save the fact that the "marks" for his good conduct and industrious work would not represent the curtailing of his detention, but the permission of indulgences, and the accumulation of such small per centage of his earnings, as might enable him eventually to leave the workhouse with means to emigrate or start afresh in industry. The modification of such details would be by no means difficult; and the reformatory aspect a system of the kind would give to workhouses, would be every way desirable rather than the contrary as regards the class in question, i. e., the able-bodied paupers, who, except under rare calamity, are brought to such a state by vice or idleness. That everything beyond the barest necessaries should be earned by such persons by hard labour—that at every turn they should find steadiness, sobriety, and industry their sole means of obtaining any share of comfort or liberty—would be the very greatest benefit which could be conferred on them. At the same time, for the better sort, whom misfortune may have driven to the workhouse, the possibility of earning and laying by somewhat, if ever so little, towards future restoration to freedom, would be the most desirable stimulus. The ratepayers themselves would benefit by the spur thus given to both classes of paupers to perform their allotted labours, and then profit by extra tasks; and the whole workhouse would be changed from a place where the idle become more idle and the degraded more degraded, to one where the faults which brought men there would meet their fittest punishment and cure, and where new habits of temperance and industry might be formed even for the most apparently hopeless characters.*

The modifications which we have here ventured to suggest concerning the whole arrangements of workhouses may be thus resumed:—

1, 2. The workhouse proper (or place of labour for male and female paupers) to be reformed by the introduction of a system of marks and fractional payment of labour.

3, 4. The casual wards in poor districts of London to be enlarged.

5, 6. The hospital for curable and incurable male and female patients to be reformed under a commission of physicians, and afterwards regularly inspected.

7, 8. The asylum for the aged supported in all possible cases by charges on the relatives who could maintain the inmates.

9—16. The male and female blind, deaf and

* In the splendid workhouse of Monte Domini, in Florence, I have seen the inmates engaged in all manner of trades: blacksmith work, iron-bed making, weaving, carpentering, cabinet making, locksmith's work, book binding, wood carving, mattress making, boot and shoe making of all kinds, and artificial flower making. In every case the workmen or workwomen received a certain share of the remuneration of their labour; and no heartier scene of work I ever witnessed anywhere. The director assured me that there were no complaints of interference with other tradesmen in the town, nor any jealousy of the boys being taught as much as possible.

dumb, insane, and idiot asylums all emptied, and their inmates sent to the county asylums for their respective afflictions, and supported therein at the cost of the rates.

17—20. The boys', girls', and infants' schools, and the nursery also emptied; the children being placed out in families from infancy, and educated in ordinary day-schools with other children; the rates paying their nurses and guardians under proper inspection, and the educational fund their schooling.

21, 22. The lying-in hospital and penitentiary to be transferred to such institutions as are above described.

These plans would involve in some cases more, in others less, expense than the present system. The reformed workhouse, we believe, would in the end be an economy as effecting a repression of pauperism. The reformed hospital would involve considerable outlay, which might or might not be balanced by the speedier cure of patients. The blind, deaf and dumb, insane, and idiotic would cost more, boarded in the county asylums, their wants being better supplied. The infants might perhaps cost more out at nurse than in the workhouse; the boys and girls boarded out as proposed, would cost less, and (by far less often returning as paupers) would vastly lighten the rates. The lying-in hospital and penitentiary for fallen women, transferred to such an institution as has been suggested, would be nearly by half taken from the ratepayers and laid upon male offenders.

On the whole perhaps, therefore, we may consider the results of such changes would be to leave the rates much as they find them. As in some cases, however, they might involve considerable extra cost, the question of the equalization of rates over large areas would doubtless need to be considered. The palpable injustice, however, of the present system—the rich parishes in London paying next to nothing, and the poor being overwhelmed with their rates—renders it certain that ere long some such changes must be effected; and with such equalization the universal benefit of any scheme tending to the *general* repression of pauperism would inevitably be experienced. The Parliamentary inquiry on this subject is more satisfactory in its results on this point than on any other. The Committee report (p. 44)—

"That much evidence was adduced showing the unequal pressure of the charge for the relief of the poor in different parts of the metropolitan district; and various plans were submitted to your Committee for the equalization of the poor-rate; and your Committee recommend the general question of extending the area of rating to the further consideration of the House; but the circumstances of the metropolis are so peculiar, that in any legislation to extend the area of charge or management, it would be necessary to have regard to those circumstances."*

On the subject of the law of Settlement, nearly connected as it is with the equalization of rates, we shall not attempt to enter. Complaints from all parts of the kingdom of the evil results on the working classes of the present state of the law, are making themselves heard—and, we may be assured, will eventually obtain redress; whilst the history of the Bills proposed and rejected, the Reports and Committees concerned in the question since the Ninth Report of the Commissioners in 1843, is proof of the extreme intricacy and difficulty of the question. The existing law, resulting from a series of Acts of Parliament passed and amended from the origin of the Poor-laws in 1601 to 1662, 1685, 1691, 1697, 1795, 1834, and 1847, is a mass of entanglement whose most obvious result is to shackle the unhappy labourer, and to make it the interest of every landholder to prevent him from enjoying the comforts of a separate cottage. If he have resided three years uninterruptedly in one parish, it is on the rates of the Union in which that parish is situated that he is chargeable. If he have not resided three years in the parish in which he becomes a pauper, he is sent back (except under peculiar circumstances of a £10 holding or an apprentice-

* A Bill was introduced by Messrs Ayrton and John Locke, as early as 1859, for the equalization of poor-rates in the metropolitan districts. It failed, however, to obtain a second reading.

ship) to any parish where he did so reside; or failing such, to any parish where his father or grandfather so resided; or to the parish where he or his father or grandfather were born. How few even of educated people understand this complicated law! How few poor labouring men and women can know how to regulate their conduct thereby, so as, amid all their hard struggles for existence, to combine the obtaining of employment and the avoiding of some unlucky movement which will bring on them, in their old age, a sentence almost equivalent to a penal transportation! Still worse is the evil which arises from the temptation thus held out to landholders and farmers to keep their parishes clear of all resident labourers who might in time come upon them for support. All England has been lately roused to indignation at the accounts of the hovels used by the poor in Norfolk and elsewhere; and philanthropists are seeking earnestly the means to correct the evil, and discover the true economical principle by which decent cottages for workmen may be a fair investment of capital. But till the Law of Settlement is altered there can be but partial benefit from any such schemes. The landlord's interest is not to have labourers' cottages on his land at all, even supposing they paid him six or eight per cent. for their cost of erection. Half-a-dozen paupers chargeable on his rates would swallow up such profit on a score of cottages. If we suppose an entire parish to belong to a single squire, or to ten farmers, then, if the squire or the farmers can contrive (as they may easily do) to prevent any working man from acquiring his three years' right of settlement on their parish, they keep themselves free of the greater part of the burden of the poor-rates—an exemption cheaply gained at the inconvenience (to them very small, to the poor labourer very great) of obliging him to walk every day to and from his work two or three miles to the nearest village. In this village, which is his sole resource, of course the rates are disproportionately high, the dwellings crowded, and the whole vile system of poor lodgings in full play. Why is all this wrong and wretchedness, and all the sanitary and moral evils thence derived? Simply because the law of settlement has so bungled in its original good intention of making it the interest of every parish to repress pauperism in its own bounds, that it has actually created a fictitious and monstrous interest in the whole class of landholders to drive the labourer off their property into villages, where every condition of difficulty of work, high price of lodging, and bad sanitary arrangement, tends to force him to those vices wherein pauperism has its origin.

The remedy urged before now seems surely simple enough: that for the existing cumbrous legislation should be substituted a short and simple Act of Parliament, making the support of the pauper chargeable not on the parish in which he has *resided*, but on that in which he has *worked*, either last before he comes on the rates, or last for any stipulated and easily-remembered term of years. Thus the interest of the landholder to keep the labourer far off would be changed for one to keep him as close as possible to his work (thus obtaining from him a better day's labour); seeing that in any case, if he become chargeable on the rates, he will equally be obliged to contribute to his support. And for the labourer himself, he will be freed at once from all harassing anxiety and doubt respecting his future relief, should he be driven to seek for it.

The further step of making such charges common to large areas,* would remove the remaining source of evil—the interest of landlords to turn their lands to grass, and employ as few hands as possible in their farming operations. It would also permit, by the added rates thus levied on richer ratepayers, who have hitherto escaped most

* In the country, probably, the Unions now existing would suffice for the purpose above stated. In towns, where there is nearly always a rich quarter and a poor quarter, rich Unions and poor Unions, the whole town ought assuredly to be placed under some common system of taxation. No anomaly can be more absurd than that which now obtains in all the large cities of England, where the poor support the whole weight of the poor, and the rich support nothing at all. Permission to bring in a Bill to substitute Union for parish rating was asked in the House by Mr Bernard, February 17th of the present year; but being opposed on the ground of the expected Report of the Committee of Inquiry, was not insisted on by the proposer.

easily, the introduction of those improvements in the whole system of workhouse management, the necessity of which we hope we have in some measure demonstrated in the preceding pages.*

* I am happy to state that since this article was written, a Bill has been passed, laying a charge upon the district of the Metropolitan Board of Works to provide for all the casual poor up to the 1st April next—the Poor-Law Guardians to supply refuges and relief, and the Metropolitan Board of Works to levy a rate on the whole Metropolis to defray the cost. Thus we are provided at all events against a repetition of the terrible scenes of last winter.

March, 1865. Mr Villiers' Bill for the substitution of Union for parish rating is now before the House, and, if passed, will doubtless be a great step in the right direction. The law for the relief of casual poor has also been re-enacted.

THE RIGHTS OF MAN

AND

THE CLAIMS OF BRUTES.

Reprinted from Fraser's Magazine, November, 1863.

There is a beautiful Eastern story to this purpose:—A mighty king of old built for himself the most magnificent city the world ever saw. The towers of the city were of marble, and the walls of eternal granite, with an hundred gates of brass; and in the centre of the city, by the side of an ever-flowing river, stood the palace of the king, which dazzled the eyes of the beholder with its beauty, and in whose garden there was a tree whose leaves were of emeralds and whose fruit of rubies.

But the king and his people, of whose power and riches there were no end, were wicked exceedingly, and given up to cruelty and iniquity. Therefore Allah sent a drought upon their land, and for seven years there rained no rain; and the river was dried up, and the fountains failed, and the cattle perished; and the women wailed in the streets, and the hearts of the young men failed them utterly. Then said the wise men and the elders unto the king: "Send now, we pray thee, unto the prophet who dwelleth in the land of Israel, in the cave under the mountain of Carmel, and behold he will procure us rain from the Lord." Then the king hearkened unto his wise men, and sent messengers with precious gifts unto the prophet, that he should send them rain. And the messengers went up out of the glorious city, and travelled even unto Carmel, and came to the cave wherein the prophet dwelt; and they fell down at his feet and offered him gifts, saying unto him, "O my lord, send us rain!" Then the prophet caused three great clouds to rise up out of the sea, even the sea of Tarshish, whereby he dwelt; and the first cloud was white as the fleece of the lamb, and the second cloud was red like blood, and the third cloud was black as night. And when the messengers saw the third cloud they cried with a loud voice, "O my lord, give us the black cloud." Then the prophet said, "Be it unto you as you have desired, ye sons of Belial." And the messengers marvelled at him, and saluted him, and returned unto their king.

Then the king and all his wise men and his mighty men, and all the city, both great and small, went out to meet the messengers; and the messengers fell down on their faces before the king and said, "O king, we have seen the prophet of Israel that dwelleth in Carmel, by the sea, and he offered unto us three clouds to go over our land—a white cloud, a red cloud, and a black cloud; and we chose the black cloud, to the end that the rain might fall, even the heavy rain, upon the earth." Then the king, and all the wise men, and the mighty men, and all the people, both small and great, shouted for joy, and said, "Ye choose well, O messengers.

The black cloud—let the black cloud come over our land!"

And behold, while they yet shouted, there arose afar off, from the way of the sea, a mighty cloud, and it was black even as the night when the moon shineth not nor any star; and as the cloud arose the face of the sun was hid, and the darkness overspread the earth, and the birds flew to the thick branches, and the wild beasts came forth, till the roar of the lion was heard even by the people of the mighty city. And the king, and his wise men, and his men of war, and all the multitude, both small and great, fell on their faces and lifted up their hands to the cloud and cried, "The rain! the rain!"

Then the cloud opened over the city and over all the people, and out of it came the SARSAR, the ice-cold Wind of Death; and it smote the king, and his wise men, and his men of war, and all the people, both small and great, and they died. There they died even as they lay upon the earth, with their hands lifted to the cloud, and the words in their mouths—"The rain!—give us the rain!"

And of that king and nation no man remembered anything, nor could the city be found any more; but the land became a desert, and the wild beasts made their dens in the cedar chambers, and the reeds rustled where the river had rolled, and the birds of the air lodged in the tree of emeralds, and plucked at the ruby fruit.

But there dwelt one man alone in that city—he

only was left when the king, and his wise men, and his men of war, and all the people perished; and he dwelt there alone, and gave himself to prayer, and heeded not the gold, nor the marble palaces, nor the precious stones, but prayed night and day. And the years passed away, and the generations of mankind changed, and still he dwelt there alone; and his beard and hair were white as snow, and his eyes were glittering like a sword, but his strength failed not, nor lacked he anything, but prayed seven times a day and seven times every night to Allah the Gracious and Merciful for forgiveness of his sins.

Then after a thousand years, when the river had changed its course, and the granite walls of the city had fallen down, and the thick trees grew in the courts of the palaces, and the owls and the hyenas lodged in the holy places of the temple, there came a servant of God, whose eyes were opened that he might find the city, and he entered in through the broken gates of brass, and came unto the fig-tree by the fountain, where dwelt the man of prayer—the solitary man; and the solitary man lifted up his eyes, and when he saw the servant of God he fell on his face, and returned thanks that he had seen again the countenance of a man. Then the servant of God wept for pity, and said, "O my brother, how camest thou to dwell here alone?" And the solitary man, the man of prayer, answered and said, "O servant of God, in a fortunate hour art thou come unto me; and blessed be He that sent thee, for now may

I die, and my sins be forgiven. Behold, I was one of the wicked men of this city, sons of Belial were we all, and thought not of God, but only of our own lusts, and our palaces, and our high feasts, and our beautiful women; and my brethren were cruel also, and scourged their slaves oftentimes, and tortured their prisoners of war, and put their cattle to death with evil treatment. And it came to pass that I saw a camel bound upon my father's grave, and left to perish with hunger; and she knew me, and looked me in the face and groaned, and strove to lick my hands. Then was I moved with compassion, and loosened her and let her go free, and drove her into the rich pastures. And for this that I showed mercy to the camel hath the Lord showed mercy unto me; and when all my brethren went down to destruction in the day of His wrath, when the Sarsar came forth out of the black cloud and slew them all, then was I saved, to the end that I might repent. Lo! a thousand years have I prayed in solitude, till the bones of my brethren are dust, and the thick trees grow in their palaces, and the roar of the lion is heard in their chambers of cedar; and no voice of man have I heard nor human face have I seen till thou hast visited me. And now know I that I have not prayed in vain, but that my sins are forgiven, and that I may die in peace. Therefore, I pray thee, lay thine hand upon me, and let me feel the hand of a man, and say for me the prayer of departure, and let me die." And the servant of God did as the solitary man desired, and blessed him; and the shadows of death came over him like the twilight, and his eyes ceased to shine brightly, and he laid him down with his hand in the hand of the servant of God, and blessed God with a few words, and died in peace. And the servant of God buried him there under the fig-tree by the fountain, and wept over him, and went out of the city through the broken gates of brass, and returned not, neither looked back. And no man from that day forth has beheld it, neither entered there, nor knoweth any man where that city is to found; but the wilderness hath swallowed it up, and the wild beasts have made it their home, because of the wickedness of the people and their oppressions upon man and upon beast in the sight of the Lord.

There is a Western story, not quite so beautiful and with a somewhat different moral—a story which may be found by the diligent reader in the *Times* and other journals for the months of July and August, in the year of Grace one thousand eight hundred and sixty-three. This Western apologue runs somewhat to the following purpose:—

There was a certain great and lordly city whose prince was among the powerful of the earth, and for whose nod whole nations waited obediently. And this city, which had aforetime been a great and vast city, was by this prince still further exalted and adorned, till it was wonderful to behold. And there were in that city royal palaces, with pictures and statues innumerable, and gardens wherein were all manner of beasts of the field and fowls of the air; and temples were there, all bedaubed with gold, whereof the chief were dedicated, not to Allah the Gracious, the Merciful, but to two women, whose names were Miriam of Nazareth and Miriam of Magdala. And of the streets of that great city there were no end, for they were all made by the power of the prince; and every poor man's house was pulled down, and every rich man's house destroyed, so that those great streets might traverse the city, which became even as the cities of old under their tyrants—like unto Babylon, and unto Persepolis, and Tadmor of the Waste. Then men boasted of that great and wonderful city, and said it was the centre of the world, and that the buildings thereof were all on one great plan, even as the world which Allah has made. But they who made this boast were blind and fallible; for in the world of Allah nought is uniform or monotonous, nor does one tree resemble another tree, nor one mountain another mountain, but the great plan of them all is endless variety, and the unity thereof is the opposite of uniformity. But the works of men, the tyrants and the priests, who have built cities and temples, and made laws, and established false religions, these all have wrought to produce uniformity without variety; and these are they whose labours this great city resembles, rather than the blessed creations of Allah.

And in this city dwelt many wise men and learned, among the most learned of the earth: and there were delicate women, and men who wore soft raiment, and fared sumptuously every day. And all the people of the city believed that they were the most learned, and delicate, and refined people in all the world; and that elsewhere men were brutal and stupid, and women coarse and evil entreated; and that save in their city there was no civilization.

Now it came to pass that in that city a strange thing was found. Amid all the proud palaces, and delicious gardens, and halls for feasting, and places for singing men and singing women, and for dancing and all manner of luxurious delights—and among the gilded temples dedicated to Miriam of Nazareth and Miriam of Magdala—among all these places there were certain buildings set apart for a purpose of another kind. Many wise men assembled there, and many learned men, and men adorned with tokens of the favour of the great prince, and with the ensigns of a noble order called that of Honour; and these men, with their disciples (who also were youths of the better sort, and habited ever in well-ordered garments), employed themselves in these public buildings* at frequent intervals, week after week, and year after year, in the form and manner following: They took a number of tame and inoffensive animals—but principally those noblest and most sensitive

* Videlicet The School of Medicine, the College of France, the Faculty of Sciences, and the Veterinary College at Allfort.

animals, horses—and having bound them carefully for their own safety, proceeded to cut, hew, saw, gouge, bore, and lacerate the flesh, bones, marrow, heart, and brains of the creatures groaning helpless at their feet. And in so orderly and perfect a fashion was this accomplished, that these wise men, and learned men, and honourable men discovered that a horse could be made to suffer for ten hours, and to undergo sixty-four different modes of torture before he died. Wherefore to this uttermost limit permitted by the Creator did they regularly push their cutting and hacking, delivering each horse into the hands of eight inexperienced students to practise upon him in turn during the ten hours.* This, therefore, they did in that great city, not deigning to relieve the pains they were inflicting by the beneficial fluid whereby all suffering may be alleviated, and not even heeding to put out of their agonies at the last the poor mangled remnants of creatures on which they had expended their tortures three score and four.

And the people of this city still boasted and said, "Behold, we are the most wise, and the most brave, and the most polished people on the face of the earth, and our city is the centre of civilization and of humanity."

These Eastern and Western tales have a strangely-different character assuredly. The state of men's

* The *Times*, Sept. 5th (or 6th), 1863.

minds, when they could imagine that a single act of mercy to a brute would procure the salvation of the doer in the midst of the destruction of his city, is curiously contrasted with that other state when they can calmly contemplate hideous tortures perpetrated regularly, and as a matter of business, upon hundreds of animals every year, and continue to uphold the torturers in esteem, and in high public functions, as the instructors of youth. We do not seem to have advanced much over the Moslem by our eighteen centuries of Christianity, so far as this matter is concerned.

The question, however, of Cruelty to the Brutes is one not to be hastily dismissed, nor can the recital of any barbarities be admitted to determine it in all its bearings. In quoting the above Eastern apologue, and recording the terrible fact of contemporary Parisian manners, we beg to disclaim all intention of treating the subject by that method of mere appeal to the feelings by which nearly every question of morals can be distorted and prejudiced. The infliction of pain is a thing naturally so revolting to the cultivated mind, that any description of it inevitably arouses strong sentiments of dislike, if not of horror; and were we to proceed no further to explain the motives and causes of such inflictions, vivid pictures of all penal—and even of all surgical—treatment might easily be drawn, so as to call forth reprobation upon the heads of the greatest benefactors of humanity. In the following pages we shall endeavour to reach the ground of the whole controversy by arriving at some answer to the fundamental question, "What *is* Cruelty to Animals? What are the duties of man as regards the welfare of the brutes, and how are they to be ranked in comparison with the duties he owes to his human fellow-creatures?" The search for the solution of these problems will fortunately absolve us from the painful task of entering into any description of the cruelties committed against animals either in France or England, or discussing special acts of public lecturers or private students of physiology. In all such cases it is the vagueness of popular moral opinion in which evil finds its great defence; and so long as cruel experiments are only rebuked by the denunciations of excited sentiment, so long will the perpetrators pass by contemptuously the ignorant blame of those who "understand nothing of the necessities of the case, or of the interests of science," or (at the best) will draw a veil of secresy over the disgusting mysteries of their operating tables. A different result would be obtained if society in general could be brought to form a sound and clear opinion of the limits wherein the sufferings of animals may lawfully be inflicted for the benefit of mankind, and could then pronounce with calm and dispassionate judgment its severest censure and condemnation upon every act which should transgress these limits, and therefore deserve the opprobrium of "cruelty."

The world owes to Bishop Butler the exposition of that ultimate ground of moral obligation on whose broad basis stand our duties to all living beings, rational and irrational. He says that if any creature be sentient—i. e., capable of suffering pain or enjoying pleasure—it is cause sufficient why we should refrain from inflicting pain, and should bestow on it pleasure when we may. That is enough. We need go no further to seek for a primary ground of obligation for mercy and kindness. Many other motives may, and do, come in to enhance and modify this obligation; but, standing by itself, it is sufficient. If we could divest ourselves of every other idea, and even admit the dreadful hypothesis that neither man nor brute had any Creator, but came into existence by some concourse of unconscious forces; yet even then—in a sunless, hopeless, Fatherless world—there would still remain the same duty, if the creature could feel pain, to avoid inflicting it; if it could feel pleasure, to bestow it. We cannot get below this principle. It is an ultimate canon of natural law—a *necessary* moral law (in metaphysical parlance)—since we cannot even conceive the contrary, nor figure to our imaginations a world or a condition of things wherein the obligation could be suspended or reversed.

Let us endeavour to arrive at a clear analysis of such natural obligations:—

First. In the case of rational, moral beings—what are our necessary obligations towards them?

We have seen that as they are sentient beings, we are bound to avoid their pain and seek their pleasure; but as they are more than sentient, and also rational and moral beings, other and higher obligations are added to those which concern their pain and pleasure. The highest end of a merely sentient being is enjoyment of pleasure and freedom from pain, i. e., Happiness; but the highest end of a rational and moral being is Virtue. Thus, as we are bound to seek the sentient being's happiness because he is capable of happiness, so we are bound to seek the moral being's virtue because he is capable of virtue. Here, also, we have reached an ultimate obligation. And inasmuch as virtue immeasurably transcends happiness, so must moral interests transcend sentient interests; and the being who is both moral and sentient, demands that his moral interests be primarily consulted, and his sentient interests secondarily; and the being who is only sentient and not moral is placed altogether subordinately, and can only claim that his interests be regarded after those of the moral being have been fulfilled. To this simple obligation, to seek the virtue of all beings capable of virtue, there are, of course, added many religious and fraternal motives of the greatest force and sanctity in enhancing our duty of aiding our fellow men. But the original ground (as in the former case) is sufficient of itself. Were there no Divine Author of virtue, no immortality of blessedness for the virtuous soul, yet still the fact that a being could attain to virtue would constitute an obligation to seek his virtue.

The great ends, then, of the obligation of man to his rational fellow-creature is, in the first place, to seek his Virtue, and in the second place his Happiness. To the virtue he can conduce, and the happiness he can produce—both in limited degrees, which degrees are the sole bounds (theoretically) of his obligations.

But, practically, the powers of any human being, either to conduce to the virtue or produce the happiness of mankind, are limited, not only by the influence he can exercise on any one, but by the numbers on whom he can, in his narrow sphere, exercise any influence at all. Secondary moral obligations here come into play, requiring that in that necessarily narrow sphere of his labours there shall be precedence in his benevolence given to certain persons above others. If a man's powers permitted him to aid the virtue and happiness of all mankind—of all equally—he would be bound to do so. As this is impossible, he must partition his benevolent cares on certain obvious principles of selection—propinquity of blood, contract of marriage, debts of gratitude, &c. Roughly speaking, these secondary obligations may be described as regulating that benevolence be first shown to those nearest to us, and afterwards to those more remote. They cannot be lawfully interpreted to abolish the claims of more remote objects of benevolence, but only to subordinate them; that is, when any degree of equality exists between the wants of the nearer and further claimants, the nearer has the precedence and preference. But when the want of the nearest claimant is altogether trifling, and the want of the remoter claimant urgent and vital, the prior claims of the first cannot be held to supersede those of the second, which would in effect amount to their entire abolition.

These (we fear, somewhat tedious) analyses of principles, lead us to the right point for considering the obligations owed by man to the lower animals. The brutes are sentient, but not moral creatures, therefore our concern is solely with their happiness. To what does this claim amount? If we had absolute power we should desire to relieve all animals from all pain and want, and we should bestow on them such pleasures as their humble natures can receive. Obviously we can practically do little more than meet these obligations towards the animals with whom we come in contact by refraining from causing them suffering, and supplying those which belong to us with proper food and shelter. The life of a brute, having no moral purpose, can best be understood ethically as representing the sum of its pleasures; and the obligation, therefore, of producing the pleasures of sentient creatures must be reduced, in their case, to the abstinence from unnecessary destruction of life. Such, then, are our duties towards the brute, simply considered, without reference to the human race.

But the claims of the brutes on us for happiness must necessarily be subordinated not only to human claims for moral aid, but for human claims for happiness also. First, the happiness of animals is a vastly lower and smaller thing than the happiness of man; secondly, as all the interests of man touch upon moral grounds, they assume higher importance than those of un-moral beings; and lastly, that race of man to which we belong must have over us claims of precedence superior to any other race, were it even angelic, which should be more remote. So clear and so wide is this line of demarcation between our duties to man and to the brutes that it appears almost an impertinence thus to analyze it; and we may doubtless safely proceed in our argument, assuming it as granted on all hands that there is an absolute subordination between the claims of the animal and those of man. The whole lower creation is for ever and utterly subordinated to the higher.

What then remains of the obligation to consider the pain and pleasure of the sentient but un-moral animals? Is there any space left for it in the crowd of human duties? Surely there is a little space. Claims which are subordinated to higher claims are not (as we have already said) therefore abolished. Here is an error common both to our views of the relative claims of different human beings, and of the relative claims of brutes and men. There is in both cases a point where the rights of the secondary claimant come into the field, else were there in morals the anomaly of moral obligations which should never oblige any one. Where is this point to be found?

We have already said that in regulating the precedency of human claims, the point is found where there ceases to be any kind of equality between the wants of the two claimants. Where the wants are equal (or anything like equal) the nearest comes first, the remoter afterwards. If a father need bread to save him from starvation, and a friend need it also for the same purpose, the father's claims must come first. But if the father need it only to amuse himself by throwing it to fowls on the river, and the friend need it to save him from death, then the father's claims go to the ground, and the friend's become paramount. This principle is continually neglected in human affairs, and the neglect causes great moral errors. The parent, husband, wife, or child whom affection and duty both direct to make their nearest and dearest the object of their "precedency of benevolence," continually fall under the temptation to make them their exclusive objects, and evade other obligations under the delusion that they are all merged in the one primary obligation. The same thing takes place in the case of animals. Men say, "Human obligations come before all obligations to the brutes. Let us wait till all human beings are virtuous and happy, and then it will be time to attend to the brutes." But we are no more morally justified in the one case than in the other, neither in merging all human duties in duties to one individual, nor in waiting to consider our obligations to the animals to those Greek kalends when all human wants will be abundantly supplied.

The point where the inferior claim of the brute, as of the man, must come into the field, can only be in each case where there ceases to be any kind of equality between the superior and inferior claims. We must consider carefully what can constitute the relative claims of beings of such different rank. Passing below the last human claimant on our benevolence, we find a "great gulf fixed." With the rationality and moral freedom of the agent, life itself has so far altered its value that we no longer recognize in it any of the sanctity which pertained to the life of a man; nor can the creature's comfort or enjoyment of any kind be put in the balance. We can in no case say that the claim of life for the brute is the same thing as the claim of life for a man; nay, even of security, or food, or comfort of any kind for the man. Everything which could be fairly interpreted to be a want for the man must have precedence over even the life of the animal. But here we must stop. Those cruel impulses of destruction, which we may call wantonness in a man, have no claims to be weighed against the brute's life and welfare. His gluttonous tastes, his caprices, his indolence, have no claims. Here the claims of the brute come on the field. Our obligations to consider its humble happiness must appear here or nowhere. They are postponed utterly to man's *wants*. They stand good against his *wantonness*. Practically, where does the principle lead us? Simply to this—that we may slay cattle for food, and take the fowls of the air and the fish of the sea to supply our table; but that we may not (for example) torture calves to produce white meat, nor slash living salmon to make them more delicate, nor nail fowls to the fireside to give them diseased livers. We may use horses and asses in our ploughs and our carriages, but we have no right to starve and torture our poor brute servants for our avarice or malignity. We may clear every inhabited country of wild beasts and noxious reptiles and insects whose existence would imperil our security or militate against our health or cleanliness, or who would devour our own proper food; but we have no right to go into untrodden deserts to take away the lives of creatures who there have their proper home, nor to kill in our own country harmless things like sea-gulls and frogs for the mere gratification of our destructive propensities.

And further. Besides these limits to the taking of life, there are limits to the infliction of pain. Here, again, if the pain be necessary, if the life demanded by human wants cannot be taken without the infliction of some degree of pain; or if (without killing a brute) we are obliged to put it to some suffering, to fetter it for our security, or for any similiar reason, here, also, we may be justified. But though we may thus inflict pain for our want, we are no more justified in inflicting it than in taking life for our wantonness. If from the odious delight in witnessing suffering, or from furious tempers, or parsimony, or idle curiosity, we put an animal to needless torture, we stand condemned; we have offended against the law requiring us to refrain from inflicting pain on any being which, by its sentient nature, is sensible to pain.

These views are surely almost self-evident. To affirm the contrary and maintain that we have a right to take animal life in mere wantonness, or to inflict needless torture upon animals, is to deny that a sentient being has any claims whatever, or that his capacity for suffering pain and enjoying pleasure ought to determine in any way our conduct towards him. For if that capacity for enjoyment is not to protect his life (i. e., the whole sum of his pleasures) against our wanton destruction, nor his capacity for pain protect his nervous frame from our infliction of needless torture, there is nothing left to be imagined of occasion wherein his claims could be valid.

The line then which we are seeking must be drawn here or nowhere. Animal's lives (i. e., their whole sum of pleasures) may be taken for man's wants, even if those wants be ever so small, but not for his wantonness; nor may they be taken in any case with needless infliction of pain.

We shall assume that the reader will concede

this principle. It remains to test its application to the controversy which concerns us at present—the right of men to put animals to torture for the sake of (what they claim to be) the interests of Science. We must endeavour to discuss this question very calmly, and not allow ourselves to be carried away by the natural indignation caused by pictures of agony. Almost similar pictures of human agony might be drawn from the scenes in any military hospital, and yet would argue nothing against the goodness of the operator.

"Science" is a great and sacred word. When we are called on to consider its "interests" we are considering the cause of that Truth which is one of the three great portals whereby man may enter the temple of God. Physical science, the knowledge of God's material creation, is in its highest sense a holy thing—the revelation of God's power, wisdom, love, through the universe of inorganic matter and organic life. The love of Truth for its own sake, irrespective of the utility of its applications, has here one of its noblest fields; and no love of the Beautiful by the artist, nor of the Good by the philanthropist, can surpass it in sanctity, or claim, on moral grounds, a larger liberty.

Where then are we to rank "the interests of science," among human wants?—or wantonnesses? Surely among the wants deserving of fullest privilege. Man, in his highest capacity as a rational being, hungers for truth as the food of his soul, even as he hungers for meat for his body; and the wants of the soul must ever be placed in higher rank than those of the body. He has a right to seek truth as he has a right to seek natural food, and may obtain it equally lawfully by the same measures. Thus we arrive at the conclusion that man has a right to take animal life for the purposes of science as he would take it for food, or security, or health. And this, be it remembered, is strictly for science, as science, apart from the contingent utility which may result from any discovered truths. When men go about explaining the probable use which may be derived from a scientific experiment, they are employing supererogatory argument. The scientific truth, as a truth, is an end in itself: the derivable utility affords another and supplementary argument.

Of course, when it happens, as in the case of anatomical researches, that every discovered truth is likely in a high degree to contribute to the restoration of human health and the salvation of human life, then the supplementary argument hence derived for the prosecution of such researches is proportioned to the whole value of human health and life, and deserves the highest recognition. For all purposes of reasoning, however, we may carry with us the full admission that the interests of science alone, as science, are enough to justify a man in taking away the life of any animal.

We may take animal life (that is, the whole

sum of the animal's pleasures) for the interests of science; but we must take it with "no needless infliction of pain." Now, unhappily, until lately, nearly all experiments of science were inevitably accompanied by the infliction of torture. It was not so much the creature's life which the experimenter required as its endurance of all manner of lacerations and "vivisections." It must be owned that here was a trying problem. Should science (it was asked) turn aside in her royal progress and forego her claims for the sake of some miserable brute or reptile—say of the frog, which Marshall Hall dared to call "God's gift to the physiologist"? Or should the torture of a thousand animals be held as nothing in the balance against the supreme interests of man? It would seem that in such a conflict, such an "antinomy of duties," as Kant would have named it, our sympathies would have been with the man who relinquished his experiment at the instigations of mercy; but that, at the same time, we could not presume to censure the man who pursued it unrelentingly. Be it remembered, however, that here and everywhere it can only be in the *true* interests of science that such sacrifices can be justified at all. Of this we shall say more anon.

But this whole phase of the question may now be put aside for ever. The most beneficent discovery of ages—the discovery for which the sages of old would have offered hecatombs, and yet for which no *Te Deum* has ascended from the churches of

Christendom as for many a bloody victory—the great discovery of perfect anæsthetics, has altered the whole condition of the case between the man of science and the brutes. It is at the option of the physiologist, by the use of chloroform, to perform nearly every experiment he can desire without the infliction of any pain whatever. With the exception of the problems connected with the nerves of sensation, he can test at will any scientific truth at the cost, perhaps, of life, but never of torture.

How stands the case now? Surely that such experiments as may be required by science at the cost of animal life may be freely made at such cost; and that the experiments which require processes naturally involving torture, may be freely performed with the use of anæsthetics and consequent avoidance of torture,—*but not otherwise.* Here is the line which Providence has drawn for us in these latter days as clear as daylight. There is in our hands the means of obviating the torture while reserving the interests of science; and we are inexcusable if from indolence, parsimony, or any other motive, we fail to use it. The experiment then becomes unlawful to us, and falls under the condemnation of wanton cruelty. Let us see precisely what these two conditions involve; firstly, that the life we are going to take is really demanded by science; secondly, that the pain of the experiment shall be removed by anæsthetics.

For animal life to be really demanded by science

we must conclude that it is wanted either, firstly, for the discovery of some new truth; or, secondly, for the establishment of some questionable fact; or, thirdly, for general instruction. Thus an anatomist may kill a bird or beast to discover or ascertain the facts of its structure, and the natural historian may kill it to affix its place in zoology or ornithology, or the toxicologist may kill it to preserve it in a museum for general instruction. All these reasons for taking the lives of animals must be held valid. But, where there is no anticipation of discovering a new truth, where there is no questionable fact to be ascertained, and where general instruction can be obtained perfectly without the sacrifice of fresh life, then there remains no justification for the act. It passes under the censure of wanton destruction.

Secondly, that we may consider the conditions for the justification of torturing experiments fulfilled, we must demand that in every case in which the production of severe pain is involved, the experimenter shall employ chloroform or some other anæsthetic with such sufficient care as to obviate the pain. No excuse of trouble or expense can be admitted; for if the individual or Society be unwilling, or unable, to undergo such needful trouble and expense, they are disqualified from undertaking experiments which cannot lawfully be performed save under such conditions. Here then stands the case against the vivisectionists. Have they done that which in itself is lawful under lawful conditions? Have they taken the lives of brutes only when the interests of science really demanded them? and have they performed painful experiments always under the influence of anæsthetics? If they have observed these conditions, they must stand morally exempt from blame, and the popular outcry against them deserves to be disregarded as ignorant and futile. If they have transgressed these conditions, then they must stand morally convicted of the heinous offence of Cruelty, and the indignation and disgust of mankind would be amply justified against them.

We cannot pretend to bring forward evidence of the infraction of these conditions by the societies and individuals who have been accused of cruelty in vivisection. The subject has been discussed in all the leading journals of the country, and facts have been alleged of sufficient gravity and supported by ample authority to justify in full the anxious investigation of the case by men of humanity. Viewing the evidence before us, it appears impossible to doubt that in France, for years back, a vast number of horses and dogs have been dissected alive and submitted to every conceivable operation for the instruction of pupils in anatomy and veterinary surgery, and that no chloroform has been in use on these occasions. On the other hand, in England, it is affirmed, seemingly on good authority, that vivisections are comparatively rare, and are performed only by scientific men for the ascertainment of physiologic facts, and usually with the exhibition of chloroform.

If these facts be so, it appears beyond question that the French system has terribly transgressed the limits of morality in this matter. Dead horses and dogs would have served the purpose of instruction to the pupils in anatomy as well as living ones; and the whole mass of torture involved in their living dissection might have been spared. If for the purpose of instructing their pupils in the surgery of the living fibre, it may have been necessary to perform some operations on animals before death, yet of those actually performed daily at Allfort (64 on each horse) the great majority are (like the removal of the hoof) wholly useless, and present no kind of compensating benefit for the acute torture they inflict, inasmuch as the operations cannot be copied in the human subject, nor would they ever be used by any owner in the case of a horse. As to the primary motives justifying such taking of life for purposes of science, they cannot be alleged in the case at all; for there is no attempt at discovering any new fact, or ascertaining any doubtful one, ever propounded. These points have been clearly demonstrated in the French Academy; and in the *Séance* of August 25, 1863, M. Dubois proposed a motion, whereby the evils in question would have thenceforth been forbidden, the pupils instructed on dead bodies, and the dissection of living animals confined to special cases of the discovery or verification of new facts. He proposed that three replies should be made to the questions asked by Government on the subject, to the following effect:—

"1. The Academy, without dwelling on the injurious form of the documents that have been submitted to it, acknowledges that abuses have been introduced into the practice of vivisection.

"2. To prevent these abuses, the Academy expresses the wish that, henceforward, vivisections may be exclusively reserved to the research of new facts or the verification of doubtful ones; and that, consequently, they may be no more practised in the public or private courses (of lectures) for the demonstration of facts already established by science.

"3. The Academy equally expresses the wish that the pupils at the schools of veterinary medicine may henceforward be exercised in the practice of operations on dead bodies, and no more on living horses."

As this Report was negatived by a majority in the Academy, and the Report actually adopted evaded the questions presented, and left the whole matter in its original condition, we are under the painful necessity of still leaving at the door of the men of science in France the terrible charge of perpetrating and sanctioning the agonizing deaths of multitudes of highly sensitive animals, wholly without justification from the real interests of science.

Further, the condition on which painful experiments can be lawfully made (namely, the use of anæsthetics) being, to all appearance, altogether rejected in the case of the French vivisections, the last justification is withdrawn, and the case stands as an exemplification of the greatest possible offence to be committed towards the animals, without any extenuating circumstances. The most highly organized and most friendly creatures are put to the death of uttermost and most prolonged agony, entirely without justification, and with the habitual neglect of that precaution by which all their sufferings might have been obviated. When we say that this great moral offence has been committed for years, and is still committed, in defiance of remonstrance, by the splendidly-endowed scientific associations of one of the most civilized countries in the world, we seem to have reached the last term of condemnation which useless, wanton, deliberate, and exquisite cruelty can incur.

In the preceding pages we have endeavoured to examine this question from the purely moral side, and as a problem of Ethics separable both from religious considerations, and from natural sentiments of pity or disgust. Solely as a matter of *moral duty*, imperative on us as rational free agents, we have (it is hoped) demonstrated that the claims of animals must be regarded so far as to cause us to respect their lives when no human want, but only wantonness, asks their destruction; and also that the infliction of torturing experiments upon them can only be justified when accompanied by the use of anæsthetics. Offences against these principles we have condemned on purely ethical grounds, and as infractions of the immutable laws of morality.

But it is impossible to regard a subject of this kind solely from the bare stand-point of ethics. Man is something else beside the agent of a "categoric imperative." He is also a creature of affections and sympathies; and, above all, he is a religious being, whose acts and feelings bear a certain relation to his Creator.

Now, as to the affections and sympathies of man, there are many species of animals on which they are naturally bestowed in a greater or less degree, and to kill or torture such animals is not only an offence against the laws of morality, but against the instincts of humanity and the feelings of the heart. So strongly has this been felt, that a great philosopher has actually asserted that the ground of our duty of mercy to the animals was not founded on their sentient nature, but on our sensibilities; and that cruelty was forbidden, not because it tortured the animal, but because it brutalized the man.* Here, however, he committed (as Bentham well showed) an enormous error, and ignored the true

* This sentence is a paraphrase of Macaulay's excellent epigram; that the Puritans forbade bear-baiting, "not because it caused pain to the brute, but because it caused pleasure to the man."

principle laid down by Butler. Such a doctrine, if admitted, would introduce the same hateful system of morals towards the brutes as that which has too often polluted human charity,—causing it to be performed, not for the benefit of the receiver, but the moral and spiritual interest of the giver. Each duty must be done for its own sake, not for the sake of any other object, however desirable; nay, in truth, no duty can be fulfilled truly (in both sentiment and action) save disinterestedly. The attempt to produce our own moral culture out of our humanity or beneficence is, *by the hypothesis*, absurd. Only disinterested and single-hearted actions really warm and enlarge the soul, not self-regardful ones. We are bound to consider the welfare of the brutes for their sakes, not ours, and because they are so constituted as to suffer and enjoy. That is the moral principle of the case.

Humane feelings, however, towards the brutes, though not the ground of our obligations towards them, form a natural tie which cannot be rudely broken without doing violence to many of the finer attributes of our nature. If a man be condemned in the court of morality for selling a faithful horse or dog to the vivisectionists, he would surely also be condemned for that act in the sentiments of every man of refined feelings. There is a story extant, so hideous that we hesitate to tell it, of a certain man of science who performed on his dog what he was pleased to term *une expérience morale*.

He tortured it for days in a peculiarly horrible manner, to try when the animal's affection would be overcome by his cruelty. The result proved that the dog died without ceasing to show his humble devotion to the man (or monster, we should say) who put him to such a test. The indignation which this fiendish act arouses in our minds is not solely a moral reprobation: it partakes also of the bitterness provoked by an outrage upon the affections.

The sentiment of tenderness to the brutes is of course not only inferior in sacredness to the moral principle, but also unlike it in being a very variable matter. Different nations and different individuals have it in very diverse degrees. The inquiry into its extent and influence would doubtless afford an interesting chapter in the study of human nature. We should find, as a rule, the more highly cultivated nations feeling the sentiment most vividly; but to this rule there would be many exceptions. The Arab's care for horses, the Turk's care for cats, are probably unparalleled elsewhere. But on the other hand, we find the Greeks, even in Homer's time, able to relish the sweet tale of Argus; while the whole magnificent literature of the Hebrews contains no passage, save in the story of Tobit, to imply any friendly feelings towards the animals. The singular commands in the Pentateuch, not to "muzzle the ox which treadeth out the corn," and not to "seethe a kid in its mother's milk," suggests rather the design of the legislator to soften the hard natures of the Israelites than to protect the animals from suffering, inasmuch as neither of the acts forbidden involved any real cruelty. In Hindoo literature, again, there appear to be perpetual tender references to the lower creatures. In the *Mahabharata*, in particular, there is an exquisite story of the hero who insisted on the admission of his faithful dog along with himself into heaven, and refused to accept the offers of Indra to conduct him there without it. At last the dog transforms himself into Yamen, god of Death, who has followed the hero's steps through the world, and now leaves him with a blessing to enter Paradise, free from the penalty of mortality.* As might naturally be expected, the condition of animals is much modified in countries where any of them are either supposed to be Divine beings, or else the abodes of human souls undergoing metempsychosis. This latter doctrine, involving such low and ludicrous circumstances as the transmigration (represented in a Theban tomb) of the gluttonous man into the pig, has perhaps met on that account with more contempt among us than its moral character deserves. Among the multitudinous superstitions of mankind, and fantastic dreams concerning the "undiscovered country, from whose bourne no traveller returns," not by any means the worst is that which

* See the *résumé* of the poem in Mrs Spiers' (now Mrs Manning's) admirable book, *Ancient India*.

would represent the future punishment for sinking our human nature in cruelty, sensuality, or sloth, to be the loss of that human nature for a time, and the incarnation of the sinful soul in some cruel, or sensual, or slothful brute. Between this idea (combined, as it always is, with the prospect of final restoration) and the doctrine of a burning cave of everlasting blasphemy and despair, it may be thought that the notions of Pythagoras and the originators of the Egyptian and Hindoo theologies do not suffer by comparison. Probably, however, the results of neither doctrine concerning the future would have essentially conduced to human virtue; and as to the influence of that of the metempsychosis on the conduct of men towards the brutes, its humanizing effects have doubtless been counterbalanced by the introduction of vegetarian errors, and consequent discouragement of animal life; and also by inducing a degree of care for some favoured brutes, infringing monstrously upon the rights of mankind. The writer's father was witness, during the old Mahratta wars, of various revolting scenes of famine, wherein the sacred cows of the Hindoo temples were standing gorged to repletion beside huge vessels of rice devoted to their use, while the starving population lay dying and dead of hunger all around.

Turning from nations to classes, we find as a rule that the most cultivated are the most merciful. But here also there are exceptions. In

England it is the half-brutalized and sottish carter, or the degraded and filthy dealer in "marine stores," who is brought up before the magistrate for furiously flogging his stubborn horse, or skinning alive some miserable cat. In France, alas! it is men of science —men belonging to the learned professions—who disembowel living horses and open the brains of dogs.

In the case of individuals, the presence or absence of tenderness for animals appears to constitute a very curious test of character. Its connection with benevolence towards mankind is of the inverse sort in too many instances. Few earnest philanthropists care at all for animals, or have any special sympathies with favourite dogs, horses, or birds; and they often seem to resent the care of others for such creatures as a defrauding of human claims. When the proposal was made for opening that very unassuming little institution in Islington* for the shelter of Lost Dogs, the outcry raised on the part of human charity was greater than has ever greeted the erection of one of the gin-palaces, or casinos, or other conservatories of vice in the kingdom. The objectors did not recognize the great law of human nature by which mercy begets mercy, even as "revenge and wrong bring forth their kind," and that the "merciful man" may not seldom have *become* merciful by beginning with

* Now at Hollingsworth Street, Holloway—well deserving of a visit.

mercy to "his beast." If it had no result whatever on human feelings, it would be hard to say that keeping a kennel for a few starving brutes was a much worse expenditure of money than sundry others with which the rich gentlemen of England indulge themselves.

But if the strong feelings of philanthropists for human claimants are somewhat chill as regards the animals, there is, on the other hand, a more deplorable inclination among all who have a tendency to misanthropy to bestow on animals an amount of affection very visibly distorted from its rightful human channels. Every Timon in the world has his dog; every embittered old maid her cat, or parrot. They do not love these creatures so much because the dog, cat, or parrot fills up the measure of their affections, as because they have withdrawn their affections from humanity, and pour them out on the brutes in the place of better objects. This kind of love for animals has in it somewhat truly painful to witness. It cannot be defended in any manner, yet our pity may fairly be given to a condition of heart which reveals a past of intense suffering, and is in itself a state of disease of the affections. We are inclined to feel contemptuous, or perhaps a little resentful, when in a world full of human woes and wants, a vast amount of tenderness and compassion is lavished upon some over-fed spaniel, dying of the results of excessive indulgence; or a legacy, which might have afforded education to a child, is devoted to the maintenance of a parrot. We are disgusted when we hear of a lady comforting a mother on the death of her only daughter, by saying, "I felt just the same when my Fido died." But resentment and contempt are no right sentiments for such sorrowful exhibitions of moral malady any more than for the depraved appetite of physical disease. Probably the worst form of this distortion of the affections, and one for which no excuse can be made, is to be found when the pride of the over-indulged men and women of wealth and rank keeps them aloof from their human fellow-creatures, and leads them to lavish on their animal favourites the care and tenderness they would disdain to display to a human being. The lady of fashion, who leaves her child unvisited for days in its nursery, under the care of menials, while she watches the feeding of her spaniel, and covers it with caresses,—is about as odious a specimen of humanity as may easily be found.

On the other hand, there are cases of intense love for animals in persons obliged to lead a solitary life which are among the most affecting incidents in the world. In Le Maître's beautiful story of *Le Lépreux de la Cité d'Aoste* (founded entirely on facts verified on the spot to the present day), the outcast leper and his sister are recorded to have dwelt in the ruined tower outside the city for many years of their suffering lives, utterly cut off from human intercourse. One day a poor little cur, starving and homeless, wandered into their secluded garden. They received it with delight, and the sister fed it, and made it her constant companion and favourite. After some years the sister died, and the leper was left utterly and for ever alone, save for the presence of the little dog, which gave him the only semblance of affection left for him to hope for in the world; and by its caresses and intelligence served to beguile his days and nights of ceaseless suffering. One day the poor animal strayed out of his garden towards the town. It was recognized as the leper's dog, and the people were seized with the alarm that it would carry the infection of his disease into the town. Fear is the most cruel of all things. They stoned and beat the poor creature till it only escaped from them at last to crawl back to its master and expire at his feet. He who would not sympathize with the leper's grief, must have a heart hardened indeed.

Again, there is a most remarkable story (recorded, we believe, a few years ago, in a paper in the *Quarterly Review*) of a French convict who was long the terror of the prison authorities by his violence and audacity. Time after time he had broken out and made savage assaults on his jailers. Stripes and chains had been multiplied year after year; and he was habitually confined in an underground cell, from whence he was only taken to work with his fellow-convicts in the prison yard: but his ferocity long remained untamed. At last it was observed that he grew rather more calm and docile, without apparent cause for the change, till one day, when he was working with his comrades, a large rat suddenly leaped from the breast of his coat and ran across the yard. Naturally the cry was raised to kill the rat, and the men were preparing to throw stones at it, when the convict, hitherto so ferocious, with a sudden outburst of feeling implored them to desist, and allow him to recover his strange favourite. The prison officials for once were guided by a happy compassion, and suffered him to call back his rat, which came to his voice, and nestled back in his dress. The convict's gratitude was as strong as his rebellious disposition had hitherto proved, and from that day he proved submissive and orderly. After some years he became the trusted assistant of the jailers, and finally the poor fellow was killed in defending them against a mutiny of the other convicts. The love of that humblest creature finding a place in his rough heart had changed his whole character. Who shall limit the miracles to be wrought by affection, when the love of a *rat* could transform a man?

But whatever result a general review might give us of the amount of tenderness of nations and classes of men for animals, there can be little doubt that it would prove to be a real characteristic of humanity, and possessed of a definite place among the sentiments of our nature. On the other hand, the affection and devotion of many species of animals for man are matters of too great notoriety to need more than passing reference. The dog, horse, elephant, cat, seal, and many species of birds, show these feelings in the most unmistakable manner; in some cases marking their love by truly heroic self-sacrifice, or by dying of grief for the loss of their masters. Probably many other species of beasts and birds would prove capable, on experiment, of similar attachment. The tie established in such instances between a man and the brute who gives him his unbounded devotion, is unquestionably one of great tenderness. The poor dog's love is a thing so beautiful that to despise it is to do violence to every softer instinct. The man is in so far below the brute if the brute can give him a pure, disinterested, devoted love, and he can give back no tenderness and pity in return. Cowper said well—

> "I would not have that man to be my friend
> Who needlessly sets foot upon a worm."

The human affections of one who could feel no emotions of pity for the animal which attached itself to him must be of little worth, and partake largely of egotism or mere selfish passion. Woe to the woman or the child who should depend on such a man.

To choose for objects of cruel experiments animals endowed with the wondrous power of love, is not then only a moral offence, viewed in the light of a needless torture of sentient creatures; it is also a sin against all the instincts of tenderness and pure sentiment. We are justified not only in condemning it on moral grounds, but in revolting against it in the name of the common heart of humanity.

There remains one grave and solemn side of this question which we have some hesitation in approaching. Man and brutes are not mere creatures of chance. Sentiments of pity are not matters of arbitrary taste. Moral laws do not alone bind us with a sacred obligation of mercy. The MAKER of man is also the Maker of all the tribes of earth and air and waters. Our Lord is their Lord also. We rule the animal creation, not as irresponsible sovereigns, but as the vicegerents of God.

The position of the brutes in the scale of creation would appear to be that of the complement of the mighty whole. We cannot suppose that the material universe of suns and planets was created for irrational and unmoral beings, but rather to be the habitation of various orders of intelligences endowed with that moral freedom by which they may attain to virtue and approach to God in ever-growing likeness and love. If we may presume to speculate on the awful designs of the Supreme Architect, we almost inevitably come to this conclusion, that these world-houses were all built to be, sooner or later, in the million millenniums of their existence, the abodes of living souls. Be this as it may regarding the other worlds in the universe, we must at least believe that here (where such beings actually exist) their palace-home of plains and hills and woods and waters, with all its libraries of wisdom, its galleries of beauty, has been built for them, and not for their humble fellow-lodgers, the brutes and the fowls, the insects and the fish. They are, we must conclude, the complement and filling-up of the great design. Some of them are the servants appointed for our use; all of them are made to be happy—to fill the world with their innocent delight. We cannot think that any of them, any sentient creature, was made primarily for another creature's benefit, but first for its own happiness, and then afterwards to "second too some other use." Thus we believe the world was made for Man,—the end of whose creation is Virtue and eternal union with God; and the complement of the plan are the Brutes,—whose end is such Happiness as their natures may permit.

If this be so, our relation to the whole animal creation is simply that of *fellow-creatures*, of a rank so much higher, that our interests must always have precedence. But to some orders of animals we are in a much nearer relation, for these are the servants given us expressly by God, and fitted with powers and instincts precisely suiting them to meet our wants. The camel, horse, ass, elephant, the cow, sheep, goat, dog, cat, and many species of fowls, are all so constituted as to supply us with what we need in the way of services, food, clothing, and protection. Our use or misuse of these servants is a matter in which it is impossible to conceive that we are irresponsible, or that we do not offend the merciful Creator when, instead of profiting by His gifts, we use our superior power to torture and destroy the creatures He has made both to serve us, and to be happy also. If there be one moral offence which more than another seems directly an offence against God, it is this wanton infliction of pain upon His creatures. He, the Good One, has made them to be happy, but leaves us our awful gift of freedom to use or to misuse towards them. In a word, He places them absolutely in our charge. If we break this trust, and torture them, what is our posture towards Him? Surely as sins of the flesh sink man below humanity, so sins of cruelty throw him into the very converse and antagonism of Deity; he becomes not a mere Brute, but a Fiend.

These would seem to be the simple facts of our relation to the animals, viewed from the religious point of view, on the hypothesis that our usual ideas concerning the lower creation are correct, that brutes have no germ of a moral nature, no prospect of immortality, and that between us and them there are no other ties but those of fellow-creaturehood. It may be that a more advanced mental philosophy, and further researches in science, may modify these ideas. It may be that we shall come to see that sentient life and consciousness and self-consciousness are mysterious powers working upward through all the orders of organic existence; that there are rudiments in the sagacious elephant and the affectionate dog of moral faculties which we need not consign hopelessly to annihilation. It may be that we shall find that man himself, in all the glory of his reason, has sprung, in the far-off ages of the primeval world, not from the "clod of the valley" any more than from Deucalion's stones, but from some yet-undiscovered creature which once roamed the forests of the elder world, and through whom he stands allied in blood to all the beasts of the field. It may be we shall find all these things; and finding them we shall not degrade man, but only elevate the brute. By such ideas, should science ever ratify them, we shall certainly arrive at new and vivid interests in the animal creation, and the brutes will receive at our hands (we must needs believe) some more tender consideration. But these are, as yet, all doubtful speculations, and we do not need to rest a feather's weight of argument upon them to prove that as religious beings we are bound to show mercy to all God's creatures.

God has made all the domestic animals with special adaptations to our use; but there is one species whose purpose is manifestly so peculiarly beneficent, that we cannot pass over it in forming an estimate of our relation to the lower creatures. Many beasts and birds are capable of attaching themselves to man, but the dog is endowed with a capacity for loving his master with a devotion whose parallel we must seek only in the records of the purest human friendship. There is no phenomenon in all the wondrous field of natural history more marvellous than this; and the beaver's architecture, the bee's geometry, may justly be ranked second to the exquisite instinct by which the dog has been rendered capable of such quick and vivid sympathy, such disinterested and self-sacrificing devotion. Nowhere, would it seem, do we come on clearer traces of the tender mercies of the Universal Father, and of His thoughtful provision (if we may so express it) for His children's wants, than in these instincts given to the dog to make him the friend of man, and enable his humble companionship to soothe the aching and cheer the solitary heart. In the various vicissitudes of human life, Providence has found it needful to allot to thousands years of loneliness, and days filled with the anguish of bereaved, or separated, or deceived affection. At the best, numbers of us must lack (amid, perhaps, much true friendship) that special tenderness of unquestioning and caressing love which children might supply. But even here that same Providence has, in a measure, supplied and forestalled the want of our hearts even as it supplies the wants of our physical nature for food and rest. As a mother might give to her child a toy to replace some unsuitable companion, so has the dog been given to us, and fitted to be our gentle play-fellow. How does he so marvellously understand our happy moods, and bound beside us with his joyful gambols? And how does he, in a moment, comprehend when we are sad—he who sheds no tears, nor shows any of our marks of grief —and try to lick the listless hand, and nestle to our side, as if to prove to us that his humble devotion will never fail us? How does it come to pass that his affection for his own species, and attachment to his home, and care for his food and safety, are all secondary with him to the love of his master; and that he leaves his companions and his abode without a sign of regret, and flings himself into any danger of robbers, or angry seas, to save him; and, finally, will often refuse all food, and die of starvation upon his grave? These are wondrous instincts—wondrous powers of pure disinterested love, whose existence in a creature so suitable in other ways to be the companion and guardian of man, is surely as much an evidence of the Creator's goodness as almost any other in the range of natural theology.

Nor is it some costly animal, whose support only the rich man could afford, or some delicate one, unable to live in different climates, to which such instincts have been given. Over all the globe, from north to south, the canine race can live where man can live, from the Esquimaux's hut to the kraal of the Hottentot; nor are there many so poor but that they may enjoy its possession. From the king who distrusts the friendship of his venal courtiers, to the blind beggar in his uttermost desolation, there are few whose deceived or lonely hearts cannot find some humble comfort in the true attachment of a dog.

Nay, may we go yet a step further? May we say that in these dumb companions God has placed beside us, in some sense, the emblems of what our own devotion might be to Him who is *our* Master; on whom we depend for all things; and from whose hand we also ought to take our joys and chastisement with the same unwavering faith and grateful love? It may be so; and we, the oft-offending children of that great Father, may look on the blameless and loving servants He has given us—servants who obey us so readily, and trust us so unreservedly—and find in them more than companions, even monitors also.

But we must not pursue these themes. Still less can we turn now to argue as to the right of men to subject creatures like these to hideous experiments and agonizing tortures. God help us not only to have mercy on His creatures, but to love them also in their place, and bless Him for their service to us, and for the happiness which He, the Lord of all, has not disdained to bestow upon them. We shall be the nearer to Him for doing so; for well did Coleridge say:—

> "He prayeth well who loveth well
> Both man, and bird, and beast;
> He prayeth best who loveth best
> All creatures great and small;
> For the dear God who loveth us,
> He makes and loves them all."

THE MORALS OF LITERATURE.

Reprinted from Fraser's Magazine, July, 1864.

THERE are many questions which present themselves from time to time concerning the Morals of Literature—questions of great interest, but not always of easy solution. We are not speaking of such literary misdemeanors as plagiarism, calumny, blasphemy, indecency—things which must have been recognized as offences ever since literature existed. Rather do we refer to modes of writing whose ethical character is sometimes doubtful, or which, at all events, has not yet been branded with the opprobrium which delinquency against the principles of justice, truth, delicacy, or charity would deserve. The ever-increasing depth and fulness of the stream of books and periodicals in our time, carrries us more and more frequently against these dubious shoals and quicksands of literature; and it would seem in every way desirable that they should be duly surveyed, and marked down in our charts as dangerous or otherwise. On the one hand, it is to be wished that actions really infringing the principles of morality, should meet with universal condemnation—a condemnation for which no commercial success of the offending works should compensate. On the other hand, it is no less to be wished, that the fear of transgressing, where there is no true cause for blame, should not fetter the author, or prevent him from giving to the world whatever he may have to teach.

The due discussion and settlement of these questions would be a work of great magnitude and of signal utility. Without any pretension to attempt its achievement, we propose only, in this paper, to throw out a few suggestive questions which may indicate briefly the nature of the task we desire to see performed.

1. In Biography. Where are the limits to the proper exposure to the public of the thoughts, feelings, and actions of the subject of the biography, and of those with whom he was connected?

We shall all allow, in generalities, that, if architecture should have its "seven lamps" for illumination, literature should be guided at least by the five holy ones of Truth, Purity, Simplicity, Loving-Kindness, and Reverence. But, practically, the claims of Truth are in continual collision with those of at least two of the rest: with Kindness, as regards the revelation of error and wrong; and with Reverence, as regards the violation of the sanctities of the inner life. In many cases the biographer may most justly feel at a loss to decide which guide he is to follow—the principle of such abstract truth as should require him to tell (so far as he knows it) "the truth, the whole truth, and nothing but the truth," concerning his subject and all connected with him; or the principle of kindness which shall adopt the rule, "de mortuis nil nisi bonum;" or, lastly, the principle of reverence, which shall warn him from dealing with whole departments of life most essential for a thorough comprehension of character. We all know how deplorably many biographers have erred in their solution of this problem. We have "Lives" which "lie like an epitaph," and are mere eulogies, as inane as the portraits of Queen Elizabeth, without a shadow in her face. These are written on behalf of kindness, and at the expense of truth. They are utterly useless; tending rather to nauseate the reader of the over-sweetened subject; and only misleading us in the great science of humanity, of which each separate biography ought to be what a rock is to the geologist, and an elementary substance to the chemist. The only excuse for them is when they arise from that hero-worship, whose law it is to dazzle the mental eye and render, not only spots but huge stains and blurs invisible, or transformed to radiant stars. Such biographies, written with sound vision, would be altogether unpardonable.

Again we have "Lives" (but they are more rare), wherein all the errors and offences of the subject are stated plainly enough; and if truth be infringed, it is on the side of severity, not mercy. Nearly always such biographies sin against charity, being dictated by active hate; and the reader's spirit of justice calls out for the champion (who sooner or later is sure to appear), to defend the helpless dead from the attacks of his calumniator. In our day it seems as if every character in history, who had been held up to opprobrium, is thus obtaining honourable rehabilitation. The literary pillory is always succeeded by the literary wreath. If there should be Comtistes in the twentieth century, their Calendar of heroes and saints will be at least half filled with the damned of history, till we have the month of Judas, the week of Nero, and the day of St Guy Fawkes.

Again,—and this is what concerns us most just now,—we have "Lives" written with the manifest desire to do every justice to the subject; to set forth alike the virtues and the defects, in a manner at once true and kindly. But another great law is broken—the law of reverence. The man's most secret life, his most private memoranda, his letters, written in the heat of passion or remorse, to his closest intimates—are violated and thrown open to the world. The public have got the truth; but they have lost something almost equally precious—the sense of the sanctity of the heart and soul's secrets. Or rather, we may say, that a special and individual truth has been insured by the sacrifice of the universal principle of truthfulness and confidence between man and man, whereby we trust each other with things sacred. The injury done by such a biography cannot easily be measured. There is first the rude violence done to the common feeling of the sacredness of the inner life—a violence which destroys its delicate beauty, like a blow on a woman's face. Then there is the loss of confidence in the security of all written and spoken confessions of feeling, whereby many a heart may be led to hide a wound which might have been healed by the hands of wiser friendship. Lastly, and worst, the most secret outpourings of the heart become entangled in a web of self-consciousness in youth, and in later life are utterly checked and arrested. The young man or woman who has read one of these biographies, can hardly write a diary touching on the inward life (a task otherwise most useful for self-knowledge), without a poisonous under-current of reflections as to the effect it would produce if hereafter published; like the one which he has perused, and which was equally, no doubt, intended by the writer to be kept secret. Even a child (as we have known) may be thus instructed in miserable double-mindedness and vanity. One who had been duly indoctrinated in the juvenile forms of this pernicious literature, asked of her guardian (an acquaintance of the writer), the ominous question, "Auntie, don't you think I am good enough to be put in a tract?"

What is a biographer to do to avoid splitting on these rocks?—to be at once true, kind, and reverent of inner sanctities? Must biography be reduced to a mere dry statement of the most ordinary and public facts of life; such a résumé as a newspaper-writer holds in his bureau, ready to print the day any man of note expires, and telling the world only of his birth, marriage, and death, his battles, speeches, books, honours, and last will and testament? This would be to cut off from us something more than a delightful branch of literature. It would be (to use our former simile), to forbid the geologist to examine below the surface of his rock; the chemist to analyze his element. "The noblest study of mankind" would hereby for ever be arrested. Such a sacrifice can hardly be demanded. If we could consult the departed as to how they would desire the records of their earthly career to be written, we may feel assured they would not ask of us to eliminate from them aught which might really guide or help the living; any

> "Footsteps which perchance another,
> Sailing o'er life's solemn main,
> A forlorn and fainting brother,
> Seeing, may take heart again."

But the question is just in this one point: What *is* good for the living to read? No man, we believe firmly, was ever the better, morally, for any knowledge gained at the cost of the violation of any real sanctity in the heart of his brother, be that brother still in the flesh, or long since gone home to God. We do not accomplish any good for the world by sacrificing either our own or others' secrets in this way. When the things "spoken in the ear" of faithful and tender friendship, or confided to pages never meant but for the writer's eye alone, come to "be proclaimed upon the housetops" of the public press,—it is a portent of moral ruin, not a process of reformation; be those things never so good and so profound.

Perhaps we may find some clue to the right principle of biographical reticence, by ascending to some larger generalities of literature. All literature should be guided by truth—a certain kind of artistic and moral truth even in fiction, a more literal and material veracity in history, description, science, and biography. What do we mean by such veracity of the latter class? Surely it is the simple rule of all truth—THE JUST EXPRESSION OF OUR IMPRESSION.

Our impression may be more or less nearly identical with absolute objective fact, but the faithful rendering of such impression in the manner we conceive best calculated to convey it to another is our truth—that which each of us "troweth." Now in describing a person, place, or event, in literature as well as in common speech, it is clear our duty is to strive to render our impression of such person, place, or event, thus faithfully or honestly. We are not called upon to tell everything we know, to describe every detail of feature and character, or of scenery or action; but only so to write as that the whole of our description, be it short or long, shall be the just expression of the sum of impressions the person, place, or event has made upon us. Nothing is implied in the ordinary engagements of the author to the reader, more or less than this. Of course, cases may arise when a further engagement may be formally or tacitly given to insert every detail; but this must always be exceptional, or else literature would be reduced to a *procès verbal*, or a catalogue. It is, in fact, the same principle which prevails in art, and makes a portrait by Titian something different from a gigantic painted photograph. What is it which the true artist, the painter or sculptor, really seeks to accomplish? Is it not "the just expression of his impression?" He does not seek to give a mere literal transcript of the object before him, but to take it, as it were, whole and entire, and cast it afresh in the crucible of his own mind. Either this, and this alone, must be the supreme aim and achievement of art, or else, if it be not so, a mirror (could its images be made durable) would be better than any portraits of Raphael's or Titian's; and Madame Tussaud's wax-works superior to a statue of Phidias. There is no third excellence conceivable. Art is either mere imitation—and then the meanest imitation, so that it be accurate, is the best art—or else it is something beyond imitation, and is the "just expression" of the artist's fullest and most perfect "impression."

How does all this apply to literature? Surely in this way: that the pen no more than the pencil should aim at a mere reproduction of material fact; but should render *that*—and something more. A fine landscape-painter gathers up all the features of his scene in his mind, and throws them on his canvas glorified and individualized; so that as he saw that mountain or forest, others may see it henceforth for ever. As we all know, this is produced by no servile copying of every rock or tree, every blade of the grass, every leaf of the wood. When modern artists, honestly seeking truth, have laboriously accomplished such servile copies, they have missed their aim, and made something which is no "expression of their impression" at all, something less like their impression than a few free touches of a master's brush would have produced. All this must apply to the author as to the painter. His business is first to obtain a vivid and true impression, and then so to express it as shall best convey the same to the reader. Is this to be done best by a record of sensations and ideas produced by the scene, or by a dry literal catalogue of objects and facts? Shall, for instance, the present writer describe the view before her eyes, by telling of gardens sloping down through grassy glades to the sea, the deep shadows of the ilex lying heavy on the ground, and the stone-pines standing out in lovely outlines against the sky and dazzling waters, and palms and oranges and cypresses blending with the blossoming apricot and almond in masses of glorious colouring; of the fountain playing close by, as fountains only play in Italy; the birds singing in the joy of opening spring, and the calm and soft Mediterranean beating gently like the pulsations of a peaceful heart against the low, tideless shore? No words can convey perfectly the richness and the softness of the scene; but would an accurate and minute account of each tree and clump and shelving bank do any better? Ought we to say "there are first 369 orange trees in a garden of half an acre, then a jet d'eau six feet high, then 500 yards of slope, descending at the incline of two feet in a hundred, on a lime-stone soil; the grass is unfitted for hay, the trees of no value as timber, but worth somewhat as fuel?" It is quite clear that the latter class of description may be desirable, if we want to purchase the house and garden to which it refers; but it is not literature, but business—a surveyor's or valuator's report, not a piece of literary or artistic composition. In like manner, if we should need to go to law about anything, we may desire a sworn information, or *procès verbal*, describing it minutely. But all these are necessities extraneous to literature, and true literature should make no pretence to fulfil their requirements. The veracity of the writer is engaged to this, and this only,—that his *impression* be reproduced in his work. Of course, according to the nature of the case, there may be a moral obligation involved in the care taken to make that impression co-ordinate with the facts; but this is another matter to literary veracity.

To apply all this to biography. It seems clear (if the principles above-stated be true), that the biographer's office is to render justly his impression of his subject's life and character, in the way of Art—not in the way of a Report of the one, or a sworn Information of the other. He is then under no obligation to enter upon details which motives of kindness or of reverence may induce him to pass over in silence, provided always that the impression he has derived from any such details known to him, be fairly rendered by his general description of his subject. He must make his hero neither better nor worse than such facts prove him to have been.

This principle would, we apprehend, relieve biographers of one class of their difficulties,—the impression, namely, that they are called upon when they undertake a biography, to share with the public all they know concerning their subject, and to reproduce the material facts, in crude literature, on which their judgment has been formed. When all is done, however, it must be avowed that other and great difficulties will often remain, with which nothing but consummate good taste can enable an author to deal. If publicity given to things which ought to be kept secret is a great evil and mischief, on the other hand the concealment of things calculated to afford deep insight into human nature, to warn or to encourage, is no less truly a great loss and injury to the world.

One of the many sorrows of youth, to which later life brings comfort, is the impression that we are alone in our struggles, our trials, and our sins. Sometimes it is a morbid vanity which makes us hug the idea of our lot being quite unparalleled. More often, perhaps, it is a very innocent and natural ignorance of the inner circle of other homes and other lives which makes us feel we are differently constituted from our kind. Then comes a real danger from an imaginary fact. "It is not good for man to be alone" (even in fancy) in the world. Everything becomes unhealthy—the greatest truths seem unreal, as the isolated consciousness works without its natural aid of sympathy from other minds possessed of similar consciousness. Struggles seem hopeless when we do not know that any other soul has ever striven and conquered in the same fight. Above all, sins assume sometimes the most portentous and giant shapes, before which we stand paralyzed with fear and shame, abandoning, perhaps, all hope and effort for our own recovery, till in some blessed moment we learn that one who has since become a saint on earth or an angel in heaven, fell once under the same Apollyon who has crushed us, and then rose up and slew him, and passed on "singing softly," on the celestial way. Then the demon who seemed to hide the whole horizon of our lives, and blot out the very sun with his shadow, shrinks to a tangible hideous fact—bad and black enough, Heaven knows! but a fact which, with God's great help, we will drive off our path for evermore. It cannot be doubted that books revealing deep moral and religious experiences are in these ways of immense utility. Especially are they so to us, to whom the guiding (and also contaminating and self-desecrating) practice of the confessional is unknown, and especially also in our day, when new phases of intellectual creed disturb the spiritual life in a thousand ways, and make half the thoughtful youth of the land pass through a stage wherein (as their teachers inform them) they have no right to claim the sympathy of the good now alive, or to appropriate the experience of the pious of old. How the few books which appeared twenty years ago—*Arnold's Life, Sterling's Life, Blanco White's Life,* and told us that good and sincere men had felt our doubts, and struggled through our trials; how they poured light and comfort into our hearts! How many men and women, now calm and happy in rational faith, may be thankful for having had the intolerable solitude of their hearts in youth dissipated for ever by books like these! It is quite clear that whatever may be demanded of us, the sacrifice of that which gives its value to books of this class cannot be required. Their subjects would be the last to desire it. Here then, in fact, lies the test of the biographer's capacity for his work. Can he retain what he ought to retain, and exclude what he ought to exclude, with regard at once to the interests of the living and the sacredness of the dead?

Besides these religious sanctities of life, there are the domestic and friendly ones, whose violation is hardly a less offence. Of course the consent of the parties in question is usually the test of justifiable publicity here; but what is to be done when the exculpation of one is the blame of another? There are difficult dilemmas here also.

2. Fiction has a veracity of its own to preserve. How far is it lawful, for instance, in fiction, to introduce real persons known to the writer, draw the portrait sufficiently exact to make them recognizable, and then add purely imaginary features of character or actions or opinions, which the reader shall henceforth inextricably associate with the real person? We are all ready to condemn such a practice utterly, when plainly described; but it is done every day, in fact, and that by writers of high reputation. In what the Germans call *Tendenz* novels (novels with a purpose), it is, in fact, the regular custom to take for the type of some opinion to be preached up or preached down, somebody who may be fairly identified therewith, and then having duly labelled and ticketed his unhappy specimen, the novelist,—inasmuch as he is a novelist and not a biographer,—proceeds to draw from his imagination facts and adventures and ideas, to be attributed to the specimen in his story, and woven in as neatly as may be with the description drawn from actual life. We have seen one of these, wherein it was intended to demolish a certain too hardy thinker, and wherein he was accordingly first identified unmistakeably with a certain character in the book, and then *that* character was made responsible for

the opinions of a totally different and antagonistic thinker, and (in that capacity) easily and triumphantly annihilated! These things remind us continually of Archbishop Whately's excellent simile between the practices of ancient heathens towards Christian martyrs, and those of modern theological critics to their subjects—"they both dress their victims in the skins of wild beasts, so as completely to disguise them, and then set the dogs to tear them to pieces."

Again: Fiction may avoid the sin of thus misrepresenting individuals, but is it justified in maligning human nature itself? Reading certain classes of literature, very popular in England just now, it would seem as if nobody were offended at pictures of life which would make us all a set of crawling worms unfit to be suffered to exist, much less to be made subjects of a work of art. If men be all mean and interested and worldly-minded, then it is no more proper to make them subjects of fiction than wasps, toads, and maggots. It is a marvellous thing how the admiration for the mere *savoir faire* of the clever writer, painter, sculptor, blinds men to the question whether their art is exercised on a fitting or an unfitting subject—i. e., whether it is worth something or nothing at all. The more people become amateurs of style, cognoscenti, or even practical artists themselves, so much greater seems the danger of their forgetting the whole scope and meaning of art in their criticism of the more or less successful way in which the effort is made to render any meaning whatever.

In Shelley's *Essay in Defence of Poetry* there is an admirable distinction between the different sorts of utility. There is an utility of the higher and of the lower kind; an ultimate and absolute utility, and a secondary and subordinate utility. The first concerns the great final ends of our existence, the second the temporary purposes of our present condition. The first utility promotes our welfare as men and women, immortal and rational moral agents; the second supplies our needs, and aids our prosperity as merchants, soldiers, sailors, bricklayers, and seamstresses, wanting food, clothing, shelter, wealth, health, pleasure, power, fame, or any other earthly good. Of course, that which aids the higher and moral part of us, also in a certain way elevates and aids the lower; and of course, all which aids the lower to its natural and true well-being, serves to afford a sounder basis for the higher. But the classification is a real and most valuable one, affording us a clue to many labyrinthine problems of social science, and reconciling the eternal quarrel between the Thinkers and the Workers, the *Aurora Leighs* of the world and the practical philanthropists. In like manner in art (the arts of writing, painting, sculpture, architecture), there are two utilities, the lower utility of giving expression to the thought, and the higher utility which lies in the thought itself. The first is very needful—just as the support of our animal life, and supply of our lower wants, is needful for all higher purposes. The body must be cared for first, and then the soul. But the reason why the body itself exists is, we humbly believe, to afford a basis and scaffolding for the higher life of the soul; and assuredly art exists only to afford expression to thought. Thus, then, in every work of art there are two things to be measured: the expression, which may be good, bad, or indifferent; and the thought expressed, which also may be good, bad, or indifferent. Clearly the best art is the best thought best expressed; but when this cannot be attained, what is the next best thing? Is it a bad or indifferent thought well expressed, or a good thought badly or indifferently expressed? Reason says, "The good, beautiful, noble thought, however imperfectly expressed." Popular judgment would seem to say the bad, vulgar, commonplace thought well expressed. Thus, in Painting and Sculpture we continually hear cried up as marvels the clever representation of subjects essentially base, and even gross; and in Literature we find enormous value attached to the sharp delineation of meanness, or the bold portraiture of vice. Surely the sound estimate of such works would rather lead us to deplore that the power of forcible expression had been attained by those who have no thoughts which ought to be expressed at all? All power misused is a sorrowful sight; the greater the power the more sorrowful. Lucifer is only the ideal of archangelic genius and might, applying his strength to work evil, and by his insight turning all human woe and sin into the sport of his Mephistophelic sneers. Great art, applied to degrade and libel humanity, is not Divine, but devilish. If we regard mankind with specially illumined eyes, we must do so either more like God, with a greater than human pity and tenderness and sympathy, or more like a demon, with greater than human scorn and cruelty and contempt. Viewed calmly there is something infinitely horrible in this latter character. We have a right to judge the man whose genius raises him above us,—but whose lovelessness sinks him below the humblest affectionate child,—as men may hereafter judge some giant creature born of human race, but yet no human being; a creature stronger and wiser than we, as we are stronger and wiser than our unknown progenitors, half-men, half-brutes, who roamed the forest of the primeval world with the cave-bear and the mastodon—a creature whose power and skill should be guided by no justice, tempered by no pity; who should vivisect our living hearts as wretches now vivisect the noble horse and loving dog, for mere scientific curiosity, and should pride himself in the art wherewith he laid bare every quivering nerve and throbbing vein. Such a creature would strike us with horror and hate. Why are we to regard a great writer with adoring admiration, because he can with his pen tear open all the wounds, expose all the diseases of humanity—not only untouched by compassion, unmoved to any effort to heal or save, but glorying in his own mighty gifts, and busy only to "build up the pyramid" of his own self-worshipped personality? Genius so employed is not human, far less is it Divine.

"Is it not then competent to art to seize on every subject, every phase of existence, and bring it out into the light under its magic glasses?"

"No," we answer fearlessly, it is *not* competent to art to choose subjects base or gross. The office of art is to express thought; but it must be good and noble thought, or the art is prostituted. Men first fall into the delusion that all that is real is a subject of art, and then that nothing is real except the ugly and the mean.

Of course, so long as nature is in question—inanimate nature, brute nature, or human nature which is really nature at all,—there can be nothing unfit or beneath art. It is the distortion of the natural into the artificial which makes a thing or a person an unfit subject for art, whether of the pen or the pencil.

Writing down individuals is pretty generally admitted to be wrong; writing down classes or nations, though less condemned, is yet hardly defended; but writing down the human race generally, seems to escape all blame. To describe society as nothing better than a mass-meeting of knaves and fools—of corrupters and corrupted—this is considered as witty and profound as it would be thought silly and wicked to describe the inhabitants of a special village in such a way. To paint human life without its background of immortality, or its sunlight of religion, is deemed as just and proper as it would be said to be profane and false to assert that a single individual had died beyond hope of heaven, or lived without a ray of God's love. What result can authors expect from books written with such views of existence as these? Surely, at best, to call forth a few bitter and joyless laughs, and then to leave behind them that sense of distrust and contempt for our brother men, which is about the greatest curse any unfortunate heart can carry through the world.

3. In Criticism. What is the duty of the critic towards the author he reviews? Is he at liberty to make a book a mere peg, which he may cut and fit at his discretion, to enable him to hang thereon more conveniently his own ideas?

It would seem that the critic bears to the author very much the relation which the merchant bears to the farmer or the manufacturer. He is the medium between the producer and the consumer, and is bound to act fairly towards both parties. Of course, when he is a gifted man, the critic does more than this, and himself produces a high branch literature: but he is bound never to do less. The task for which he makes himself responsible is to do justice to both sides; to give the reader a really fair idea of what the writer says. It is a simple question of honesty, whether he fulfils this duty or not. He is a juryman, sworn to bring in a true verdict; and if he say "guilty," when in his conscience he thinks the author not guilty, or *vice versa,* he is forsworn. The same principle of truth laid down before, applies here also. The critic is bound by literary veracity to give the "just expression of his impression." The correctness of the impression is what makes him more or less intellectually fit for his office. The fairness of the expression of that impression is what makes him morally honest or otherwise in the discharge of it.

Now, what shall we say to the literary morality of our time in respect to this matter? Of the multitude of criticisms which issue every week from the periodical press, how many are conscientiously written? how many are the "just expression of the writer's impression" of the books reviewed? Of course, thank Heaven! the majority are meant, in a certain but not very strict way, to fulfil this principle. There is a common justice and fairness here in the world, as elsewhere; and no one imagines reviewers to be a peculiarly unrighteous order of the community. But is such justice universally done? If, indeed, a book have no particular tendency at all, whether religious, poetical, or social; if the writer have managed to escape touching any of the dozen red-hot ploughshares which lie for ordeal in every path of literature, then, indeed, he may be tolerably sure of a just review. But how does it happen that when we read a book which is not of this colourless sort—which has some definite principles, and aims at some definite purpose—how does it happen, we repeat, that we know beforehand with such singular foresight, that the said book will be praised in such and such a Review, and pulled to pieces in such another? The phenomenon is inexplicable, if we maintain the perfect judicial fairness of the critical press. It betrays our profound convictions that, in the long run, prejudice always conquers truth; for *some* cause (one side or the other) must needs be sound, and supported by sound arguments; and yet we feel assured beforehand that *no* arguments will make it go down with its opponents. Happily, however, a very great change is taking place in the whole tone of such criticism. The higher journals are manifestly swayed by a desire to exercise, if not the impartiality of a judge, yet at least the consideration of a gentleman even for an enemy or an inferior. To look back on the old reviews in *Blackwood* or the *Quarterly*, where an "infidel" like Shelley, or a radical like Godwin, was to be annihilated, is like passing from a field of civilized warfare, where cannon and bayonets do the work, and where, when the fight is over, the wounded are cared for and the slain decently buried,—to the onslaught of Choctaws and Ojibbeways, tearing and screaming, and striking their foes with poisoned arrows and clubs and stones, and finally marching off, brandishing their scalps, and performing a war-dance to their own entire satisfaction.

"Nous avons changé tout cela." Critics can rarely now be charged before the court-martial of literature with "conduct unbecoming an officer and a gentleman." They are fair and worthy soldiers, if not all Bayards and Du Guesclins. But there is yet one trick of unlawful warfare common among them. They do not abuse, or vilify, or use personalities against an author of whom they disapprove; but they persist in seeing in his book what they think ought to be in it,—by no means what he has really put there. A species of traditional natural history has long been current, in which the Tory, the Democrat, the High-Churchman, the Freethinker, the Strong-minded Woman, the sentimental Philanthropist, and many other beasts and beastesses, assume recognized forms, much like the heraldic two-headed eagle, the fork-tailed lion, the pelican wounding itself to feed its young with its blood, and other equally veracious creatures. Regular modes of treatment of these animals have long been established, and constitute a most convenient art—somewhat conventional, indeed, but saving a world of trouble and study. Thus, when a man wants to paint a carriage-panel, or engrave a seal, he does not go to the Zoological Gardens, and copy a real eagle or lion or pelican, but sketches quite happily, out of his moral consciousness, the two heads and the forked tail and the sharp beak and bleeding breast. So the reviewer, having briefly ascertained by a glance with what sort of beast he has to do, proceeds to write his critique *currente calamo,* describing his Tory eagle, or Infidel roaring lion, or Philanthropic pelican, without any further notice of the poor animals who are screaming in their cages for better recognition—"I have not got two heads!—nor I two tails! nor do I ever pick myself to pieces!"

To judge a book fairly, a critic is assuredly bound to try first really to understand what the author means, and then, having understood him, he may, if he can, refute and expose the fallacy of his arguments. But how high a tone of criticism does this involve?—how much candour, and self-denial, and intelligence in the critic! Yet no man has a right to undertake the office at all, who is not morally and intellectually prepared to fulfil it in such a spirit. To make his own article brilliant and readable; to launch a few sharp sayings at an opponent; to perform, in the two or three pages allotted for his critique, a set of literary *tours de force,* with epigrams for pirouettes, and sarcasms for wit, may be all very natural and excusable; but a reviewer is engaged, before all this, to do justice both to the author he reviews and the reader who will learn from him of his book; and he has no right to perform his *pas seul* before the audience till he has done that duty. What would the old Israelites have said to their "spies" if, instead of bringing back the grapes of Eshkol, they had returned with specimens of the centipedes of the wilderness of Marsaba, the tail of a panther from Ajalon, and some apples of Sodom from the Dead Sea shore? This is, after all, the sort of report many a reviewer gives of the books he undertakes to examine. He finds the centipede, and the panther, and the fruit of ashes. They are all really in the work; but to discover them he passes by many a vineyard and oliveyard and cornfield and flowery plain, and gives, in effect, though not in literal words, an absolutely false impression of what may be, after all, "a land flowing with milk and honey."

Not less unjust is the practice which is the converse of this dispraise of inimical books, namely, the over-praise of those which are on the critic's side of politics or religion; or the works of his private friends. How arguments, poor and false, are pronounced sound and forcible; how low sentiments and garbled quotations, and all the other literary sins, are condoned by partial confessors of this class, there is no need to tell. Moses told us it was wrong to bear false witness against our neighbour; but after three millenniums, very few of us think it harm to bear witness, just a little bit untrue, in his favour.

Such are a few of the more obvious questions which recur every day concerning literary morality. The subject may, perhaps, be resumed in a future article, and other problems discussed which seem no less to require adjustment.

THE HIERARCHY OF ART.

Reprinted from Fraser's Magazine, January and March, 1865.

THE sacred service of the Beautiful has three orders in its priesthood. There are artists of the first and highest rank—poets, architects, sculptors, painters, composers of music. There are artists of the secondary order, dramatic performers, translators, copyists of architecture, of sculpture, and of painting; engravers, performers of music. There are artists, lastly, of the third rank, who are merely dilettanti.

Primary Art is *creative*, and is directly derived from God's revelation of the Beautiful through His works. It is original in the only sense applicable to human things, and deserves the name of creative, because its achievements, though only copies and combinations of the works of God, are yet fresh creations as Art. We call the works of God, however beautiful and truly artistic, Nature. We call man's copy of them at first hand, Art. The man has created Art out of what before was Nature. The epithet Creator, Maker (ποιητής), is ancient as Art itself, having from the first commended itself to the deep intuitions of the Greeks; and we may still retain it, while confessing that its meaning in the primary sense, as applied to the Great First Cause, recedes further and further from the reach of our philosophy.

The value of creative Art is determined by two conditions: 1st, by the extent and fulness with which the artist has received the Divine revelation of Beauty in Nature; 2nd, by the faithfulness with which he has recorded that which he has received.

He who has been permitted to pierce to the inner secrets of Nature, and embrace with eagle glance the wide horizon of her glory, and who having thus enjoyed the Seer's privilege, can paint his vision for the sight of other men,—that man is the supreme creative artist, the high-priest of Art. But he who only sits at Nature's feet and gathers a single flower, and gives it again to his fellows in its truth and beauty, he also belongs to the same order of primary artists. He is, in his degree, also a true priest of the Beautiful.

Secondary Art is *reproductive*. It does not derive its inspiration directly from the Divine revelation of Beauty in the world of matter or the world of man, but from the beautiful works of the creator-artist. It occupies towards these primary works of Art a position almost exactly analogous to that which they do to the original works of Nature. Such Art is justly called secondary. All inspiration which is not drawn directly from God's revelation of the Beautiful in Nature, but only indirectly through the medium of the primary artist's works, is necessarily subordinate. It may be excellent of its kind, and deserving of high estimation—as when it enables the secondary artist to take the gold of the original artist's thought, and cast it afresh from the crucible of his own mind into an entirely new form of beauty, (for example, when a great actor reproduces the conception of the poet). Or it may be very poor and humble, as when it merely reaches to an accurate repetition of the original artist's work, (for example, in the copies of statues and pictures). But in every case it must remain in a different order from primary Art, and ought not to be confounded with, or judged beside it.

A difficulty of distinguishing the two orders seems, at first sight, to arise in the case of that large sphere of art which illustrates historical events and characters. Such events and characters can only be known to the poet, sculptor, or painter through testimony. Is he therefore to be reckoned only of the secondary order when he illustrates these? Not so, assuredly, for the testimony from which he draws his knowledge is not Art, but History, i. e., the recorded science of human nature. Even if it happen to be preserved in artistic form (as in poetry), it is not as poetry, but as history, that it has supplied his inspiration. The case only becomes intricate and the line uncertain, where history blends with mythical and wholly imaginative creations in supplying the art-subject. To determine the value of a reproductive artist's work, three conditions are to be marked:

1st, the intrinsic excellence of the work he chooses to reproduce; 2nd, the extent to which he has reproduced in fresh form, and not merely copied, the work in question; 3rd, by the perfection of his own achievement, as itself a work of Art, judged independently from the original.

Tertiary Art may be so denominated when it is only *receptive*. It does not either create or reproduce, but merely passively receives inspiration, either at first-hand from Nature's beauty, or at second-hand from the creator-artist, or at third-hand from the reproducer. The man who thus receives beauty, even though he never give it forth again in any form of Art, has his place in the temple of the Beautiful; and his rank in the third order of her priesthood is determined, 1st, by the excellence of that beauty of Nature or Art whose inspiration he is able to receive; 2nd, by the fulness of his comprehension and the delicacy and subtlety of his appreciation of such beauty of Nature or Art.

All these three orders of Art-service—primary, secondary, and tertiary,—or creative, reproductive, and receptive, have their corresponding failures and errors resulting in the production of bad or untrue Art.

Bad primary Art results either, 1st, from the artist's choice of natural subjects which do not reveal beauty; 2nd, from his failure to translate real natural beauty into beautiful Art; 3rd, from his taking his subject of primary Art, not from

Nature, but from the inspiration of some original artist before him. This last is the offence of plagiarism, or the pretence of making creative art, where the art is only imitative and reproductive.

Bad secondary Art results either, 1st, from the artist's choice of bad primary Art to reproduce; 2nd, from his failure to reproduce what he copies in a work which shall both preserve the merits of the original, and be itself a true work of art.

Bad tertiary Art results either, 1st, from mistake as to what is really beautiful in Nature or Art; 2nd, from incompleteness of æsthetic sense, leading to an over-valuation of the lesser beauty and an under-valuation of the greater.

In a large and general way, regarding the two first orders of Art, the primary and the secondary, it may be affirmed that their value, if good, is determined, 1st, by the beauty of the thing they express; 2nd, by the perfection of the expression.

Perfect Art would be the most perfect expression of the most beautiful thing. Imperfect Art is found wherever there is either imperfection in expression or defect of beauty in the thing expressed. Finally, where the thing expressed is not beautiful, and the expression also a failure, there is no Art at all—the work ceases to have pretensions to the title.

Such, in brief, are the relations of the three orders of the hierarchy of the Beautiful, one to another. It will be of interest to pursue the analysis of these relations in detail through the different branches of art in which they are developed. The classification of primary or original arts need not detain us long in this undertaking, except so far as it is needful to notice that poetry stands in a double position towards all forms of Art. It is *an* art—and, for many reasons, to be ranked the first of arts; but it is also the pervading spirit of all other arts, in which the element of poetry has the largest and most important share. Poetry expressed through the medium of language (to which we rightly give the name *par éminence*, because by language can it be most widely and perfectly expressed), is only one form of poetry. There is a poetry expressed in architecture, a poetry expressed in sculpture, in painting, and in music; and all these deserve to be estimated according to their value as poetry. Deduct the element of poetry from any art, and a mere *caput mortuum*—a body without a soul—will remain. Of the three elements needful to constitute a true work of Art, namely, poetry, science, and mechanical skill, poetry is that which gives the essential art-character to the other two, which, without it, may achieve miracles of handicraft, yet never make a true work of Art. They form the body—poetry the spirit, of Art.

What, then, in this sense, do we mean by poetry? A few pages back the word was used in the profound signification which the marvellous insight of the Greeks induced them to give it. The "poet" was the maker—the Creator-artist. Does not this reach to the root of the matter? In so far as the artist has done that which makes him a creator, i. e., in which he has received God's revelation of the beautiful through Nature, and has faithfully transferred it to Art, in so far he is a poet. He is a great poet if he have received this widely and recorded it powerfully; but he is still a true, albeit lesser poet, if he have received even a single lesson and recorded it faithfully. The element of poetry, in all cases, is the element of Divine Beauty. God—the Source of all goodness, truth, and beauty—reveals Goodness to the conscience, Truth to the intellect, and Beauty to the æsthetic nature of His creatures. As a man becomes a saint in proportion as he receives the revelation of goodness to his conscience, and reproduces it in his life,—as he becomes a philosopher in proportion as he receives the revelation of truth in his intellect, and reproduces it in science,—so, likewise, he becomes a poet in proportion as he receives the revelation of beauty to his æsthetic nature, and reproduces it in Art. Just in so far, and no further, than as a man has partaken most deeply of that spirit of God revealed in the beauty of Nature, just so far, and no further, are his works high and true poetry. All poetry is God's poetry.

> "God Himself is the great Poet,
> And the Real is His song."

As man's inward ear receives the divine echoes of that eternal psalm, and his lips learn to repeat it in clear utterance for the joy of his fellow-men, in so far he is a poet.

To turn, however, from this grand universal aspect of poetry, to its rank among the arts in the restricted sense of poetry expressed in language. Even here it is generally admitted to be the first of arts, in right of its instrument, its scope, and its durability. Language, as an instrument of art, is superior to the marble of the architect and of the sculptor, and the pigment of the painter, in being immeasurably more delicate and of more varied powers. It stands properly, indeed, as the medium between mind and nature, and is itself half immaterial. It is the *Logos* whose father is spiritual, and whose mother corporeal—the threads which the soul draws out of itself to weave its web of thought. Only with the notes of the musician can it suffer comparison; and these, if even more delicate and ethereally expressive than language (i. e., expressive of thoughts too tenuous, evanescent, and transcendant for language), are, on the other hand, so inferior in respect of definitiveness and certainty, that the balance may still be left with language, in its high service as an instrument of poetry.

Again, the scope of poetry is far beyond the narrow spheres to which the art of the architect, sculptor, painter, and even musician are confined. It is conterminous only with the necessary bonds of all human things—namely, with the capacities of the mind of man. To the utmost horizon of thought, in the highest empyrean of aspiration, poetry sustains her flight. Temples no builder could dream, forms no sculptor could chisel, colours no limner could paint, belong to her alone. No Michael Angelo has conceived such domes as Milton has reared in imperishable verse; no Rembrandt has painted with such lurid hues as those which shadow Dante's "Hell;" no sculptor carved such opulent form as that of Shakspeare's Cleopatra. The true poet sees all history as one epic Odyssey of our humanity,—tempest-driven, spectre-haunted, Circe-tempted,—yet brought *home* at last; and to him creation itself is a divine drama of Prometheus Unbound, with the immensity of space for its stage, and eternal time for its hour of action.

And again, poetry is more durable than any other of the arts. Architecture and sculpture alone can vie with it in this respect; and the Theban temples and the Sphinx may indeed overshadow us from an antiquity higher than that of Homer and Job. But when every stone of Egypt's colossal fanes and statues lies buried under the desert sands, men will still read the tale of "Achilles' wrath," and, in some yet unborn tongue, will renew again and yet again the wail of the Chaldæan patriarch.

True poetry is immortal. Once born into the consciousness of the human race, it can never die again; nay, it partakes in a manner of the omnipresence, as well as eternity, of its great first Author. It is ubiquitous; and, while the temple, the statue, the picture, can only be in one spot of earth; and even music itself must depend for a voice on material aids (costly and laborious almost in the proportion of its power), poetry alone may gush from every human lip, and spring in every human heart a fresh fountain of ever-living joy. There is no home so lonely, no wintry waste so desolate, no dungeon-cell so dark, but poetry may therein speak to the soul she loves, to cheer, to bless, and to ennoble.

Poetry, then, we may surely admit, is the most perfect, the most comprehensive, and the most durable of the Arts. A great poet—a true creator-artist in language—stands at the summit of the hierarchy of art. There is no order above his own, or equal to it. He is the supreme pontiff in the temple of the Beautiful.

But, if poetry be the greatest of the original arts, it follows that its various reproductions ought to hold similar rank among the secondary arts—that is, so far as they are capable of being real reproductions, and not servile copies. We have therefore to consider next the three forms under which poetry may be reproduced—namely, 1. Dramatic acting, including operatic singing and expressive dancing; 2. Recitation—singing, or vocal reading; 3. Translation. A few words must suffice for each.

Dramatic acting is the greatest of all reproductive arts; first (as above said) because it reproduces the greatest original art, i. e., poetry. Secondly, because in accomplishing this purpose, it is furthest from servile copying and nearest to an original art. In this last respect, it is more justly defined as an embodiment, in material form, of the semi-spiritual language of the poet, than as a similar reproduction with the copies made of statues and paintings. The creator-poet, indeed, brought into being the character of his drama—the Hamlet or the Macbeth. But he left it a purely mental *eidolon*, a denizen of the world of souls, revealed to the senses only through the medium of language. The actor then took up the task—if not of creating, yet of incarnating. The poet's disembodied thought became the actor's living man. Nay, more, the actor performs this work not by means of any material artistic instrument, marble or pigment, or words or musical sounds. He makes *himself* his instrument, and transforms himself, body and soul, into the poet's creation. He takes the incorporeal idea, and, by wondrous sorcery, clothes it in his own flesh and blood. He *is*, for that high hour, Hamlet or Macbeth.

In some ways acting may be considered rather as a combination of arts, than a mere reproduction of any one of them. Poetry, painting, and sculpture are all joined together by a true dramatic actor—and even music is added to the number by the operatic performer. Campbell, in lines more philosophically analytic than befits poetry, yet singularly elegant and accurate, defines the matter well:

"For ill can poetry express
Full many a train of thought sublime,
And painting, mute and motionless,
Steals but a glance from time.
But by the mighty actor brought
Illusion's perfect triumphs come,
Verse ceases to be voiceless thought,
And painting to be dumb."

Operatic singing—the actor singing his part as well as acting it—includes, as we have just said, again another art—namely, music. The operatic singer, who is at the same time a good actor, stands at once as reproducer of the musician and the poet. Unhappily, in such combinations, the interests of poetry being nearly always sacrificed to those of music, the operatic singer, whose *libretto* is a mere tissue of rhymes spun to suit the composer and carry out the plot, can hardly be considered as holding the place of reproducer to the poet, but only to the musician. When the case is otherwise, however, as in Oratorios founded on the sublime poetry of the Bible, the art becomes truly magnificent. No preacher has, probably, ever touched so many hearts with such profound emotion as Madame Lind Goldschmidt, interpreting at once Handel and Isaiah.

Again, the art of Dancing bears to other dramatic arts, a position which has been unjustly degraded, owing to the miserable modern substitution of *tours de force* in the dancers for grace, and the frequency with which it (more than perhaps any other Art) has been misapplied to immoral ends.

Taken in its true and right use, dancing may lay claim to a rank very closely allied indeed to dramatic acting. It is not mere dumb-show and pantomime—acting seeking to express itself, as well as it may, without the aid of words. As such it would deserve small honour; for it is not the business of art to achieve its purposes under self-constituted difficulties, but to make each work as perfect as possible with all the means in its power. Dancing is rather poetry expressed in motion—emotions having in them the essential element of poetry, finding utterance, not in vocal sounds, but in the expression of the whole body, every limb and every feature playing its part. Such dancing (as, for example, that of Taglioni in the sweet prose-poem of *Undine*) is truly a reproductive art, and a most refined one. It is evanescent, like all the dramatic arts, but, for the moment, vividly beautiful. If *poses plastiques* be reproductions of sculpture, or living sculptures; and *tableaux vivants* be reproductions of painting; dancing unites both of these, and adds to them the poetry of motion. Within its sphere—a narrow one, yet perhaps never yet fairly filled,—it affords a combination varied as that of the operatic singer; and to those numerous men and women in whom the eye is more keenly awake to grace than the ear to harmony, dancing is itself a kind of music. The celestial "dance" of the planetary orbs, and the music of the spheres, are one and the same.

Dancing of course has other uses besides this special one of reproducing a poetic thought or drama upon the stage. Its simpler form, that of giving expression to one or other natural human emotion, joy, love, rage, victorious triumph, or the like, has existed probably in every country in the world, from the remotest time to our own. Sometimes it hardly ascends to the rank of an art, however rude. There is little of either poetry, science, or skill in it, any more than in the sportive leapings of young colts and kittens, or the angry rushing of a herd of buffaloes. Such are the mere jumpings of children and savages, and the war-dances of Red Indians and the Amazons of Dahomey. At other times it becomes an art, partaking much of poetry, and somewhat also of science and skill. Such was, doubtless, the Pyrrhic dance of the graceful Greeks, and such are now the national dances of Europe—the Waltz, the Mazurka, the Tarantella, the Cachucha, the Highland Fling, and many more, all of which have doubtless some highly poetic idea at their source, from which, in the lapse of ages, they have developed appropriate expressive emotions, and then become stereotyped in tradition. In this respect they bear a complete resemblance to national tunes, which, when really deserving the name, are (like our own National Anthem) slowly developed as expressions of a popular feeling, and then permanently fixed and adopted. The most singular line of sentiment for dancing to express, is undoubtedly the religious; and it is perhaps a proof of the deep root in human nature whence the art of dancing springs, that it should even have extended itself to the sphere of the religious emotions. David dancing before the sacred ark of Israel; the old heathen dances in honour of the gods; and the existing dances of the Moslem Dervishes, are all instances of this fact. It has even been asserted (I know not on what authority), that to this day solemn dances by young acolytes form a portion of the Catholic service, on special festivities, in some cathedrals in Spain. The Welsh Jumpers certainly make their grotesque leaps into the air the distinctive ceremony of their sect. Into these details and their very remote relation to art, it is not our business now to enter.

To return. The dramatic actor, or operatic singer or dancer, is (as we have seen) enabled to bear to the poet a relation which no other reproductive artist does to his original, and of course it is only the dramatic poet who can receive such aid. The epic poet can only be reproduced by a reciter or vocal reader, and the lyric poet by a singer, reciter, or reader. Here we have inferior and more distant relationships between the secondary and primary artists. There is no longer a transformation of the whole man into the creation of the poet; there is merely a rendering in voice what the poet has left in written language, or it may be as first himself recited aloud to the singer or second reciter. Yet, though doubtless inferior to acting, the reproducing of poetry by means of reading, reciting, or singing, may be a very high form of secondary art, embodying the thought of the poet so far as may be accomplished by vocal sounds, in a manner demanding real genius. When the results of such readings, recitings, or singings, are extremely powerful impressions, we may argue that the performer has need of even greater skill than the actor, since he produces a similar impression with very much less complete instrumentality. This is a principle, however, which, applied in every case of art, can only call for our recognition of the artist's personal skill and ingenuity. The value of art, as such, can never be estimated with reference to the special mechanical difficulties overcome in each achievement, but only according to the intrinsic beauty and perfection of the work itself. A poem written in an uncouth dialect, a statue carved directly from the block without a clay model, a picture painted with a man's foot instead of his hands, a piece of music played on one string of a violin—all such achievements as these may be more or less curious or admirable, as instances of ingenuity. But their value as art must simply depend on the fact of whether the poem is good in itself, in spite of its dialect; the statue, picture, music, intrinsically good and correct, however they were carved, painted, or performed.*

* It is curious that Galileo should have fallen into the fallacy

Besides recitation, vocal reading, and singing, poetry is reproduced by an entirely different process of secondary Art, namely, by translation. Here is perhaps the typical instance of Reproductive Art, for there is no new art brought in, as in the case of the dramatic performer; nor is the work a mere copy, as in the case of merely imitative sculpture and painting. True artistic translation requires the secondary artist to take the thought of his original, and cast it afresh in a new mould, i. e., in a different language. The completeness with which this is done, the perfection with which "the true thought,

of actually setting up a standard of perfection in art, by which it should be valued in the ratio of the difficulties it overcomes—an error essentially vulgar and leading to all the absurd misjudgments we constantly hear of, such as the *furore* for Paganini's one-string sonata, rather than for his really excellent ordinary performance, and the popular value set on such tricks of marble-cutting, as Veiled Women and the Pompeian Mother. The most tasteless person can understand the conquest of a mechanical difficulty, which is of the same nature as the daily achievements of the factory and the work-room applied to a different purpose; but the creation of a real work of Art—a true revelation of the Beautiful—is quite another matter, and out of the sphere of their cognizance. In an original letter of Galileo's to Carlo Cigoli, recently published in a pamphlet "Nel Trecentesimo Natalizio di Galileo," the great philosopher argues in this deplorable way: "As to what sculptors argue that Nature moulds men but does not paint them, I reply that she makes them not less by painting than sculpture, because she both sculpts and colours; but that is their (the sculptors') imperfection and a thing which detracts from the value of sculpture; because the farther are the means by which a thing is imitated from the thing itself, so much more the imitation is marvellous."

the whole thought, and nothing but the thought," are so rendered, and the perfection of his own poem as itself a work of Art, constitute the merits of the translator.

Language, we have already described as half spiritual, half material, an efflux of the soul which it makes its instrument of thought. Now, in strict accuracy, there are as many languages in the world as there are souls who speak in them. The same vocal sound does not mean the same thing in the mouth of two different persons. If it express even a more material object, the idea of that object existing in the mind of the child or clown, and of the man who thoroughly understands its nature and properties, and its relation to other objects, is not alike. A daisy to an infant means a little white thing out of which chains can be made; a daisy to a botanist is a flower of a certain class and order; a daisy to a farmer is a weed, showing such and such conditions of his ground; a daisy to a poet is a

> Wee crimson-tipped flower,

from which he can draw the most exalted lessons of philosophy. When we leave material objects, and speak of sentiments and passions, the diversity between one word and another is still more marked. The joy, grief, love, and fear of a hero and a coward, of a great and wise man and a mean and vicious one, are totally different things. Colours, sounds, tastes, and odours, are certainly various to the senses of some persons—very probably are so to us all. It is only in the most rough and imperfect manner that the same words, then, can be said to convey to all the same impression. Much more wide is the variance where language itself is changed, and we have to seek for synonyms in words of another tongue. Here the variance of individuals has become the diversity of race and nation, divided by the furrow of centuries. As each word born of the souls of one race bears with it the character of that race; so each born of another bears another physiognomy. Could we thoroughly imbibe the genius of twenty languages, we should find each of them apart and individual, and the individuality of each would bear direct relationship to the character of the nation from whose lips it came. And though such analysis as this is beyond our powers, yet, so much of the distinction in question is patent and unmistakeable, that the most superficial acquaintance with a second language reveals to the learner, always with some surprise, a new conception of the genius of the people by whom it is spoken. It may be truly said that only by knowing their language it is possible to gain a conception of that essential spirit of a people, which, like the perfume of a flower, exhales through spoken words.

Now if this view of language be true, the task of perfectly translating a poem, out of one language into another, is obviously impossible. There are no such things, in truth, as synonymous words—nor do any combination of the words of one language produce a real synonym with those of another. Let us take the commonest instance, and confine our comparison to four modern European tongues. Will anybody pretend that the tender and sentimental German "Lieben," the deep, warm English "Love," the passionate Italian "Amare," and the frivolous French "Aimer," are the same verbs? Is it the same word which can only be applied, like our own, to one of the great sentiments of humanity—to the love of lovers, parents, friends; the love of nature, or the love of God; and a word which, like the French, is equally suitable to express approval of a piquant sauce and a becoming bonnet?

The task of a translator of poetry may be likened to that of a reproducer of painting, who executes his work with a different kind of material from that of the original. He has to turn oils into water-colours, or body colour into chalks. No one colour at his disposal is the equivalent of another in the original work. He must create a similar effect with a different material and (in many respects) by a different process, corresponding to the wholly different genius and construction of each language. It must be owned that we have here a task of stupendous difficulty, in which the highest reproductive genius can hardly do more than approximately succeed. Where much of the beauty of the poet is essentially verbal—i. e., when in the mysterious sorcery of genius he makes the very sound of his words express, as music does, the thoughts in his mind—then indeed the work of translation may seem hopeless. In that region of shadowy evanescent feeling, where such poetry lifts us, amid gleams of iridescent light seeming to open up glimpses into unknown worlds of glory and of agony—amid odours of Paradise, recalling what we might deem antenatal realms of joy having no counterpart on earth—there the true poet is the sole great sorcerer. The translator is but a false wizard who waves his wand in mimicry, but whom no "spirits from the vasty deep" of our human nature will obey. We stand coldly and critically by, and ask: "How came these words to pass once over the souls of men like a rushing mighty wind, bearing Pentecostal tongues of fire, henceforth to speak from a thousand lips? We hear nothing but dry, dead phrases. There is some delusion here!"

But when the poetry, though breathed through fitting words, is essentially a poetry of thought—above all, when it has a form of rhythm immediately related to thought (as in the case of Hebrew poetry), then the task of the translator ceases to be impracticable. His rendering of the same thoughts in other, if still in fitting words, is also true poetry. The power possessed over us by the original poet is wielded again, with hardly diminished strength, by the reproducer; and Job, and David, and Isaiah, translated into the tongues of nations yet to be, will still lift the souls of men, even as of yore they lifted them, on the old Chaldean plains, or amid the desert hills of Palestine.

Such, very briefly sketched, is the great primary art of Poetry; and such are the secondary arts of its Reproduction in Dramatic performance, Reading or Recitation, and Translation. It remains to speak of the tertiary art connected with poetry, namely, the Reception of Poetry, either through nature or through art.

It is hard to believe that there are human beings above infancy and cannibalism who have absolutely no sense of poetry in Nature or Art;—men to whom "the primrose on the river's brim" is a "yellow primrose" and no more; and to whom Homer, and Dante, and Shakespeare, and Byron, and Burns, and Tennyson all speak as idle wind. Whether there be any such men, in whom the æsthetic sense is as wholly wanting as intellect to the idiot, and eyesight to the blind, it concerns us not to inquire closely. One thing is certain—there do exist thousands in whom that sense is so feebly developed, or so crushed down by the weight of earthly cares and labours, that it remains for all their lives almost as though it were not. The joys and elevating influences it is calculated to bring are to them unknown, as much as the sweetness of the fields under the sky of spring is unknown to one whose years have passed in the black depths of the toilsome mine. They have been saying, "What shall we eat, and what shall we drink, and wherewithal shall we be clothed?" till they have forgotten ever once to consider the lilies of the field, or listen to the voice of the heavens proclaiming the glory of God. Again, there are happier men and women who intensely feel the beauty of the world and the enchantment of art, although they are unable to reproduce in any way what they feel, or transmit their joy to another. These last are the true receivers of Art—the ultimate grade in the hierarchy of the Beautiful; and to them the primary and secondary artists address themselves as their proper audience. The wave of beauty which began in a thought of God and successively passed through the material world, and through the souls of the poet and the reproducer, reaches their heart as its strand, and there breaks and dies. Without their sympathy and their comprehension, Art would be the lonely play of the artist by himself, of which ere long he needs must weary. For a brief space only could Art so exist. Human sympathy—not fame, or renown, or base earthy rewards, but the true fellow-feeling and delight of kindred hearts—is to Art what the rain and the dew are to the flower; and the greatest and proudest artist the world has seen is dependent for his very inspiration, for the energy which enabled him to carry out his grandest idea, to the consciousness that there waited for him the humble sympathies of those who themselves could never write a line of poetry, or chisel a block, or hold the brush of a painter.

The more numerous and the more perfectly

trained are those who thus fill the third order of art, the greater is the encouragement of the highest forms of primary and secondary art; and for this cause alone we might desire to extend the taste qualifying men for such an office. In a still higher sense, however, the same extension is to be earnestly sought for the joy and elevation of those who themselves receive its benefits. Not for any ulterior object whatever, not to make our children seem well educated, or to teach the poor this or that good moral or religious lesson to be learned through verse, are we to strive to disseminate a love for poetry. It is enough that poetry—the poetry of Nature and the poetry of Art alike—are *God's revelations of the Beautiful.* As such they are holy: as such they are good for the soul of every creature He has made. When we have aided a man to acquire a high and pure taste for poetry, we may be assured we have aided him to somewhat more than a refined and blameless pleasure:—we have aided him to receive a Revelation of God.

Having now briefly discussed the supreme art of Poetry and its reproductions and receptions, it is our next duty to consider that primary art which, with its reproductions, may be considered to stand next after poetry. The fair decision of the claims of the various arts to this position would involve considerable discussion, and carry us away from our proper subject of the relation of the secondary to the primary arts. Architecture, Sculpture, and Painting, each for various reasons, may be estimated as next to poetry in excellence. It will be more convenient, however, for the present, to place these great arts in a later group by themselves, and to consider next to Poetry, the art of Music, which is far more nearly related to it than the others.

MUSIC has for its medium, not language, but inarticulate sounds—or at least, sounds which, if articulate, are so independently of music. The music in them does not (as in the case of poetry) depend on their articulation. With the seven notes of the scale and all their varied gradations and combinations, the musician expresses his thoughts even as the painter expresses his by the seven colours and their gradations and combinations. But the musician's thought is only a thought, or feeling—the ideas and impressions of a human soul—its joy, pain, love, or fury under certain imagined conditions—which he strives to express in his notes, and thus convey to the soul of his auditor. The whole transaction belongs to the psychical world, and barely descends to use as the medium of mind and mind the most ethereal and sublimated form of material force—namely, the mere undulations of sound in the atmosphere. The painter, on the contrary, save in ideal painting, strives to reproduce an actual tangible reality, a scene once beheld by bodily eyes; and his medium of effecting this is a whole repertory of material instruments—pigments, and brush, and canvas. It is in accordance with this far more tenuous and ethereal nature of music, that it should be transitory and evanescent, dying away with the undulations of air which are its media, and only reproduced to die again as soon. No one either could, or would, prolong the existence of a sound beyond a brief moment; and even the compositions of music which, being suited for continual repetition, might seem to claim an immortality like that of written poetry, appear, by some well-befitting fatality, to have always failed to secure it. An antiquity of some centuries for a few simple tones, is all, I believe, which can be allotted to any music now existing, and we habitually speak of music as "old" at an age, which for any other art would be comparatively recent.

How does the fact that music is only the expression of a human thought or feeling—and not of any material object in nature—correspond with the assertion with which we began, namely, that all true primary art is derived directly from "God's revelation of the Beautiful through His works?" It corresponds perfectly, inasmuch as the thoughts and feelings of man, which form the proper themes of music, are all beautiful, all divine revelations. Music cannot deal with ignoble, mean, or ugly thoughts and sentiments, with petty cares, or base, rancorous, or envious feelings, but only with what is noble or sublime, or at least simple and uncorrupt. There is a music of innocent gaiety, of joy, of gloom, of grief, of love, of triumph, of divine aspiration, and resignation. But there is no music of envy, of worldliness, of cowardice, of spite, of all the base and ugly things which grow in the neglected places of our hearts. Music paints the flowers in those gardens, from the rose and the lily to the frailest blossom whose perishing beauty fades as it opens in the evening air. But the weeds, the noxious and poisonous parasites and fungi of the soul, the stinging-nettles and toad-stools, she will not paint. They are no subject for her art.

The more purely *human* is any feeling the more fit it is for music. But what is this, but to say that the more distinctly it is a "revelation of God, through His works"—(that is, through His greatest work—namely, man)—the more it is a subject for the art of music? It must be divine, i. e., natural, and it must be beautiful, i. e., noble, or, at least, innocent, in that human world to which it belongs. But to say that it must be divine and beautiful is to say it must answer to our original definition of art; "the revelation of the beautiful by God through His works."

The poet deals with both the world of matter and the world of man. He may, if he please, write whole poems of pure landscape with no human interest introduced. Or he may write a poem which shall begin and end with the study of a human soul. The more there is of human in his work (provided he be equal to the higher task), the loftier will be his achievement. But the musician deals exclusively (as we have said) with human sentiment, aiming, even when he touches on landscape, to express not the landscape itself, but the impression such a landscape has made on a human mind. He does not describe seas and mountains, and flowery vales, but the feelings of awe, or wonder, or delight which seas and mountains and valleys are qualified to produce in him who beholds them. This purely ideal aim of the art assuredly lifts it into a most exalted sphere. A great composer, such as Beethoven, or Mozart, or Handel, is an artist whose subject is the most transcendent—namely, all the higher phases of human thought and passion—and whose medium is the most ethereal and refined, namely, the shadowy fluctuations of inarticulate sound. He sits in his study, and there (in the strictest artistic sense) *creates* in thought the whole storm of melody which mortal ears have never yet heard, but which by-and-by will roll over the world, bursting the bars of a thousand hearts and bearing souls unnumbered "upon the seraph-wings of ecstacy." Through that composer's soul the feelings and thoughts of our humanity move as in some awful procession, and one after another, he heralds them and proclaims them afar. His power, of its kind, is supreme and unique; no other artist may unlock the treasure-home of memory, or open the graves of long-buried sorrows, or throw back the portals of heaven, with such a mighty hand as he.

But the musician's power, great as it is, has three fatal limitations. First, there are natural limits to the things he can express. Second, there are limits, natural and accidental, to the powers of men to understand his form of expression even when most perfect. Lastly, his power does not rest entirely with himself, as do the powers of the poet, the sculptor, and the painter. Even if he be able to perform his own compositions, and thus add the art of the reproducer to his own, it is a very small matter in music; a few hours of his life, a few hundreds or thousands of audience, and his reproductive work reaches its bounds. His written music, however sublime, must be dumb except whenever it find a worthy interpreter.

The interpreter and Reproducer artist in music is the Performer. His relation to his original is very closely analogous to that of the vocal reader to the poet; but the performer is indispensable to the composer, while the vocal reader is not so to the poet. Written music, before performance, is comprehensible only to a most limited class among receiver artists; and even to them conveys hardly a share of the impression which it gives when actually executed by the voice or instrument; whereas written poetry not read aloud, conveys almost its full impression to the millions who can peruse it in print. The eye suffices for poetry, but only most imperfectly for music. Thus the musical performer stands to the composer in the position of an almost indispensable assistant and interpreter. He is the Aaron who must give forth to the chosen race the prophecies which Moses has received but cannot utter. He is the medium between the soul of the composer and the soul of his auditor. How high and real an art is such reproductive music, it is needless to describe. Grievous is it, then, that, instead of being the chosen life-work of a few who might fulfil it aright, and make music an enchanting influence, glorifying and elevating us at due intervals, it has become the inevitable task of every idle girl who would pretend to education; and through whose perpetual bad performance, music has been degraded and desecrated, till half its noblest spells have for ever lost their power. Music is peculiarly an art which cannot thus bear to be vulgarized. A poem, a statue, a painting is not spoiled when we have read or beheld it a thousand times. But an air of music, however beautiful, is for ever desecrated once it has become the spoil of every strumming piano-player in our drawing-rooms, and organ-grinder in the streets. It is a positive injury to the world when good music is badly played—a pain to those who are compelled to listen to it, and whom it interrupts from other pursuits, and a permanent deterioration of the power of the same music for ever. No other bad art is half so obnoxious and intrusive, nor half so injurious, as bad music; yet, in the deluded idea that some sort of refinement is to be had out of it, we go on teaching our young women by thousands to do that which it is certain not one in fifty will ever do well; and allow our streets to be infested by vagrants, whose office it is ruthlessly to murder all the most beautiful new airs as fast as they are composed.

Tertiary art in music takes two very remarkably different forms, according to the degree of æsthetic feeling and culture in the matter possessed by the individual.

A great work of music to him who really understands it, is a poem which he can read, as it were, verse by verse, following out the guidance of the composer through all his wondrous rhapsody of playful fancies, and solemn dreams, and wild unearthly joys, and desolate outcries of despair. The soul of the listener in such case is the real instrument over whose chords the musician's hand passes slowly—now touching gently the lightest, now sweeping mightily the strongest, till every string vibrates in rapture and in passion. The same music to another hearer is no such defined poem: only an influence vague and sweet like the calm of a summer's evening or the odour of flowers, leaving his natural course of thought unbroken, but by some unknown spell, glorifying and deepening it —making joy more glad, and sorrow more sorrowful, and memory more tender, and lifting the aspirations of faith and love on billows of holy melody to heaven. The soul of this listener is not the instrument of the musician, only the mirror, hitherto dimmed with dust and damp, over which he passes his hand, rendering it for one brief hour able to reflect all the gloom and the glory of mortality. Perchance, it is hardly a lesser boon which music brings to him who thus receives it as a glorifying and illuminating influence, than to him who finds in it the grandest of legible poems. In either case, and nearly to all men, music is capable, under fit conditions, of conveying great and pure pleasure, and a real ennobling influence. Shall we not learn then, at last, to scout the vile parodies which vulgarize it, as among the most offensive and mischievous of all the derelictions into which false and degraded art can fall?

Architecture differs from the other four great arts in one remarkable particular. Poetry, Music, Sculpture, and Painting, can and ought always to be exercised purely for their own sakes, and not for any ulterior purpose. The rule of *de l'art pour l'art* is clear and literal as regards them. When any of these arts is practised principally with a view to some other object beside art, their proper character is deteriorated if not destroyed—be that other object in itself never so good and laudable. The Beautiful is an end in itself, the real and only end of Art. The Good, indeed, and the True are so inseparably linked with the Beautiful that every work really attaining the Beautiful must partake of Truth and Goodness. But it is not for the sake of instilling Truth or preaching Goodness that the Beautiful should be produced. When any artist attempts to do so, and makes a poem or picture whose main purpose is to develope scientific facts or enforce moral lessons, the result is an inferior and imperfect work of art.

But this great principle which holds good through all the realms of art, and is of easy application as regards poetry, music, sculpture, and painting, is found hard to reconcile with the necessities of architecture. The number of buildings which are erected mainly as works of art, must always be trifling compared to those constructed for definite utilitarian purposes. We build houses, fortresses, churches, that we may dwell in them, use them for military operations, perform in them religious services; but not mainly or primarily to create works of architectural art. Indeed, the edifices which may be considered purely artistic are not at first sight easily discoverable. Almost every building (except such a merely fantastic thing as a modern imitation temple) has another purpose beside art. A man makes a poem, a piece of music, a statue, or a picture, because he wishes to express something beautiful, and (if he be a true artist) for no other reason. But very rarely indeed does any one erect an edifice, large or small, without having in view some other purpose beside expressing beauty in the abstract. Some want must be supplied, some event recorded, some convenience attained, by almost every building which men think of constructing. Thus for architecture, the great rule of *de l'art pour l'art* must, it appears, be taken with some modification. What may this modification be?

It would seem that the principle on which a work of architecture must be admitted to rank as pure art, or excluded from such claim, is this—When the purpose of a building is such that the architect is free to consult *Beauty before Utility*, then that building may be pure art. When the purpose is such that the architect must consult *Utility before Beauty*, then the building cannot be pure art. In the first case the purpose merely designates the character of the work, leaving the artist to the full development of whatever sense of beauty he may possess. In the second case, the purpose overrides the whole work, limiting in every direction the artist's idea of beauty by considerations altogether apart from those of art. Only those edifices which belong to the first class are to be criticised from the stand-point of pure architecture. And this class we must suppose to constitute not only true art, but the *best* art which architecture can create. Fancy temples, even such pretty ones as those in the Villa Reale, at Naples, seem always to involve some degree of folly, if not of impertinence. We intuitively expect a building to have a purpose of utility (be it only that of a cenotaph), and are not contented to learn that it exists only for its own sake as a beautiful object. If we are told a building has no reason of existence beyond its supposed beauty, we experience a sense of being trifled with, and regard the work, however graceful it may be, as in some way incongruous and idle. On the other hand, again, the purpose for which a work claiming to be architectural art is destined, must needs be an elevated one. The lower forms of utility, even were they compatible with beauty, would make high art ridiculous. A grand building destined to be a shop or shambles would have all its beauty of form nullified to the imagination by its unbeautiful purpose. But buildings devoted to religion, justice, or the memory of the mighty dead, have, in their noble purposes, elements of grandeur auxiliary in the highest degree to the effect of any beauty they may possess. Thus we arrive at the conclusion that the universal principle of all the arts, *de l'art pour l'art*, "Art for art's sake, having no other purpose," must be modified as regards architecture—"Art having the end of art (i. e., beauty) for its predominant purpose, and some elevated utility for its subordinate purpose."

The buildings which may or may not be thus classed as belonging to pure art, may now be sufficiently easily defined. All kinds of human abodes —palaces, castles, houses, cottages; all kinds of business erections—factories, warehouses, shops, markets, schools, must necessarily be excluded. The architect who designs such buildings is called upon to consider first of all the utility of his work; what the people who will inhabit his house or use his school will require for their accommodation. The walls, corridors, and chambers must be constructed of the size and form they will need, whether by so doing they accord or disaccord with the ends of art. He must make windows, *not* because the beauty of his façade will be improved by them, but because the inhabitants of his rooms will require light. He must build chimneys, *not* because chimneys are beautiful, but because the people who are to use his building will want warmth; and so on through every department. In his whole design beauty must be subordinate to use. If he transgress this principle, and endeavour to make art paramount in an edifice designed for use; and, to accomplish this end, insert much that is useless, and omit much that would have been useful, out of regard for art, he commits an egregious mistake—a similar one to that of the poet or painter who makes a poem or a picture the vehicle of moral lessons or scientific information. He errs as to the very purpose of his work; and the inhabitant of the house which has been made uncomfortable to make it architectural, or the audience in a music-hall which has been unfitted for music to suit the laws of proportion, have each a right to denounce the architect's work as a failure and an impertinence. His business was first to make a habitable house and a good hall, suited according to the principles of acoustics for hearing music. Only when he had secured comfortable habitability and unshattered sound was he at liberty to think of architectural beauty.

The scope of pure art in architecture being narrowed by the exclusion of all such buildings as we have considered, and of all those which must obviously be classed along with them, there remain only two descriptions of edifice whose position is to be determined, namely, Religious Edifices and Monuments. We will discuss these as carefully as possible.

1st. Are religious edifices susceptible of becoming works of pure art? Two very different ideas of what is a religious edifice may be traced among mankind. To the old Greek a temple was a House of the Gods, wherein the blessed and beautiful Immortals sojourned to receive the homage of men. To the modern English Protestant a church is man's place of prayer, whereto he resorts to perform exercises of devotion (more conveniently paid there than elsewhere), addressed to a Being who is equally present in all other places. Between these two opposite conceptions lie a hundred shades of belief, which have called into existence fanes intended for every form of worship, ranging from the most material to the most spiritual.

When we conceive of a temple as a house for

such a being of beauty and power as one of the old gods of Olympus, it is clear that the office of the architect would be simply to design the most perfectly beautiful house he could imagine—an ideal edifice uniting every element of grandeur and grace. In doing this, the idea of beauty would be his primary idea, just as in the case of an architect building a modern mansion, the idea of utility would be primary. Regard for convenience of worshippers would be secondary to the Greek architect, just as beauty would be secondary to the modern one. Here, then, the Greek would work in the field of pure art. His edifice would be as strictly a work of art, ruled by the principle, *de l'art pour l'art,* as that of any sculptor or painter.

On the other hand, when we conceive of a Protestant Church as a place *for the performance of human exercises of devotion,* it is clear that the office of the architect of such a church is before all things to design a building calculated to fulfil that purpose by such arrangements of size, shape, light, sound, as shall best enable the congregation to go through the offices therein to be performed. A church in which the people cannot see or hear the minister, or the minister conveniently perform his rites, or in which the music is badly heard, or light, or air, or warmth, or means of entrance and egress deficient—a church with any such defects is a failure, however beautiful its architecture may be. True, the architect, after securing these objects, ought, if possible, to add further such beauty and solemnity of style as may serve to impress the minds of the congregation with sentiments befitting religious service. But although this secondary duty of the architect might at first sight appear a primary one (and would probably be so considered by minds of the High-church type), it cannot strictly be so accounted. Protestants frequent their churches not to undergo æsthetic influences, but to join in certain forms of worship and to listen to certain predications. If they are all the time vainly struggling against adverse physical conditions, preventing them from hearing their minister, seeing their prayer-books, assuming proper postures, or enjoying such an atmosphere as may leave their lungs free from irritation, it is plain enough that the most impressive architecture can do little to solemnize their minds. The architect of such a church will have made a gross mistake in building even the most beautiful edifice with these defects. It may be added that the special requirements of a northern climate and of the more Calvinistic forms of Protestantism unite every possible difficulty and disadvantage in the way of sacred architecture, just as the climate and simple sacrifices of Greece afforded it every possible advantage and facility. A really beautiful edifice, suited to evangelical worship on an English winter's day, may be said to be an impossibility; and it is a fortunate coincidence that the same minds which prefer such worship should be usually indifferent to architectural beauty. It is a question not to be too contemptuously dismissed, whether, after all, the supposed revival of church architecture in England has not been a mistake, and whether the much-abused square chapels and churches of a century ago, with their direct and simple suitability to the actual necessities of the *cultus* to be performed in them, were not in better taste (supposing them to be handsome and grave of their kind) than all our recent mediæval imitations.

Catholic churches and cathedrals have a much nearer claim to be works of pure art than Protestant ones; and for this reason, that they resemble much more in character the Greek temple than the Protestant place of prayer. A Catholic church, in the first place, always contains the Host—believed to be a divine Presence specially located within the building; commonly, also, it is the shrine of some dead saint, over whose bones the edifice is a sacred monument. Although prayers are used, the chief religious service (namely the mass) hardly requires any arrangement for the congregation; nor even for the occasional sermon is preparation made beyond a pulpit fixed against some convenient column. The processions, for which space is wanted, afford rather scope for the architect's ideas of grandeur than any check to his fancy. When we add to all this, that in the lands where Romanism survives in splendour, the climate exonerates the builder from all care for warmth and light, we have assuredly found reasons enough why Catholic architecture has been always a great and noble Art, and Protestant architecture a very different thing.

Moslem Mosques, again, are simply *places of prayer;* but the forms of prayer to be performed therein are so simple, the climate of Mahometan countries so inexacting, that in designing them the architect is left almost wholly free to follow the guidance of beauty. He has only to plan beautiful courts, or shaded *loggie,* or great, lofty halls, where the faithful may freely enter and depart at will, finding therein ample space and perfect calm and solemnity for private devotion, or for occasional listening to some reader of the Koran. The strong religious and artistic genius of the Arab race has found accordingly in architecture the free field denied to it in sculpture. A beautiful mosque is not an ideal House of the Gods, but an ideal Outer Court of Heaven—the most solemn and grand and sacred place the architect could design.

It would detain us too long to glance at the relation to pure art held by Egyptian temples, Hindoo, Buddhist, and Guebre temples, Druid circles, and that first temple of Zion, whose architecture, could we recover it, would probably afford the most perfect instance of purely ideal art, inspired by the highest veneration. A building which should bear in architecture the rank which Isaiah bears in poetry would be a glorious fane indeed! Probably, as regards Eastern heathen temples, the architects were usually little trammelled by such utilitarian considerations as disturb those of our churches, and remained free to design as much beauty as their artistic and scientific attainments permitted them to conceive or execute.

Religious buildings, then, we conclude, may either belong to the class of pure architectural art; or have no right to aim at being works of art at all. The Parthenon was a work of pure art. A London church, designed to admit a thousand people to "sit under" a fashionable preacher, only becomes incongruous and ridiculous when it makes pretensions to being a work of art.

2. Monuments, whether actual tombs, or cenotaphs, or trophies, or memorials of any kind, are obviously at present the purest form in which we can practise architecture. Their purpose (even if it include the inhumation of a corpse) leaves the architect free to design whatever edifice may seem to him most beautiful as representing the sentiment of grief or triumph, which the monument is intended to perpetuate.*

Thus, in conclusion, we find that to judge of

* It is a singular proof how little the true principles of these matters are sought for amongst us, that it should have become a fashion of late in England to make even monuments serve a double purpose, and to attempt to combine adorning churches with coloured glass windows, and recording the memory of some departed friend. The very idea of a Monument is nullified by this ingenious device so much in favour with the clergy.

architecture as art we must exclude from view the great majority of buildings, and confine our attention to such temples, mosques, cathedrals, and monuments of all kinds as may reveal the architect's conception of beauty freely developed without regard to utilitarian aims.

How does the primary creative art of architecture which remains after such elimination meet the definition with which we started, viz., that all primary art is derived from God's revelation of the beautiful through his works? Architecture does not copy nature as poetry, sculpture, and painting do. How can we affirm it is derived from it at all?

It must be avowed that the relation between architecture and nature is not quite of the same kind as that between nature and the three great arts we have named. True that a great deal of architectural form is imitated from nature. Columns were undoubtedly copied from the stems of trees, which had originally in the primitive wooden buildings held the place of supports. The capitals were copied by the Egyptians from palms and lotus; and by the Greeks first from the simple bevelling of the wood, as in Doric—from the horns of the sacrificial rams, or the curling locks of women, in Ionic; and, lastly, for the Corinthian (according to the familiar legend told by Vitruvius of Callimachus) from the basket of toys laid over a sprouting acanthus, by a nurse mourning at a young girl's grave. Fanciful resemblances for these orders have been drawn yet further; and we are told (most erroneously) that the Doric represents the proportions of a man, the Ionic of a woman, and the Corinthian of the girl from whose tomb it took its birth. In Gothic architecture, again, the interlacing tracery of the roof may well have been suggested by the crossing branches of the forest—the columns being trunks of stately trees, and the capitals bearing bunches of grapes, nests of birds, human faces, or (as in Milan) figures of saints and angels. But these and all other details of ornament, obviously copied from natural objects, cannot be really said to prove architecture a derivation from nature in the sense in which sculpture and painting are so. Much of what is most beautiful in architecture is also the most remote from any transcript of natural beauty, either literal or idealized. Rather is there a formal repetition and conventional representation of such objects as are copied, altogether adverse to nature. The relation of architecture to nature must be quite other than this, to give it the rank it actually holds among the primary arts. What may this true relation be?

In discussing the subject of Music we arrived at the conclusion that it represented nature inasmuch as it represented *human* nature, the passions and sentiments of the soul of man; and of these such only as are beautiful—in other words, it was a true primary art by being "directly derived from God's revelation through nature,"—the nature of His highest creature. Now, it would appear that architecture is similarly thus derived from the Beautiful *in human nature only*. It represents a certain number of the sentiments natural to man, which are beautiful in themselves, and which find in it an expression, if not similar to that they find in music, yet of parallel power. The impression, for instance, of Religious Awe conveyed by an oratorio of Handel, and the same impression conveyed by the interior of Milan Cathedral, are probably as nearly equivalent to the individual susceptive of their respective influences, as the power of any two arts well may be. It must be noticed, however, that the sentiments capable of being represented in architecture are exceedingly restricted in number, compared to those at the disposal of the musical composer; and that though both are limited to beautiful sentiments, excluding all things mean and base, the architect is compelled to choose among beautiful feelings the few which can be rendered by his art. Religious Awe, Solemnity, Praise, bright and fanciful Joy, Triumph, Mourning, may be said nearly to exhaust the list of the sentiments reproducible by architecture.*

* As examples of each we may instance the earlier Egyptian temples, such Druid remains as Karnak and Stonehenge, and such Christian churches as the Holy Sepulchre, San Lazaro at Cyprus, San Lorenzo at Rome, Winchester, &c., as displaying profound religious Awe. The mosques of Cairo and of India, the Parthenon, the Pæstum temples, the Pantheon, all partake of both Solemnity and glorifying Praise, the latter sentiment being altogether embodied in the majestic splendour of St Peter's, the

The primary art of Architecture, judged by the foregoing principles, will in all cases have its value determined, first, by the beauty and grandeur of the natural human sentiment which the architect has reproduced; secondly, by the power with which such sentiment has been so embodied, and the extent to which the building will impress the spectator with the same sentiment; thirdly, by the adherence to those principles of proportion and balance which obtain throughout nature, and being founded on the laws of gravitation and dynamics, apply equally to all works either of art or nature. The *poetry* of

church which is in Architecture what the Te Deum is in Music. Again, the feeling of Joy, full of bright and playful fancy, was represented by graceful fanes like that of Vesta in Rome, or the marvellous octagon at Baalbec, and perhaps by some of the pagodas of the East. Triumph has had its arches, trophies, and columns from the days of Sesostris to our own, the solemn prostyle temple of Nemesis at Rhamnus (whose statue was formed of the block Xerxes had brought to make his own trophy), being its gravest type, and the airy little poem in marble to Apteral Victory on the Athenian Acropolis, its lightest fancy. For Mourning, alas! there is no age or land where death has not left his mark, and where some grave—from the cairn and barrow of the savage, to the Lycian Mausoleum or Egyptian Pyramid—does not represent that ever-recurring sentiment of humanity.

Marvellous indeed is it that it should be within the power of architecture to reproduce all these feelings through such means as are at our disposal—the arrangement of walls and columns and arches, the play of light and shade, and the interchange of forms graceful or massive. Not more marvellous, however, than the familiar magic of music, which by quicker or slower movements of sharper or lower sounds, touches every chord of our hearts.

the architecture will be determined by the first and second conditions — the *science* and *skill* of the architect by the third.

Secondary or Reproductive Architecture is of far more difficult definition than any other form of secondary art. The line between it and Primary or Creative Architecture is exceedingly hard to draw, for the questions might be equally asked: Is there any architecture wholly original? and, is there any architecture merely reproduced? So very large a share of the art is engrossed by what we have just described as its scientific as distinguished from its poetic elements, and this scientific part is so necessarily traditional, that to ordinary eyes one building may almost seem to have grown out of another, in a sort of Darwinian succession, by "natural selection," in unbroken series since the first primates of our race, half gorillas, half men, built themselves wigwams in the forests of a forgotten world. Each style has been gradually developed—the Greek from the Egyptian, the Saracenic from the Greek, the Norman and early English from the Saracenic, and from them again the decorated, perpendicular, and Tudor, in regular succession — till the Palladian (descending by another pedigree through the Roman from the same Greek origin) met again the northern line of tradition and completed, as it would seem, the circle of our inventions, seeing that Europe has been well-nigh barren of new architecture ever since. Yet in each transition, and in each instance of each style, there was assuredly room for the true artist, while using the science of his predecessors, to embody fresh poetry in his work. The likeness between buildings of the same country and age is after all only the same kind of likeness which may be found between the poems, paintings, or musical airs of any one epoch and nation. It only betrays the general taste then and there prevailing. Hence primary architecture must be accounted such as reveals some fresh poetical feeling—some new ideas of beauty derived directly from the human sentiments in the architect's mind. The architect must say something to the spectator—something which has not been said in the same way before—something which is a revelation of a natural and beautiful human sentiment. He must make awe, joy, praise, triumph, or mourning, express themselves through his work as they have not hitherto been expressed through any previous work of architecture. True secondary architecture must be such as reproduces primary architecture, retaining all its beauty, and repeating its expression of the same sentiments. To effect such reproduction by servile copying would manifestly merit small praise; and the variances of position, materials, and climate, are all so great that actual imitation in architecture is less feasible than in any other art. A successful reproduction of a fine edifice must needs involve a very considerable share of taste and skill, or we find in its stead such a caricature of a Greek temple as the Parisian Madeleine—the flowing and undulating lines of the original changed for hard, sharp angles; and the glistening white marble replaced by whity-brown columns, built up in pitiful little drums, like a pile of pieces from a backgammon-table, and making, with the flutings, a cross-bar like a tartan plaid.

The merit of secondary architectural art of course must be determined like other secondary arts; first by the beauty of the original it reproduces; secondly, by the perfection with which the poetry of the original is translated and its science and skill successfully revealed.

Artists of the tertiary or Receptive order in architecture are numerous enough, so far as a rudimentary sense of architectural grandeur may go; but very few in the degree of a thoroughly cultivated sense of the art. Almost every one is susceptible of some influence from majestic buildings; but the delicate appreciation of their special beauties is a thing rarely to be found. Receptive art in architecture may be estimated, first, by the character of the work whose impression is felt; secondly, by the strength and fulness of the impression; thirdly, by the technical knowledge of the science of architecture, and discrimination of taste in judging of its application. This last condition (as happens in all arts) continually is mistaken for the complete receptive sense itself; and those who can discuss fluently the merits of the details of a structure, and the strict appropriateness of the decorations of the different styles, assume the position of connoisseurs in architecture, when their minds and hearts remain wholly unmoved by the poetry which speaks through the entire edifice. Another not less common error is that which discloses itself by the frequent observation, "I admire Classic architecture; I do not care for Gothic," or *vice versâ*. The different styles express different things—different beautiful human sentiments. The receptive sense of architecture should make a man able to read and sympathize with each varied expression, as with the grave and gay moods of a poet, and to comprehend alike the high Joy of the old Athenian, uttered through the matchless symmetry and perfection of form of his temples, between whose white columns the blue sky of Greece and the dancing waves of Salamis are gleaming; and the solemn Awe of the mediæval Christian, spoken through the vast, dim cathedrals of uncertain form and overwhelming grandeur, whose dull grey stones repeat the gloom of the cold and cloudy North. Each is beautiful in its place; and to be dead to the impression of either is to lack the power of receiving the art of architecture.

Sculpture holds among the great arts a position easy to be defined. Its office is to reproduce the Beauty revealed in nature *through form*. With this alone it is concerned, and among such beautiful forms its dignity demands that it should choose the highest only. The human form, supreme in beauty, occupies it primarily; then such combinations as fancy may create, by uniting the human and the animal, as for example, in centaurs, fauns, satyrs, angels, and sphinxes, and the human-headed bulls and lions of the Assyrians. Lastly, in actual animals of the highest class, horses, lions, leopards, &c. Below these (although the cow of Myron was greatly admired by the ancients, and Alcibiades' dog and the wild boar of the Mercato Nuovo of Florence by ourselves), the beauty of the lower creatures is hardly great enough to suffice for the dignity of sculpture, except as accessories to the human figure.

The beauty revealed through form by the sculptor is not exclusively physical beauty. The beautiful or grand passions and sentiments of human nature—and even those of animal nature—are also his domain. The ἦθος (expression), as the old Greeks called such revelation of passion or sentiment either made through action, or traits of emotion on the countenance of a statue, is a large part of the sculptor's art; indeed, no statue could be considered a true work of Art which was deficient in such expression. But the limits of this expression are to the sculptor exceedingly narrow as compared to those of other artists. He is bounded far more than the poet, musician, or painter, as to the passions or sentiments he may attempt to represent at all: and even among those which are at his option to use, he is called upon to exercise the strictest reticence in the representation, lest he transgress the limits, not merely of the Beautiful, but of the Dignified. "Expression," says Winckelmann, "changes the features of the face, and consequently alters those forms which constitute beauty. The greater the change the more unfavourable it is to beauty." Therefore expression, instead of being driven as by the dramatist to the utmost verge of veracity, must by the sculptor be confined to the very calmest and most chastened indication. Jupiter makes Olympus tremble, but only, as Homer says, "by the bending of his eyebrows." Apollo's wrath against the Python he slays is revealed only by the open, breathing nostril, in the statue in the Vatican. Even Niobe's maternal anguish only changes her to stony despair; and Laöcoon in his agony strives for self-control as much as for relief.

As a means of reproducing his subjects, the sculptor has at his disposal either the perfect Statue "in the round;" or Relief, which may be so high as to be nearly complete statuary, or of middle height, or bas-relief, or again *intaglio-rilevato*, or perfect *intaglio*. For size he has no limit to his art from such *colossi* as that of Rhodes and the Sphinx, and the statue of Carlo Borromeo, to the tiniest coin or gem on which his design can be executed. For material he has clay, wax, wood, marble, stone, ivory, and metal, and their imitations and substitutes. Here we come on the great mechanical peculiarity of the art. Only through the means of a perfectly ductile material (such as clay or wax) is it possible for the sculptor to produce his most perfect forms at their first creation. But these materials, which alone meet the necessity of creation, are generally unfitted to be permanently preserved. It is needful, therefore, to copy the image into the durable material, in which it is finally to be kept, and wherein its beauty can be thoroughly displayed. The relation, then, of the original model to the finished statue is unique among the arts. It is the work of Art itself—the sculptor's direct derivation from nature brought to the highest perfection within his power. Yet it is not this which the world beholds, but its copy, which the sculptor may either execute himself, or may, if he so please, confide to any one capable of thoroughly reproducing his model (if any such can be found). The sculptor has done his task when he has realized in form the beauty he designed. It may or may not be desirable for him to be himself the marble-cutter, and finish the completed statue with his own hands; but if he do so, it will only make him the reproducer and copyist of his own work—the marble will be the *replica* by the master of the original model. Between the architect who merely designs his edifice on paper, and never touches stone or slate, and the painter, who actually does his work with his own brush, the sculptor thus holds a half-way position. He shares accordingly with the architect, the poet, and the musician the advantage that his work may be indefinitely multiplied without his interference. He shares with the painter, at his option, the actual manipulation of his work.

Sculpture is truly creative and original when it is directly derived from the beauty revealed through Nature. It may belong to either of the two classes —that of individual Portraiture, which professedly aims to represent only a single real personage whose lineaments are known to us,—or to that of Ideal art, which aims to represent either a purely imaginary being, or one whose actual features are unknown. But the lines between these two classes of sculpture are less far apart than is commonly conceived; for there can be no good portrait which does not partake of the ideal, nor any good ideal which has not been faithfully derived in its parts from Nature. The difference lies in this, that the portrait statue should assemble the traits of the individual it represents in all his higher moods and sentiments, so that it should serve as a likeness for him, not at one special place or time, but everywhere and at all times, and even (if we may speculate so far) bear a resemblance to whatever form we can conceive his spirit to wear in any future state of existence. The ideal statue, on the other hand, should assemble the traits, not of one person, but of many persons, in whom the special character desired to be represented should be peculiarly developed.*

* The selection of the most beautiful parts, and their harmonious union in one figure, produced ideal beauty, which is

Even in the case of animal sculpture a certain idealization is required—a selection of the finest possible forms for each feature and limb. The sculptor's duty is to see with illumined eyes the beauty scattered it may be through many forms; or, as in the case of the portrait statue, revealed in gleams by one form, and then to collect all such scattered rays into one focus. Be it noticed also that in admitting the class of Portrait Statues to rank as works of Art, it can only be under the restriction that they should be portraits of persons, beautiful either in form or expression. The one sole object of pure Art being to create beauty, the admission of any such aim as the recording of the features of an individual for the sake of affection or curiosity, can by no means be recognized as contributing to a work of Art.

As to the strict originality of a work of sculpture, it is clear that it must be determined, as above stated, strictly by the fact of the sculptor having personally studied from Nature, and not by the fact of any other sculptor having, or not having, studied

therefore no metaphysical abstraction; so that the ideal is not found in every part of the human figure taken separately, but can be ascribed to it only as a whole; for beauties as great as any of those which art has ever produced can be found singly in Nature —but in the entire figure Nature must yield to Art. . . . . By the Ideal is to be understood merely the highest possible beauty of the whole figure, which can hardly exist in Nature in the same high degree in which it appears in some statues.—Winckelmann's *Hist. Ancient Art*, chap. ii.

from the same Nature before him. No man's work ceases to be original because he beholds in Nature the same beauty which another beheld previously, or because his insight leads him to find the supreme excellence of that same particular natural beauty also discovered to be best by past artists. Nothing, for instance, can be more idle and ignorant than to reproach a modern sculptor with being merely an imitator of the Greeks, if at the same time it can be shown that he only draws his inspiration from the same ever fresh natural beauty which their consummate taste made them discover twenty ages ago to be the highest of all. On the other hand, if a modern sculptor, instead of seeking inspiration from Nature, merely tries to obtain it at second-hand, either from the Greeks or any other artists, he ceases to be a creator, and becomes an imitator. The reproach against him is justified.

The value of a work of sculpture will be determined, first, by the inherent *beauty* of its subject,—in which consists the Poetry of the work; secondly, by the *perfection* with which such beauty is rendered,—in which consist the Science and Skill of the work. The best of all statues would be one representing the highest beauty, with absolute accuracy as to anatomy, and absolute perfection as to manipulation.

Secondary or Reproductive Sculpture is the nearest allied to its primary of all secondary arts. The original sculptor himself is commonly for half his time only a reproducer in marble of his own designs: and if he delegate that office to another who shall finish for him the rough outline left by the stone-cutters on the block into a perfect copy of the model, that other must be, so far as science or skill is concerned, in some degree a sculptor too. Even for the poetry of his original he must have much taste to execute his work to perfection. The difficulty of achieving such a task well is proved by the facility with which real art-critics distinguish ancient copies of sculpture from originals—even when the originals no longer exist for comparison. The disproportion between the perfection of the design and the incompleteness of the performance, with the failures of details, at once demonstrates that the copyist was unequal to the undertaking of really producing the original. Gem engraving, cameo cutting, the making of coins and medals from the designs of sculptors, are all forms of secondary or reproductive sculpture of various artistic value. Of all of them the merits must be determined,— First, by the beauty of the original work which they copy; secondly, by the perfection with which they reproduce its beauty; thirdly, by the degree in which the reproduction differs from a mere copy, and aspires to translate the original into a new language of art.

Tertiary or Receptive Art is more rare in sculpture than in any other art; especially is it so in England. Instead of judging statues by their resemblance to beautiful human forms, we guess at what human forms may be from the few statues within our observation. And this ignorance (inevitable in our climate and with our civilization) by no means stops short at the anatomical merits of sculpture. We are equally in the dark as to its Poetry. At our International Exhibitions it is not a little deplorable to behold jostling crowds gathered round some second-rate work, and listen to the enthusiastic remarks they make—on what? On the feeling displayed? the beauty of the face or figure? or life-like attitude? Nothing of the kind. On the cleverness with which marble is made to look like a crape veil, or a piece of lace, or a shower of pumice-stones, or (in one notable instance) a rush-bottomed chair! Oh, triumph of the majestic art of Phidias and Praxiteles and Michael Angelo—a rush-bottomed chair! We have reached the bathos of receptive sculpture, and can no further descend. To see the beauty of the most beautiful statues—to feel all that the sculptor means us to feel, and then appreciate the technical merits of his work—these are the conditions of true receptiveness in sculpture. How far we are from a general enjoyment thereof it is needless to tell.

PAINTING is the last great Art—the embodiment of the Beauty revealed in nature, both through Form and Colour. The scope of this Art is far wider than that of either of those we have been last considering, inasmuch as it embraces, first, the Beautiful in human nature—both the beauty of form and of colour, and also of an expression ranging through every sentiment and passion which can partake of beauty, and whose representation need not be limited within such bounds of repose as those imposed by sculpture. Secondly, animal nature,—embracing not only the higher class of beasts, but all creatures whatever which can be ranked as beautiful. Thirdly, inanimate nature,—embracing every description of beautiful landscape and sea-scape, and the buildings or ships which may enliven them; sky-scenes, interiors, special natural objects, such as trees, flowers, waterfalls—in a word, every conceivable thing which man may either see or imagine he sees, and of which Beauty may be predicated. Nay, even Beauty itself, the one great aim of all Art, may, in painting, be understood in a larger and less strict sense than elsewhere, and those humbler charms which make up the Picturesque may suffice for its requirements; although the supremest beauty is not above its reach. Painting may also deal with far larger groups and more complicated subjects than sculpture; and, while the preservation of a certain unity throughout every work of Art must be a principle applicable to all, the painter's unity embraces a wider variety than that of either sculptor or architect.

Of the various materials at the disposal of the painter, either to produce his thought in the full glory of colour, or simply to delineate in drawing, it is needless to speak. With the exception of glass-painting, it is usually exclusively with his own hand that he performs his work from commencement to completion—a speciality he holds alone among artists.

Painting claims rightly to be original and creative when the painter derives his inspiration *directly* from Nature in any one of the forms which we have indicated as within his scope. The beauty of humanity, physical and moral; the beauty of animals; the beauty of wood and wave, and sky and flower—are each and all revelations, which by truly receiving and faithfully reproducing, he becomes a creator of Art. That which before was Nature (i.e., the Art of God), he reproduces in Art, (the Art of man). All that has been said regarding the ideal in sculpture applies equally to painting. The painter may either make a portrait of an individual, or a tree, or a landscape, or a professedly ideal picture of man or angel, or forest or mountain. In the case of the portrait, he must assemble all the characteristics of his subject which are fit for painting from every different glimpse of them he has obtained. In the case of the ideal work, he must assemble from all the sources at his disposal the features of person or landscape suitable to afford the most beautiful conception of the figure or place he designs to create. Falling below this standard, and making portraits possessing no beauty of form or expression, or ideal works not assembling beautiful or picturesque natural features, the painter falls below real Art—his work, as Art, is worthless.

Beauty is revealed by the Creator of all things in so transcendent a manner through the lovely shapes, and rich and varied hues of nature, that we are all accustomed to speak of beauty pre-eminently as thus made known to us, and it is only by a sort of metaphor that we speak of other and invisible things being also beautiful; as, for instance, the tones of music, or the sentiments and actions of a man. The Greeks thought differently, and to them, who of all men best knew what beauty was, the "beautiful" in form and the "noble" in action and feeling were one and the same. But, alas! those human sentiments to which the term can apply are too often blended with others far from beautiful, and he who goes to them to satisfy his longing for beauty must meet many a sore disappointment. The beauty of form and colour, lesser in character though they be, are ever to be found by those who seek them, and in their enjoyment no regret or bitterness can blend. Thus the painter holds to Beauty, in the abstract, a relation more constant than perhaps any other artist; and having the command in his Art of both form and colour, he can record more phases of nature's charms than any other, save the poet alone. So familiar is all this, that when we speak of beauty we at once think of form and colour, unless some other kind of beauty is specially designated; and when we think of Art, we think simply of painting, unless architecture, or music, or sculpture be also named. Both from this cause, and because painting is, next to music, the most common of the Arts, we are accustomed to call a Painter, an Artist, *par eminence.*

The value of original works of painting must be determined, first, by the beauty of the subject—beauty either of expression, form, colour, or light and shade. Secondly, by the fidelity of the representation of such beauty. Infinite modifications of merit, it will be seen, must exist, according to the degrees in which each kind of beauty exists in the subject, and is more or less scientifically and skilfully rendered in the painting.

Secondary or Reproductive Art in painting has various branches. Engraving on steel, wood, or copper; lithographing and copying, either in the same style and material as the original, and the same process, or in other materials, and by a different process (as when an oil painting is translated into a water colour or pencil drawing, or *vice versâ*). The merits of this order of Art of course must be determined, like those of the corresponding orders of other Arts, first by the excellence of the original; secondly by the perfection with which it is reproduced.

The remarks on bad art made in discussing musical performance, apply with much diminished force to drawing and painting. Bad musical performance does no good to the performer, and is an offence and interruption, not to say a source of pain and irritation, to those who hear it. It has only the excuse of innocent uselessness in the rare cases wherein it can be practised out of hearing of any sensitive ear. But secondary Painting, even when it must be admitted to be indifferent art, when the painter has neither gifts nor culture to make it better, is at least innoxious to the community—inoffensive so long as its results are not forced into conspicuousness—and for the individual himself a method of obtaining correctness of eye and facility of expression useful in a thousand pursuits.

Finally, tertiary or Receptive Art in painting implies a gift which happily is not among the rare ones of the human race. The taste for pictures is among one of the most ancient and most widely diffused of all the attributes of man. No country offers us remains so ancient as to precede painting, no savage tribe is so barbarous as to lack pleasure in the sight of such rudimentary art as is within its comprehension. True that in the earlier ages and among half-civilized nations the same curious defect of the pictorial art may always be traced as among children. The first attempts at Art, instead of being, as we might have supposed, always direct copies of Nature, are, on the contrary, invariably composed out of the artist's "moral consciousness" of what men and trees and houses *ought* to look like in certain positions. Assyrian bas-reliefs, and Egyptian wall-paintings, and Chinese landscapes all show the very same propensity which will make any child to whom we give a pencil and a slate, draw rivers with fish half as wide as the stream; profiles of men displaying the full breadth of their chests; kings twice as tall as their subjects; and houses, gardens, and people all dancing in the air in a perspective excelling all that Hogarth could invent for absurdity. How is this universal habit to be accounted for? Surely only on the grounds that it is *the impression made on us*, and not *the thing which makes it*, which (like the musician) the painter first strives to represent; only learning by long practice to go to Nature herself for his model, and so, at last, to make on another the same impression she has made on him.

The amount of pleasure is incalculable which is given by the very humblest forms of the pictorial art to thousands of human beings who else would never know æsthetic gratification at all. To the inhabitant of the wretched mud cabin in the bogs, the rude coloured prints he fastens over his bed of straw; to the child, the gaudy pictures of his first story-book; to the pauper in the sick-ward of the work-house, the woodcut which breaks the blank wall, at which he has stared so long, with some image from the outer world of love and hope; to all of these, and many thousands more, prints of the poorest sort are sources of some of the best pleasures they experience. Each mechanical discovery which allows pictures to be multiplied and made accessible to the poor should be reckoned a definite gain to the human race of so much innocent enjoyment.

It is of course, however, in those who possess the strongest æsthetic taste, and have been able to give it the best cultivation, that the full measure of the enjoyment to be derived from painting is to be found. Among such persons the Receptive power must be determined, first, by the character of the beauty of the work they appreciate; secondly, by the science and skill of the painter which they can discriminate,—in other words, by their faculty for judging the Poetry of art, and their culture in measuring its Science and Skill. As usual here, as in other arts, the latter quality of criticism, i. e., the criticism of science and skill, usurps alone the rank of receptive art, regardless of the far loftier criticism of the poetry thereof. A *connoisseur* or *dilettante* is supposed to be a person who knows a great deal of the technical merits of pictures, and can readily name their authors. But in truth a full and deep comprehension of the meaning of the painter, a vivid delight in the beauty revealed through his work, is a part of receptiveness far above all such technical judgment.

From the beginning of this essay it has been maintained that receptive Art is not limited to the appreciation of human works of poetry, music, architecture, sculpture, and painting, but extends much further, even to the appreciation of the beauty from which they are one and all derived, to be found in Nature itself. He who only holds in the Hierarchy of Art a place in this third order, cannot indeed reproduce what he beholds, but he must also, like the primary and secondary artists, see and appreciate and love that Beauty of Nature. It is he who can best understand Art who is capable of most thoroughly admiring Nature. Nay, one of the great glories of Art is that it leads even the most ordinary and ungifted mind, through interest in the poem, the statue, or the picture, up to an interest in the natural subjects whence their creators drew their beauty. The same object which was passed by with inattentive eyes in Nature, reappears in Art invested with a new interest, by having been cast afresh in the crucible of the artist's mind, and henceforth attracts the admiration it deserves. The original artist, as the high-priest of Nature, introduces daily fresh votaries to her temple. Here is the completion of the circle. God reveals that Beauty, which is a part of His ineffable perfection, through the beautiful forms and colours and expressions of Nature. The primary artist beholds it with illumined eyes, and creates it anew in some great work of poetry, music, architecture, sculpture, or painting. Then the secondary artist sees the beauty of that work, and reproduces it—in dramatic acting, in reading, in musical performances, in copy of the building, the statue, or the picture. Lastly, the receiver is struck by the reproductive art—led up by it to seek out and study and appreciate the original

—then led higher still by that original up to Nature —and, last of all, led "by Nature up to Nature's God." Art is thus a golden chain of many links let down from heaven to draw man up to heaven again. The great Author of Beauty has willed that His children should share His own joy therein. No mere adaptation of their senses to the outer world has He provided for them in His goodness, but a true filial sympathy in works whose beauty they know is spread no less richly where their eyes may never behold it, even to the depths of the ocean.

All true Art is *religious* Art; it is religious in proportion as it is true, and as it more perfectly reproduces the beauty revealed by God through Nature. To ask that it shall specially occupy itself by direct reproduction of subjects suggested by the historical forms of religion, and to count it merely secular and profane when it passes such subjects by, and only reveals Nature in man, or Nature in a tree or a mountain, is to mistake entirely the high office of Art. It is by revealing BEAUTY that Art fulfils its purpose. Nothing more and nothing less is to be desired of it. Science may reveal Truth, and morality Goodness; but to Art alone it pertains to bring to human hearts the sense of that Beauty which is also divine. If it succeed in this aim it is religious in a higher sense than if it presented to us the loftiest subjects in the range of theology.

DECEMNOVENARIANISM.

Reprinted from Fraser's Magazine, April, 1864.

At the close of his sixty-third year, the Spirit of the Age has received the rite of baptism at the hands of a certain distinguished philosopher, whose connection with other "spirits," more or less apocryphal, renders the function peculiarly appropriate. We have all heard much concerning this "Decemnovenarianism" for a long time before he received his formidable cognomen. For good and evil he has been a byword. While by one party a mere reference to his numerals *Anno Domini* was supposed sufficient to convict all ignorance and superstition of utter anachronism and imposture; by another party a keen sarcasm was understood to be conveyed against the world at large by the hint that it has the bad taste to exist in a century so low in the chronologic scale, instead of in the artistic *cinquecento,* or those yet nobler "Ages of Faith," profanely termed the "Dark." Perhaps it may not be unprofitable to afford brief study to the question, What is this Spirit of the Nineteenth Century? How does it differ from that of other times? and is it on the whole worthy of either the laudation or disparagement with which it is commonly treated?

On the face of the matter appears a fact, which

yet is often curiously overlooked both by eulogists and depreciators. The Spirit of the Age is not singular, but dual. We have had two generations since the century began. There is Nineteenth Century *Père* and Nineteenth Century *Fils;* and they are as different from one another in principles, opinions, manners, and costume as fathers and sons usually contrive to be. Praise or blame addressed vaguely to both, must usually be unjust to one or the other. Let us try to draw the portraits of these two characters, so as to mark such differences as clearly as we may.

Men and women who enjoyed their youthful prime in the first quarter of this century, must have been as little imbued with what we commonly think the Spirit of *our* Age, as any generation in history. With the few exceptions of men, like Shelley, who held ultra free opinions, and were socially outlawed for holding them, the time was to the last degree conservative. The retreating wave of the great French Revolution carried men's minds back further than they had gone for long years towards Absolutism in politics and Traditionalism in religion. The connection between Liberty and the Guillotine, Free-thinking and a Reign of Terror presided over by a Goddess of Reason, was fresh in all men's minds. The equally intimate relation previously existing between Despotism and the Bastile, Orthodoxy and *Autos-da-fé,* was sufficiently distant to be forgotten. The Whig and Liberal of those days was more conservative than the Tory of our own; and the Tory was a being of whom no living specimen remains, any more than of the *Elephas Primigenius*. His footsteps may be tracked in a few old sand-coloured books, and his teeth lie embedded in the lower strata of *Blackwood* and the *Quarterly*. Nearly all which constitutes the most living life of our time was then unknown. Scientific theories and discoveries, and philanthropic schemes, occupied no space compared to the theatre and the card-table. Social Science, proper, was then unborn. The principle of association, with all its machinery (so familiar to us) of committees, patrons, secretaries, subscribers, meetings, and reports, was as little known as the omnibus which each society resembles in purpose and noise, and which is as common as such societies now. There existed then the "Society for the Propagation of the Gospel in Foreign Parts," and the "Society for the Discountenancing of Vice and the Promotion of the Christian Religion and Virtue." Who does not feel the verbosity of these titles proof enough that they belonged to the age when there was ample space in the world for their swelling skirts to expand, and time enough on men's hands to repeat six words where two would suffice? It is needless to point out the familiar changes wrought by Telegraphs, Steam, Chloroform, the Penny Post, and Photography, which if we could deduct from our present modes of existence, they would collapse like Nadar's balloon. These outward differences typified the inward, between our fathers' lives and ours. They were emphatically *slow* lives, in the cant sense, and in all senses. People had Leisure in those days. That constant sense of being driven—not precisely like "dumb" cattle, but cattle who must read, write, and talk more in twenty-four hours than twenty-four hours will permit, can never have been known to them, nor the curious sort of an ache, somewhere between head, chest, and stomach, which comes of such driving. People read Richardson still in country parts, and Scott was the nearest approach to "sensation" known. They dined at four o'clock so as to secure the loss of the best part of every day, even if they were not too muddled afterwards to attend to anything. Cards were played by grave ecclesiastics, and ladies of eminent virtue and "parts," at ten in the forenoon, if the day chanced to be rainy, and from six till midnight, whether it rained or shone. Drives were taken with four or even six horses, not for the purpose of going the faster, but rather for that of slow dignity. They danced minuets still in 1810: in fact life was a minuet, only now and then breaking out into some *gavotte* of masquerade or rout, or wild gambling wherein human nature avenged itself. Was all this dull to them as it seems to us? Was it really dull at all? Were those old Tories and card-players so far behind us intellectually and morally? Some doubts may be entertained on the subject.

In the first place, life among all classes in the last generation seems to have been much less a struggle than it is with us. Perhaps in the highest sense it lacked something of aspiration, something of the longing which pervades all nobler hearts now, to do some one thing, however small, towards hastening God's kingdom in the world, and striking one blow, however weak, in the battle for the Right and the True. But on the other hand it was freer far from low social ambitions and petty vanities. As the classes were more marked, and there was very little possibility of rising from one into the other, so there was only rarely an effort to do so, and all the ugly and pitiful toils and disappointments, and equally pitiful successes of what we denominate *l'art de parvenir* were saved to society. The genus Snob was either then less numerous, or like the Serpent before the Fall, had not taken to eating dirt, and being conscious of his own meanness; adding the pretence of not caring for rank to the folly of caring for it intensely. Just as now-a-days every Englishman honours his Queen, and is not ashamed to confess it; so in those times nearly every man honoured those who in the quaint old phrase of his catechism were his "betters," and made no concealment of the matter. If there were less struggles to rise into higher grades of society, and less attempts to keep up the fictitious appearances, which always accompany such struggles, it is clear that the greatest taint and misery of modern life must have been absent. Only to imagine what it would be to banish all that comes of these base efforts out of the present world is to see another order of things. Real poverty, short of absolute want, has no pain to be compared with the gnawings of these pitiful ambitions and the sacrifices which are made for them, which no sense of duty or honour alleviates or recompenses.

The principle which most largely actuated men in the last generation in these matters, seems to have been precisely the reverse of *l'art de parvenir*. It was the Art of Standing Still. *Noblesse oblige* meant that a man's actions, habits, modes of life, should be consistent with his birth; i. e., with a certain fact. The modern principle is that they should be consistent with the station which he would like to be supposed to hold; i. e., with something untrue. Even if the old notion had in it some absurdity, if it compelled its adherents to such imprudences as that of the Duke of Ormond giving away his last £40 in the world in vails to the household of the friend he had visited—it had in it something genuinely respectable. The new notion has no one element of good sentiment to redeem it from utter contemptibility. A man undergoing many privations for the old principles, could respect himself and be happy and at peace, since no discovery could involve him in disgrace. A man toiling and scheming on the new principle, must needs despise himself and live in constant fear of every chance disclosure which may throw down his hardly-erected edifice of respectability like a house of cards.

The gentleman and lady of the last generation not only led lives essentially different from ours— they stood themselves in widely different moral and mental positions. The ethics of 1800—1820, and of 1840—1860, are opposed in their very sources, so are the theologies, so are the politics, so are the æsthetics. Very briefly can we point out these contrasts.

The Morals of the last generation were all embued with the spirit of Paley, if not absolutely founded on his miserable *Moral Philosophy*. Locke's metaphysics were still dominant in England, though Kant had revolutionized Germany. It was generally accepted that we knew right and wrong only because an outward Revelation had commanded the one and forbidden the other; or else (as Bentham taught the more advanced minds) that a "lot of pleasures" could only be judged to be good or evil by their results on the "greatest happiness of the greatest number." There was "no higher law" heard of, nor was there any theoretic admission of a purely unselfish motive. It was considered quite a liberal and enlightened thing to say, "It is not the Fear of Hell, but the Hope of Heaven, which ought to guide us." Virtue was, in Paley's phrase, "doing good for the sake of eternal reward in heaven." Of course, human hearts were not really cramped to such pitiful systems. The same clergyman whom the writer has heard teaching a class of scholars that it was wrong to commit murder, *because* the Sixth Commandment forbids homicide, and scoffing at the suggestion that Conscience gave the law of the case;—that clergyman acted probably with as direct and simple adherence to his own conscience on all moral questions, as any of those who "count reason ripe by resting on the law within." The same noble old soldier who said he acted always from Hope of Heaven, probably never once in his whole life thought whether he was increasing his chances of going thither by being just, generous, and brave. False theories assimilate with difficulty in healthy human organizations, and, as the teetotallers say of alcohol, only run about the blood-vessels, and disorder the brains now and then, without ever becoming a part of the individual's own flesh and blood. Still these bad ethics were bad things, and tended to lower the tone of sentiment. Selfish principles did not shock the ear as they do now, for they were heard every Sunday, attached to all holiest sentiments and duties. God himself was said to have made man "for His own glory;" and man was to love Him (as Waterland said) because He is "more able to make us happy than all beside."* Small marvel was it then that those who could use such a word as "love" in such a sense misapplied it equally in human relationships. Marriage was a thing understood to be properly

* Waterland's *Sermon on the Nature and Kinds of Self-Love.*

contracted, if the man or woman had the means of bestowing some benefits; and statecraft, war, philanthropy, science, and art might surely be pursued by any man, avowedly for his own Fame, when it was taught that the creation of heaven and earth had had no other aim, even with Him whose "glory" could receive no increase from the hallelujahs of the universe.

There seems to have been a sharper line drawn in those days, also, than we now admit between the higher and lower kinds of virtue. The Wesleyans among the lower classes, and the friends of Lady Huntingdon and the "Clapham Sect" among the higher, were separated off from the "world" by the renunciation of social pleasures, by sobriety of dress in an age of splendour, and by a general profession of far stricter principles than were expected to regulate the behaviour of others. "Merely moral" men and women might then do a good many things, and neglect a great many duties, which in our day would hardly leave them the character of "moral" at all. Gentlemen might gamble a little, and drink a good deal; and ladies might send their children away to be nursed (visiting them once a month or so for the first two years), and play cards all day and every night; and yet obtain universal respect. In our day religious people are not so strict, and people with no profession of religion by no means so lax, as in the last generation.

Then as to Theology. Broad ideas had not

yet been broached, beyond the very small circle of Coleridge. A man must be either a "Christian" or an "Infidel." If he were a Christian and a Protestant he must hold all the doctrines of Wilberforce and Hannah More; if he were not a Christian, in this sense, then,—whether, like Priestley and Belsham, he called himself so or not, was of no consequence,—he was in the same boat with Tom Paine and Robespierre, and that boat had but one mooring. The sensational school of metaphysics, leading men to hold that only through the medium of the senses can any truth be known to man, necessarily threw the entire weight of spiritual reliance upon external revelation, and of this revelation itself on the tangible book in which it was recorded. The "Literal and Verbal" school of Scripturalists owes its existence in direct logical descent from Locke, albeit his individual creed was of the widest, and rested "miracle on doctrine, not doctrine on miracle." It was natural for men who felt convinced that all ground of faith was taken from us by a single doubt, to treat with impatience all attempts to hold fast one doctrine and let go another, and bring reason to "sit in judgment," where (on their hypothesis) she could have no jurisdiction whatever. To be offended with the cut-and-dried theology to be found in those dreary gray and brown paper-covered books, with rough edges, which appeared between 1800 and 1830, is only to show we have not nimble imagination enough to climb down out of our present position to the shelf where they inevitably had their place.

Then for Politics. That was the age of real Toryism, or rather of Conservatism, though the word was then unknown. It may be doubted whether in any previous period of English history men had been so fond of standing still. There had, of course, always existed the old glorification of the past at the expense of the present. Our charming song of the "Fine old English Gentleman" is a modernized paraphrase of one popular in the days of James I., which compared disadvantageously those very "reverend seigniors" in doublet and trunk-hosen with their nobler predecessors of Queen Elizabeth's court. Doubtless, could we go backward up the stream, we should find each generation lauding the one before it, till Arthur and his chivalry should outshine all subsequent kings and heroes, and perform feats like Ajax lifting the stone,

> Which scarce ten men could raise;
> Such men as live in these degenerate days.

After the "degenerate days" of Homer we may console ourselves, perhaps, and take courage.

But though each age has boasted of the past, it is not very clear that Englishmen ever very seriously wished to go back, or even to stand still, as regarded political rights, till the terrors of the French Revolution drove them into a phrensy of Conservative feeling. Old Tories wanted to bring back the Stuarts, old Royalists would have held

Charles on the throne, partisans of Tudors and Plantagenets, of Normans and Saxons, fought for their respective dynasties. But a thoroughly Conservative policy, on the principle, "things are good as they are—the English Constitution is perfect, and unsusceptible of improvement," was surely never adopted by any considerable party hitherto. The first quarter of the Nineteenth Century (this Century of Progress!) was the precise period of the whole national history, when men said, "Let us stand still."

If it be a fair division of society which has been sometimes made between the Have-Somethings and the Have-Nothings, then might it be said that this Conservative sentiment was essentially a sentiment of the pocket. The ethics which, as we have seen, allowed a man to place his own Happiness as his "being's end and aim," allowed him also fairly to place the happiness and well-being *of his class* before that of all other classes. The landowner held by the Corn-laws, and by every other law which suited his own interest and kept the power in his own hands; and what was more, he acknowledged he did so, and nobody said him nay. Arguments arose as to how members of Parliament, engaged for special interests, were returned; but, perhaps, we have yet to wait for the condemnation which ought to follow the attempt to return them for any special interest (as opposed to that of the whole body politic) whatsoever.

The Whig of 1820 was a bold, brave man. His desire of progress was about the same as that of the Tory of 1860. *Festina lente* was the motto of both; but the old Whig proposed to move, if it were but a few inches, and that little movement has gone on accelerating, till it has carried Tory, Whig, and Radical away in the flood. Of course, like the religious reformer, he was confounded with the extremest section of his party. To propose to enlarge the franchise by a pound-holding, and to desire to cut off the heads of all kings, were one and the same. We recollect hearing in a country-town of a meeting wherein some notable having proposed the King's health, turned round courteously to a Whig gentleman of the utmost loyalty, and gravely apologized: "No offence to *you*, I hope, Mr E——!" Anybody who wanted change was a malcontent and a rebel, and anybody who had religious doubts was an infidel. It was all clear-sailing. We must draw a line somewhere.

Again, the Æsthetics of the past generation were singularly different from our own. Classicism appeared in a certain thin and ghostly shape in the *Style de l'Empire*. All that made it beautiful of old was gone—the originality, the breadth, the freedom, the suitabilities of race and climate. There only remained a certain puny imitation which, if Pericles or Horace could have arisen and beheld, would have driven them to hide their heads again under the waters of Styx. Furniture was "classical" which had legs carved, and draperies hung as falsely and as poorly as could be conceived. Houses were "Grecian" which had a door in the middle, a window on each side, and three windows overhead. Colours were "in good taste" which were either fawn, or gray, or that peculiar blue made by mixing black and white paint. Ladies had a "Grecian bend" when they rounded their shoulders and poked their heads. Dresses were classical which had waists under the arms and such scanty skirts as (in a case known to us traditionally) compelled the wearer to go out of the room and take it off before she could sit down. That was the æsthetic taste of 1810. Refinement meant poorness, thinness—or, as ladies' maids say, "skimpiness"—of dress and habits of life. *Tremaine* was a refined book. Byron was a "most refined creature" when he went to dine with Rogers, and refused to eat anything but potatoes and vinegar, and then stole off to a tavern, and devoured a good plain dinner in private. We ourselves remember having contemplated, as a child, with awe and admiration, three young ladies who visited the paternal abode, and never ate anything, except perhaps the wing of a chicken, or a spoonful of jelly, and a little wine and water. One day some naughty schoolboys having laid a trap for these ethereal beings, caught them all three surreptitiously in the luncheon-room—one was eating cheese, another carving a round of beef, and the third (alas! "the youngest and fairest she"), to save time, had applied a huge silver tankard of beer straight to her delicate lips!

This last period of bad taste, however, is later than can be fairly laid to the door of the generation of which we have been speaking hitherto—the generation which was at its zenith in the first twenty years of the century. The ladies and gentlemen of that time were too truly such to descend often to such affectations; they were proud rather than either vain or conceited. Their manners were a second nature, and no assumed piece of acting. Let us try to recall what those manners—now passing rapidly out of the world—actually were.

Our private illusions on the subject of clothes were once dispelled somewhat unkindly by a charmingly-attired damsel, who remarked to us, "My dear, it is not a question whether you dress ill or well—you don't *dress* at all!" In like manner the present generation would not, in the eyes of the last, have good manners or bad, but simply no *manners* whatever. Manners were things half natural, half acquired by people who united good birth and good breeding; like setter dogs, who must come of a proper race, and then receive careful training. You could not teach a mastiff to set, neither would the best red spaniel pup do the business well without thorough instruction, whatever good dispositions it might show. Nature and art must combine, alike to mark the partridge or to enter a drawing-room. But the art acquired in childhood grew to the possessor; the dignified and easy walk, the noble carriage of the head, the modulated voice, the unfailing courtesy to all, the easy tact of ever ready and appropriate conversation, were as much a part of the man himself, and as little an effort as to speak his own language. Here was perhaps the greatest distinction between him and ourselves. Our manners are either bad, or spontaneously good, or else affected and artificial. His were never bad; and were neither exactly spontaneous, nor yet artificial, but educated, and (precisely speaking) *polished.* The natural substance, whatever it might be, had received the highest possible finish. There was no veneering which might rub off, or start with a little unwonted heat. It was the wood itself brought to lustrous perfection.

The difference between our fathers' manners and ours was visible in every detail; but the essential distinction seems to have lain in the art of conversation, as practised in their time and our own. If the reader has known the happiness of associating intimately with any man or woman who brought the old system into our age, he can surely never cease to regret that that exquisite tact and suavity is vanishing from society. How really delicious a thing it was! How—when its atmosphere had once wrapped us round—we felt ourselves expand in it, as sea-anemones do in warm and sheltered caves, where there is no chance of a breaker ever disturbing the surface! "Nobody is going to say anything disagreeable to anybody! Everybody's small feelings and prejudices will be remembered. Kind things will be sure to be dropped gently, calling for no reply. The speaker will consider whether what he has got to say can interest his audience, and will never pour out his egotism irrespective of their feelings." It is a vision of Paradise, like Mahomet's promise to the blessed:—" Ye shall sit on seats opposite one another. All grudges shall be taken away out of your hearts." And then this delightful conversation (we *talk* now—we rarely converse), with its careful give and take, its courteous drawing forth of the most modest in the party, its sparkling anecdotes and friendly discussion, all came to us through such organs of speech—so soft, so full and modulated! Where are those voices gone,—those female voices of the last generation? We hear sweet singers now; but hardly ever sweet talkers, sweet laughers. We talk too loud, or else fall into the atrocity of whispering to our next neighbour, so that no third person hears us. In the days of good manners, everybody talked for the whole circle, but never raised a voice beyond the pitch of sweetness and good breeding. Our words and sentences come out gurgling and spluttering like bitter ale when the cork is drawn; theirs flowed smoothly like rich wine out of their own fine old silver claret jugs. Is it not a pity that this art—which is everybody's art, which fills up all the interstices of life, and is of tenfold more importance to human happiness than all the painting, music, and sculpture in the world—should be allowed to sink into oblivion like those of making Venetian glass, or the Tyrian dye? Shall we teach children to chatter four languages and never teach them not to interrupt people who are speaking one of them? Shall we instruct young ladies to warble like nightingales, and then leave them to scream like cockatoos in small assemblies, and sit dumb as owls in large ones? There are hundreds of well-bred people now—people whom Nature has dowered with such natural tact and dignity, that nothing can have surpassed it. But for the great mass of society, the want of an education of manners, the dying out of the old traditional practice, is surely a deplorable thing. We have got back hoops, and seem on the way to get back powder. May the kind fates give us one thing more—the manners of the people who wore hoops and powder of old, and the memory of whose suave courtesy comes to us like the odour of their own *maréchale*, or of a drawing-room full of Eastern sandal-wood boxes and *pot-pourri*.

Lastly, there was one point in which we are accustomed to think that we have made vast advance over our fathers, on which it is possible they might have had something to put in as a plea *per contra*. Their practice of duelling was barbarous, was immoral, was the source of great and useless misery. But in despising it, as we have learned to do, it may be asked, have we lost nothing of the keen sense of honour which spurred them (however wrongly) to such measures? That sense of honour was often exaggerated, often purely conventional; and the duel, as a means of satisfying it, was always imperfect, and often absurd. Still, the idea that life itself was in a moment to be risked by every gentleman, at the call even of a mistaken sense of honour, that a man's truth, courage, probity, and the reputation of every woman of his family, were things infinitely more valuable than safety, and to be defended in an instant at the peril of death—these were ideas that had in them much that was ennobling to the age in which they were current. A man imbued with them might have a hundred vices, but he could hardly be wholly base or contemptible. We have given them up, and we have done rightly; nor can we suppose that in God's world the maintenance of any high moral quality really demands an immoral practice. True honour—that is, self-reverence for the humanity lodged in us, respect for ourselves, independently of the world's opinion—can live and flourish, thank Heaven! without a pistol or a rapier. But there is no small danger that in first putting away from us, and taking on ourselves to despise as barbarous, the practice which continually gave to such honour visible dominion over life and limb, we should fall into the error of undervaluing the thing itself. Let the frequenters of those clubs where the reputations of men are coolly canvassed, and the names of women bandied about in most unseemly sort, decide whether the disuse of the much-abused duel is a wholly unmixed benefit.

What is the result of this brief review of the character of the past generation? Firstly this—That in modes of life, in religion, in politics, in æsthetic taste, in manners and social laws, it was altogether different from ours, and in many respects strangely contrasted with it. If either their spirit or ours was "Decemnovenarianism," the other was something else which ought to be called by a different name. Whether the one was better or worse than the other, the Twentieth Century must decide. While we cannot doubt that

> Through the ages one increasing purpose runs,
> And the thoughts of men are widened by the process of the suns,

it will not hurt us to bear in recollection, that with narrower creeds, and poorer systems of ethics, our fathers were, perhaps, practically as religious and as faithful to duty (as they understood it) as any men are now; that their politics, if selfish, have left us a better legacy of national security than is enjoyed by the heirs of any other race in the world; and that if we may question their taste in dress and furniture, they would unhesitatingly and utterly condemn our manners and conversation.

The younger generation of the nineteenth century—this generation of our own, which we are accustomed only to think of when we talk of the Spirit of the Age—how shall we draw its distinctive qualities?

What are the ideas which permeate it and make it what it is? Are there in truth such ideas peculiar to it, or is it any material progress which has produced the apparent change? Is it Steam which has made "Decemnovenarianism," or "Decemnovenarianism" which has created Steam, and a hundred other instruments whereby to rule over the world?

Among the most delicate of all Shelley's ethereal conceptions, is that of a race of beings whose dwelling is in the minds of men,—who say to Prometheus—

"We breathe and sicken not
The atmosphere of human thought—
Be it dim and dank and grey,
Like a storm-extinguished day,
Traversed o'er by dying gleams—
Be it bright as all between
Sunny skies and windless streams;
We make there our airy tent,
Voyaging cloudlike and unpent,
Through the liquid element."

It seems to us as if such beings would find the "atmosphere of human thought" in our time and forty years ago altogether different. There is considerably more oxygen in it just now—a tension often extreme and injurious, and as widely different from the milder air of the past as a Yorkshire moor is from a Devonshire combe. The acceleration of all modes of social and intellectual life must have had great share in producing this change; but the keener thought has again invented and applied inventions in a way no previous age ever did or could have done.* It is no part of our work now to go over those stages of material progress of which steam, telegraphs, penny posts, chloroform, gas, photography, Armstrong guns, and the analysis of the solar spectrum, are the most marvellous, but perhaps hardly more widely effective than many others by which our manufactures, agriculture, and all arts of life have been revolutionized. The volume which should embody the briefest record of these achievements during their generation would be a portly tome itself. Our affair is with the *ideas*, the mental coinage, current in the Victorian age. Gold, and silver, and copper, what is it worth? and what sort of image and superscription does it bear?

The Political ideas of our age would probably, half a dozen years ago, have been pronounced by every one eminently democratic. It was a commonly received opinion that the tendency of the times, all over Europe, was in the direction of republicanism, and that it was a question of time only when these tendencies should culminate in overwhelming power. Individual Dictators, it was thought, might acquire despotic rule abroad, and our own constitutional monarchs might long retain a nominal sovereignty in England, but all aristocratic institutions were in process of slow and certain dissolution. What has become of that democratic Spirit of the Age? It

* e. g. Photography, which seems to have been discovered and used in the last century and then suffered to fall into oblivion again.

would seem that it has certainly received a check. The failure of Garibaldi and the Mazzinian party in Italy has done something—the American war much more. That war, although actually traceable to the very failure of the Great Republic to be a real Democracy, and to give civil and political rights to all the inhabitants of its territories, has yet been most illogically accepted in Europe as evidence of the failure of Democracy itself.

However this may be, and whatever other causes have tended to modify popular sentiment, it seems clear enough that it has been modified. We are not "on the high road to universal Democracy," as many averred, a few years ago, we surely were. The English Royal House and the English House of Lords will hold their places beyond any date now in sight. Republics for Greece, or for Italy, are postponed *sine die*—perhaps till the klephts of Albania and brigands of Calabria can read newspapers, and honour Themis and Nemesis, as well as the Panagia and Madonna! "Brave Swiss," are no longer quoted by any tourists who have endured their ill manners and extortions, as models for European imitation; nor is there a general desire to see England parcelled out into cantons, and represented by a Congress of Innkeepers. Have we for all this swung back the pendulum of prejudice to the Toryism of our fathers? Not at all! Liberal politics, if not democratic ones, are so universal that it may fairly be questioned if a Conservative party, which twenty years since would have been recognized as such, now exists at all. Everybody wants to go on, and to go on pretty fast. It is only a question of how the drag is to be applied to the engine. There is no longer (as there was at the beginning of the century) a handful of violent Radicals to a nation of Tories, nor—as there were a few years ago—two balanced parties, one in favour of Progress and one opposed to it. There are none so violent as the old Reformers, none so pig-headed as the old Conservatives. Parties tend continually to efface themselves, and ideas once peculiar to the Radicals now permeate all men's minds, and make England every day more and more a country of Liberals—of Liberals only.

Singularly parallel to the change in political feeling is that in religious views in England during the last few years. New sects do not arise, nor the old freer ones ostensibly add to their numbers; but the whole existing thought of the nation is gradually leavening with free ideas which sooner or later must tend to efface sects in religion like parties in politics. The process has by no means gone so far in the one case as in the other. There is still a great conservative religious party—a party with two vast separate aggregations, the High Church and the Evangelical; but it would seem as if neither of these stood as high as they did some years ago. They are formed of men, few of whom hold a prominent place in the intellectual life of the time, and none of whom hold out the promise of hereafter rising to higher influence. The younger generation we might almost compare to the sands pouring down the sides of the loose hillocks on the shore and swelling the ever-growing mass of Broad opinion below. "Young England" now is assuredly not Puseyite, still less is it Calvinist. A small portion of it only belongs to the Earlier Broad Church of Maurice and Kingsley. The far profounder school, of which the Oxford Regius Professor of Greek is the head, probably numbers at this moment more of the rising intellect of the time—the intellect which shortly must take the foremost place in politics and literature—than any other in the land. The literature of the time bears unmistakeable traces of this crumbling away of definite traditional belief, this levelling process going on in the opinions of all the most active and cultivated minds. Few of the peculiar and distinctive doctrines of the older creeds, whose influence might be traced in every line of the literature of earlier ages, seem to have a place in the history, the science, the fiction, or the higher periodical writings of our day. A Moslem or Hindu, coming to England and studying our journals and our book-shelves, would find there a Christian literature, in the sense only of a wide humanity; of a reverent and somewhat distant tone in all mention of the Divine Being; and of a peculiar modern mode of paying a warm, brief homage to the name of Christ, resembling the self-crossing of a well-feeling Romanist at the sight of a crucifix. Of the special doctrines "necessary to salvation," of Athanasius, of Luther, or of Calvin—of any recognition of either Church or Bible as a final court of appeal for metaphysics, morals, history, or physical science, he would find very little trace. A book or a periodical which assumes the orthodox doctrines, and applies them to the facts of life, is thereby immediately marked as belonging to the "religious world," and passes out of the sphere of regular literature. Thus the members of the republic of letters, at all events, must needs be classed as holding in religion the same position which thinking men generally at present hold in politics. They are Liberals, but not extreme Radicals. They desire Reform, not Revolution; and their tone towards the past is tender, rather than inimical. In so far then as literature must be held to be the vane on our spire, we must judge thereby which way the wind is blowing all around.

There is much of good, and somewhat of evil, in this religious attitude of our generation. It is good inasmuch as it is an attitude of reverence. Whatever Englishmen believe or disbelieve now, there is hardly a trace of Voltairian shallow and trivial contempt, or of the solemn sneer of that "lord of irony," Gibbon; neither are we indifferent to the whole subject, in the deplorable manner of clever Frenchmen and Italians. Let an Englishman approach ever so nearly to the dread gulf of atheism, he very seldom denies that he knows it is a gulf, terrible and dark, and that he would fain turn round and escape it. The self-conceited satisfaction in verbal quibbles, whereby the shallower races of the South are content to shut out God and Heaven from human eyes, are flimsy veils, rent asunder at once in the strong grasp of the Saxon. Is there, or is there not, a God? Is there, or is there not, a life to come? These are questions, he may perhaps admit with downcast eyes and aching heart, to be for the present beyond his solution; but he will never dismiss them with a shrug, a quibble, and a smile. Huc tells us that when a Chinese is asked his religion he considers it an imperative duty of courtesy to depreciate it, and praise that of his interlocutor: "My religion is the poor, and mean, and foolish religion of Lao-Tze. It is not nearly so good a religion as the high and exalted religion of Fo; but opinions only vary: Truth is one. We are all brothers." The difference between these Chinese and intelligent men in Southern Europe seems to be that they all equally despise the religions in whose forms they aquiesce, and each professes a stupid and unmeaning latitudinarianism. The Chinese alone speaks civilly of another's faith, while the Frenchman and the Italian insults both it and his own with absolute impartiality!

English scepticism in our time is mostly of that sort of which it may be said—

> There lives more faith in honest doubt,
> Believe me, than in half the creeds.

It is honest, serious, and arises in most cases from the sincere interest taken in the subject. Along with it (in whatever degree it may exist) there lives a strong and high moral faith; an intense belief in justice, truth, goodness, purity; higher standards of virtue, higher conceptions of what life ought to be made, nay, even a wholly new spirit of tenderness for any genuine religious feeling in other creeds and ages—these are symptoms full of largest promise. Whatever revolution in opinion may be in store, there can be no reason to fear for its ultimate results while Scepticism itself assumes such shapes as these.

On the other hand, there is an evil side to the religious attitude of the age. It is the disposition to accept as a finality that condition of hesitation and uncertainty which, in the nature of things, should be one of transition. There is an unavowed feeling current through the higher minds of the age, that a definite Faith is an unattainable good; that the larger a man's mind, and the broader his grasp of the great facts of life, so much the more cloudy must be his creed, so much the feebler must glimmer for him the ray of Light Divine whereby Earth's pathways are cheered for humbler souls. It is not merely that men do not now hope to reduce all the awful mysteries of theology to half a page of formularies. It is not merely that they have ceased to look for celestial manna of infallible doctrines, rained down by Book or Church, for mortals to gather up and be fed. They no longer hope to have any theology at all. They no longer look with filial confidence to the Father of Spirits for that bread of life without which our souls must faint and perish. Here is the real weak point of Faith, properly so called; not the faith in books or churches, but in the ultimate intuitions of human nature; those intuitions which tell us that the Creator cannot leave unsatisfied the greatest want of His noblest creature, while He openeth His hand and fulfilleth the desire of bird and brute;—those intuitions which tell us that all which has glorified and hallowed the past, which has exalted man into the martyr, and purified him into the saint,—the Religion which has been the source of everything most beautiful and everything most holy, *cannot* be a dream and a mistake.

There is a great error current in our way of viewing these things just now. Because we have discovered that we cannot attain infallible truth, we have leaped to the conclusion that we can dispense with truth altogether. Because there is no miraculous potable gold in the alchemy of the soul, we imagine we can live without natural food. In youth we plant our tree of faith in hot haste, and dig it up by the roots, and plant again and again equally fruitlessly; and then we sit down in despair, and cross our hands and say, "We will plant no more. Let the ground lie barren." But our duty is to plant, to plant deeply and firmly, perchance with much labour and many prayers, and then at last the faith will strike its roots into our hearts and grow and flourish year by year, warmed by the sun and watered by the rains of heaven, till the feeble shoot has become a mighty tree,—different from the shoot, inasmuch as it is larger and more beautiful, yet in truth the same, and developed from the same firm-set root. Then we ourselves may look back on the day of small things, when a blast of idle words could have overthrown us, and rejoice that "neither life, nor death, nor things present, nor things to come, nor height, nor depth, nor any other creature," can separate us from God, or cast our faith uprooted on the ground.

In Morals, as well as in Politics and Religion, the present generation is widely divided from the past. Theoretically it holds different opinions, and, practically, it has established a very different standard of virtue. The system of Paley and Bentham, modified and ennobled in the hands of John Stuart Mill, represents even the Happiness-test theory in a far better light; while, on the other hand, the opposite school of ethics, which sets forth virtue as the end of creation, and intuition as our moral guide, has gained ground so far that it may be said to colour our literature, almost as Paley's doctrines did those of the last generation. In particular, Divines of nearly all varieties of theological opinion have ceased to preach the miserable "Do good that you may go to heaven" sermons we used to hear, and sound a nobler note as to the motive of duty, even when their ideas concerning the origin of our knowledge of it may be ever so confined. Kingsley's apostrophe in the *Saints' Tragedy* has struck the key-note of the newer and grander lesson :—

> Is selfishness—for *time* a sin—
> Stretched out into eternity, celestial prudence ?

People interest themselves little in theories of morals, and contentedly listen to the most degrading heresies on the subject, while they are ready to call fire and flame over some infinitely small and obscure error of theology. Yet among all the ignorance and indifference on the subject, the progress towards a higher system insensibly produces beneficial practical results. The nobler principle echoed about, penetrates men's brains at last, and kindles a generous warmth in their hearts, which the meaner one was unable to touch. The duties of the rich towards the poor are assuredly understood in quite a different sense now from what they were formerly, when careless alms or ostentatious Christmas benefactions were supposed to fulfil them sufficiently. The whole movement, of which the Social Science Association is the visible type, owes its existence to the higher sense of responsibility, first to *seek out* and discover, and then to remedy the misery of the pauper and the criminal, the ignorant and the vicious. For one "Man of Ross," one Hannah More, or Mrs Fry, of the last age, there are thousands of philanthropists now devoting themselves to doing all that in their power may lie, to lift a little of the weight of the world's burden from the shoulders of the weak and the suffering. No sooner is a scheme of beneficence started than aid flows in from every quarter from unknown friends. A mere summary of the work now doing of this sort in England would fill a volume. Here is surely the "Spirit of the Age," in its very noblest development.

In many less obvious ways a change has taken place in the general manner of regarding questions of moral importance. Thirty years ago the man who should have spoken of marriages contracted for convenience as essentially immoral, would have been laughed at for his pains. In the upper classes the notion that such marriages were fit and right, and that esteem was the only thing needed to render a worldly alliance in every way good and proper, was instilled into the minds of young people as a matter of course. A young lady who declined "advantageous" proposals for the simple reason that she disliked the proposer, was considered to deserve poverty and ridicule for the rest of her life, unless in the rare case of her being in a position to command other similarly advantageous alliances. Even down to the present time, a few belated writers of fiction make their heroines do a noble action in marrying some man they abhor, to obey their fathers or oblige their mothers. All this miserable folly is going out of fashion. We are beginning to see that the canon that "marriage must hallow love" has a converse quite equally sacred, and that "love also must hallow marriage."

It is needless to point out the often-recognized changes which have occurred in the social morals of the century. Drunkenness, gambling, blasphemy, these three giant vices, have been extruded in uttermost disgrace from the circles where once they blazed in full effrontery. It is too much to be feared, however, that dishonesty and all the special sins of trade have rather gained ground upon us than lost it during the same period.

As to the Æsthetics of our age, who knows what they are? Are we Romanticists or Classicists? Is pre-Raphaelitism an accepted thing? Ought our buildings, public and private, to be Gothic, or Greek, or Italian? or something jumbled of all? or something wholly new? Should our furniture be Tudor, or Renaissance, or Louis XIV., or Style de l'Empire? When we ask these questions, we awake to the curious fact, that every preceding generation has had its style more or less marked and predominant, through all the works of the day. But our generation has no such style. There is no one thread of thought or taste running through the multitudinous shapes or colours which our houses within and without display. If a future painter wishes to give "An Interior, Temp. Q. Victoria," or a future novelist describe vividly an English house in 1864, what can either of them do in the way of architecture or furniture to give *couleur locale* to their sketches? The crinoline remains the sole original feature of the epoch!

In manners, where are we? We will not say, like the young midshipman, who was desired by his father to take notes of the manners and customs of the nations whom he visited, and who simply appended to those of the Polynesians "Manners, none; customs, beastly." We are not at all "beastly." Probably real refinement and delicacy never reached so high a point before, as among the middle and upper classes of England now. Certainly, we may doubt that cleanliness ever did so. If the conquest of India had only availed to bring us back so many exquisitely clean ladies and gentlemen, and to introduce the supreme institution of the matutinal tub, then would not the empire of Aurengzebe have fallen in vain! Still for "manners," alas! for mode of address, for conversation, for the minor courtesies of life which make all the difference between jolting down the road of life in a cart, and rolling over it in a well-swung carriage, it can hardly be denied there is a grievous falling off from the days of our fathers. Is this owing to women? A great change has certainly taken place in their position. A woman's lot is a freer, happier thing by far than it was when life's lottery offered her but the one prize of a congenial marriage, and all the rest of her chances were miserable blanks of unhappy wedlock or dreary maidenhood, pinned up in narrowest circles of conventionality. Still further may these changes go. But let us trust that however may hereafter be adjusted many questions opened now, it will never cease to be women's aim to soften and refine the manners of their time, and to claim from men that gentle courtesy which it is equally a pleasure and an honour to give and to receive. The fear that they should do otherwise seems about as well founded as that they should join in a league for the general massacre of babies,—or anything else equally congenial to their natures!

To resume. Nineteenth Century *Père* was a fine worthy gentleman in thick white cravat and blue coat. He had the narrowest political and religious creed, and the worst æsthetic taste possible. But he was brave (as some fifty well-fought battles by sea and land could testify), pious, and charitable, according to his lights, and of supreme courtesy of manners and chivalry of feeling. He left to his son (notwithstanding his foolish opinions) the English Constitution,—also a variety of hideous edifices and public monuments, and a rather greater tendency to gout than had been enjoyed by mankind before the Treaty with Portugal.

Nineteenth Century *Fils* is a young gentleman in tweed suit and wide-awake, with a cigar permanently growing out of his lips. He has the very finest aspirations in all directions, but has no particular creed as yet, political, religious, moral, or æsthetic, and no manners whatever, good, bad, or indifferent. It is earnestly hoped by the friends of this interesting youth that he may leave something better to Twentieth Century than the heritage he received from his own respected progenitors.

HADES.

Reprinted from Fraser's Magazine, March, 1864.

A SINGULAR test might be applied to the character of different nations by examining the ideas current among them concerning a future state, and noting the precise nature of the paradise they desired, and of the hell they feared. That "undiscovered country" of whose shores all our boasted science leaves us as ignorant as the Chaldean patriarch of old, has yet in all ages offered an irresistible attraction for the human imagination, and the genius of each successive race has bequeathed to us a picture wherein unconsciously it has reflected many of its own lights and shadows. Those varied *diglyphs* of heaven and hell preserved for us in history, form a gallery wherein with great advantage we may study the thoughts and feelings of the distant or bygone families of man to whom they originally belonged. We cannot obtain a better insight into any mind than by the knowledge of the objects it most earnestly desires or vehemently deprecates. Hope and Fear, the positive and the negative poles of the soul, when we have once ascertained them, cannot fail to teach us at least the bearings of its voyage over the ocean of life.

In the present paper we do not hope to discuss the subject with the learning which its due treatment would demand, and still less intend to raise any theological debates concerning the veracity of this or that particular doctrine. Our only ambition will be to point out some of the obvious deductions to be made concerning the character of a few of the greater nations of the world from the ideas commonly attributed to them concerning a future existence. Perhaps the subject may be found sufficiently interesting for some one more qualified to deal with it, to develope it more worthily hereafter.*

The first fact which strikes us in examining the various ideas which have prevailed of a future life is the great difference in the degree of interest wherewith the subject has been regarded. In some nations, as among the ancient Egyptians, it actually appears to have assumed the foreground of thought. Men and women seem to have lived constantly with a view to the degree of honour which should be bestowed upon their mummies on earth, and to the favour with which Osiris might correspondingly treat their spirits in the interval between death and the resurrection. The most stupendous of all the enor-

* Soon after the publication of this Essay a work appeared fulfilling to the uttermost the author's desire—*The Critical History of the Doctrine of a Future Life. By the Rev. W. Alger.* We possess in this admirable treatise the complete Testimony of the Human Race to the sense of Immortality. In the Appendix Mr Abbot has added references to the entire existing literature of the subject—a work of marvellous erudition.

mous piles with which they loaded the valley of the Nile, the oldest and the grandest of all human works, was only a sepulchre—the great Pyramid of Ghiza. On the other hand, among the Israelites, the whole subject of another life was thrown completely into the background for ages; and though in possession of their whole matchless literature, we are left in doubt whether the noblest minds among them even believed that there was any future for the human soul, or "any knowledge, or device, or wisdom in the grave." The absence, or at the least the coldness of this faith, in a race so deep-hearted, so pre-eminently religious, has been at all times a phenomenon so difficult of explanation as to suggest even such strange hypotheses as that of Bishop Warburton; and our surprise is further increased by the discoveries of late Egyptian archæologists tending to show how many details of their cultus the Israelites adopted from their taskmasters, while this one foremost and all-pervading idea they seem to have utterly ignored. Even among nations kindred in race and in creed, the difference concerning all things relating to death and immortality have manifestly been extreme. The Ninevites in all their various monuments have left us no trace of their ideas concerning the dead, while their neighbours the Babylonians attached that care to the rites of sepulture, which betokens strong belief in another life. To this day the indifference, not to say levity, of the Italians contrasts strangely with the tenderness and sentiment of the Germans, both Romanist and Protestant, as displayed in their cemeteries.

As a general rule, we might perhaps affirm, even in the presence of the striking exceptions above named, that there exists a relation between the greatness and civilization of each race and the strength of its consciousness of an immortal life. As we descend in the scale among half-civilized and savage tribes, the belief seems to take less and less place in their thoughts. We do not indeed reach (unless in some semi-simious race like the tree-dwellers of Ceylon) any creatures in human shape who are utterly devoid of the belief that death is not the "end-all" of a man. Short of conditions of degradation equivalent to idiotcy, there is always some notion of future wants and future employments. According to Lyell's most interesting statements concerning the human remains found in the cavern at St Acheul, even in the earliest dawn of humanity, when the dwarf and narrow-fronted fathers of the world lived in strange fraternity with the mammoth and the cave-bear—in those far-off untold millenniums—even then the dead were buried with the weapons and the food which the disembodied spirit might desire—even then it was true that it was "the creed of the human race that the soul of a man never dies."

And as we advance onward in history, and turn from the primeval tribes of the past, and the savage races still lingering in Polynesian islands or American forests, to the nobler branches of the great human family, we find continually the faith in immortality becoming clearer and more vivid as we proceed. No better evidence for the universality of that consciousness can be found than in the fact that it was certainly experienced most strongly by the three nations of antiquity whose respective types of religion and civilization were most widely distinct, and possessed the best claims to being indigenous in their far distant localities. The Brahmins, the Egyptians, and the Druidical Celts, each believed in the life to come,—and the vast literature of the Hindoos, saturated with the idea of future rewards and punishments; the stupendous monuments of the Egyptians, recording for all time their hopes of resurrection; and the testimony of their Roman conquerors to the amazing faith in immortality which nerved the disciples of the Druids, all remain to prove the vigour with which each grasped the common faith. Yet that the Brahmin took it from the Egyptian, or the Egyptian from the Druid, who will believe? Even if we admit the unlikely assumption of a pre-historic communication having existed between the races, we shall find nothing to militate against the originality of the faith. Such communications have no results when the natural consciousness of immortality is feeble in the race which should receive instruction. As we have already seen in the case of the Jews, a people may live four hundred years in bondage to the most deeply-believing nation, and may adopt from it all manner of minor opinions and ceremonies, and yet at the end remain, apparently, exceptions in the whole human race by the absence of belief in immortality corresponding to their general mental and religious development.

Among the causes which appear to affect the vividness of the consciousness of a future existence, one of the most powerful is the comparative strength of the converse sentiment, namely, the consciousness of the present life, with its enjoyments and sorrows. When this latter consciousness is extremely intense, it appears, if not to exclude the other, at least to throw it into the shade. More precisely speaking, if a man's consciousness of the present life be of that external and sensuous kind which takes him much out of his own self-consciousness, then he will rarely be inclined to push forward into the unseen future any strong forecast of his own individuality. If, on the other hand, his consciousness be of that profounder and more inward sort which leads to intense self-consciousness, then he will vehemently and imperatively call for an eternal prolongation of his individuality. In other words, the more the purely human element of self-consciousness is developed over and above the animal consciousness of mere life, pain, or pleasure, in so far will the sense of immortality be developed also. In a large way this principle is exemplified by the nations of northern and southern Europe. As a general rule among Europeans, the northern races are reflective and self-conscious, and consequently filled with a grave and solemn conviction of a future life. The southern races, on the other hand, are outward-bent, sensuous, and, even when highly intellectual, by no means given to self-analysis and self-consciousness. That sad and often morbid and ruinous thing self-anatomy,—that valetudinary habit of the soul which keeps for ever the finger on the pulse of our own emotions, till all their spontaneity and simplicity are destroyed—this is a state utterly unknown to the Greek or the Italian. Never in our lands would the old sage have taught (and been reckoned among the Seven Wise Men of the world for teaching) his famous lesson, "γνῶθη σεαυτον." The self-examination which Pythagoras enjoined for triple use every night to his disciples, he would rather have forbidden to a Teuton or a Celt with the propensity to exaggerate self-analysis into one of the most fatal diseases of the soul. The old Greeks were of an opposite temperament. To them the difficulty must have been not to forget themselves, but to remember themselves. In their bright, radiant climate, surrounded by transcendent beauty of nature and art, with the whole world of philosophy and poetry yet lying before them like a garden untrodden in the morning dew, what had they to do with the gloomy and solemn self-reflections which haunt us under our cloudy skies and in our pent-up and darkened libraries? The Greek lived in the open air—the pure, transparent air of Greece. He sat in splendid marble porticoes, or wandered through the light olive-groves of the Academe. He talked in his noble tongue, with thoughts as free as the odours which the breeze wafted from the Ægean waves or the heather of Hymettus. There was no man to bid him be silent—no solemn creed to command him to lay his finger on his lips and bow before the awful Jehovah of the Hebrew. This life was to him intensely delightful, intensely interesting, and bright, and joyous. The consequence was that a future existence took in his mind the shape of a shadowy, dim, and mournful thing. He did not disbelieve it; his high and splendid intelligence could not lack such an intuition. But he believed in it as a twilight realm, not to be compared with this bright world—a land of shadows, if not, as Job thought, "a land of darkness as darkness itself." This dim conception of Hades naturally resulted in the formation of myths of Elysium and Tartarus, singularly colourless as compared with the glowing pictures of future joys and torments drawn by other races.

Turning from the notice of the degree of faith in immortality held by different nations, to the character of that faith itself, we find the Greek representations of the beatitude of the good and the punishment of the wicked, in the one case that of a world of very tame delights—in the other one of rather childish horrors. The Elysium of the future life seems to have been a place in no way glorified beyond the actual Elysian Fields visited by every tourist to Naples, and offering an expanse of sufficiently fertile plain, with views of the lovely adjacent sea and islands. The souls of the blessed were supposed to wander for ever in similar plains, amid amaranths and asphodels; or rather we may believe that the Greek of Athens actually placed his paradise in the beautiful regions of Magna Græcia, of which report had reached his ears from travellers. Other reports from still more distant lands—perhaps from the Balearic isles, perhaps from Madeira or the Canaries—had suggested the idea of the Islands of the Happy, the Fortunatæ Insulæ of the Romans; which we shall find again in the mythology of the pagan Irish, as Innis-na-Oge, the Isle of Youth; and again, down to the sixteenth century, the common dream of all the Celtic tribes of Western Europe, the Holy Isle of St Brandan in the midst of the Atlantic. It was of these Happy Isles that Proteus is made to speak in the *Odyssey* :—

> For there in sooth man's life is easiest:
> Nor snow, nor raging storm, nor rain is there,
> But ever gently breathing gales of Zephyr
> Oceanus sends up to gladden man.
>
> *Odyssey*, iv. 565.

The penalties of Tartarus, on the other hand, are almost ridiculous, nor can we doubt that they owe their invention to the nightmares of the original mythologist, or (as he himself would have described it) that "Ephialtes was the father of Hell." The forty-nine Danaïdes, hopelessly trying to fill their vessel, full of holes; Ixion, for ever rolling his wheel; Sisyphus, perpetually pushing up the stone which as perpetually rolls back down the mountain; and, above all, Tantalus, seeking to satisfy his hunger with the fruit which for ever swings beyond his reach, and to quench his thirst from the stream which shrinks from his lips,—all these are unmistakable dreams of the incubus sort, wherein the sufferer struggles, as it seems for ages, to accomplish some ever-failing aim. In the case of Tantalus it is impossible not to suppose that some over-indulgence in goblets of "Samian" or "Chian" had suggested the penalty of his quenchless and "tantalized" thirst. But these punishments, absurd as they are, seem to have been limited to the few enormous offenders specified, and the common herd of mankind, both good and bad, were condemned to dreary miseries with which their moral deserts seem to have had no connection. The fact of their corpses remaining unburied entailed worse penalty than their own crimes; and for a reason for their sufferings on the banks of the Styx and for the brutality of Charon we look in vain. Such as it was, this mythology of Hades evidently left the nation at large with merely a mournful anticipation of the future life. If they did not all say with Euripides—

> Better, though on the worst of terms, is life,
> Than the most glorious death;

it is probable they would all have echoed the lamentations he puts into the mouth of Alcestis, that she should no more "behold the sun," but descend to the cold regions of eternal shade. There is not, I believe, a single instance of the poets—even the nobly moral Sophocles—ascribing to any hero or heroine such expressions of hope or satisfaction as would have befitted, according to our ideas, their acts of patriotism or self-devotion. Antigone herself has none, although in her he chose to impersonate the very highest of moral truths and heroic self-devotions. She, a woman, in a nation wherein women were almost what they are in Persia and Turkey now, he made the mouthpiece of that doctrine of the HIGHER LAW, which even to our day has been denied and scoffed at among people who profess to honour Daniel and the Seven Children, and the martyrs of the Twelve Persecutions. Antigone buries her brother's corpse at the penalty of her life, and then retorts on the tyrant who had forbidden his sepulture, that in disobeying him she had only followed

> The unwritten law Divine,
> Immutable, eternal,—not like those of yesterday,
> But made ere Time began.

We have here reached regions of truth which twenty-two centuries have not served to make the common property of mankind. We are yet debating whether the production of "the greatest happiness to the greatest number" be not the final test of all morality—a test which would leave poor

Antigone's self-sacrifice for the burial of her brother's corpse in the category of what Bentham, in his *Deontology*, simply styles "folly." We are yet debating whether obedience to a wicked act of Congress, like the Fugitive Slave Law, or to an irreligious military regulation, such as requires homage to idolatrous emblems, may not be the duty of a Christian citizen or a Christian soldier—a principle by which Antigone was a criminal and Creon justified in his tyranny. Nay, more. Since Antigone had no hopes (or very dim and shadowy ones) of eternal happiness to be gained for herself in heaven by her heroism, her act was actually deprived, according to Paley, of all title to virtue—for virtue, according to him, must be performed "for the sake of everlasting happiness." Nay, Waterland, that great pillar of English orthodoxy, goes further, and affirms that "to be just or grateful without future prospects has as much of moral virtue in it as folly or indiscretion has"—a doctrine fully endorsed by Robert Hall in his sermon on "Modern Infidelity." The very circumstance which in fact raised the Grecian heroine's act to the purest pitch of disinterested martyrdom has thus been held by English moralists to deprive her of all possibility of merit. Truly we are tempted sometimes, in the face of such perversity, to wish that some of the clouds which hung between the soul of the old Greek and his Elysium might so far pass before the minds of our teachers as to enable them to look elsewhere for a motive of virtue than to this bait of paradise. To exchange *this* worldliness for what Coleridge called "other-worldliness" will hardly tend to make any of us as magnanimous as Antigone.

The secondary nature of his hopes of a future life must undoubtedly have rendered the virtue of the ancient Greek and Roman peculiarly disinterested; free at all events from one of the motives which may taint at times the sacrifices of others. Indeed, when we contemplate some of their actions —say, for instance, the voluntary martyrdom of Regulus (if we may assume the veracity of the common history)—it is hardly possible to refrain from a sense of astonishment at its transcendent ethical sublimity. To give himself up from free choice to the most agonizing death rather than break his promise; and this under the belief that "better, though on the worst of terms, is life than the most glorious death," actually attains the climax of all virtue; the motive the most purely disinterested, the martyrdom the most complete and tremendous.

Perhaps another result of the dimness and gloom of the Elysium of the classic nations may be found in that desire, so common among them, and so exaggerated in our eyes, of perpetual Fame after death. When the ideas of a personal future existence were all obscure, it seems as if the innate "fond desire and longing after immortality" found vent in the hope of a prolonged reflected life in the memories of other men. It supplied that element of infinity after which in such varied ways our souls are ever craving. The same feeling which makes one man yearn for immeasurable love, another for knowledge, another for power unlimited, another for an immortality of beatitude—nay, the feeling which prompts to the sin (otherwise so unaccountable) of blasphemy and the use of infinite adjurations and imprecations —that same feeling of craving after something endless, unbounded, infinite, lay doubtless at the bottom of the Greek's and the Roman's thirst for eternal fame. Baulked of its natural vent in the hope of personal everlasting existence, it turned to this remaining ambition with (as it seems to us) a sickly and morbid desire. Assuredly no man who believed that he himself in his own individuality was the inheritor of an immortal life, could have said with Pliny that "the happiest of all possible anticipations is the secure expectation of an honourable and undying renown." From our stand-point such a wish becoming paramount would be evidence of a morbid moral condition. Whether we stigmatize the thirst for the admiration of our fellow-men as vanity, or excuse it as a natural desire for extended sympathy —in either case we must look on its assumption of the foreground of our thoughts as a degrading usurpation. To become indeed any way a motive-power over our actions, the love of approbation must have assumed unlawful proportions; and to think of it extended into eternity and become the grand ambition of life, is actually the apotheosis of vanity.

We have become so sensible of this that even the poets, to whom till lately a sort of monopoly was granted in the matter of acknowledging a desire for fame, are now as far as other men from admitting their possession of such a sentiment. With the somewhat hypocritical modesty of our modern code of proprieties, we all assume it as a matter of course that we do not think our own deeds of any kind worthy of renown, and are exceedingly surprised and not particularly delighted when it comes home to us. As to anticipating immortal fame as Pliny, Cicero, Ovid, and so many others of the ancients candidly acknowledged they did, we should pillory directly with our ridicule any man, however great, good, or gifted, who admitted entertaining such an idea. But from the stand-point of the ancients the matter might be viewed in a different light. There was a side of touching human feeling in this ambition. We can comprehend it when we read the mournful lament of Theocritus, complaining that the humblest herbs have more hope than man—

> Ah, when the mallow in the croft dies down,
> Or the pale parsley, or the crisped anise,
> Again they rise—another year they flourish.
> But we, the great, the valiant, and the wise,
> Once covered over in the hollow earth,
> Sleep a long, dreamless, unawakening sleep;

or Horace, noting that all things have a return of vivid existence, while human life passes away into a shadow—

The moon renews her horn with growing light;
But when *we* fade into the depths of night,
Where all the good, the wise, the great are laid,
Our best remains are ashes and a shade.

There is something pathetic in the longing of men who felt like this to be remembered by their fellows and honoured under the sun, while their pale and fleshless ghosts should wander mournfully by the shores of Acheron. The appeal to pause and recollect them, so common on their tombs, comes with natural earnestness from such a state of sentiment. In looking at the beautiful sepulchral bas-reliefs now collected in the temple of Theseus, I have imagined that this appeal was intended to be expressed in each group, where the dying man or woman so tenderly clasps the hands of the survivors, looking at them with a mute entreaty for remembrance, which after two thousand years yet speaks to us from the marble. Assuredly the converse idea to perpetual memory—that of immediate and absolute oblivion—is one against which every mind shrinks with abhorrence. Cruelty never reached a pitch of ingenuity greater than that described by Procopius and quoted somewhere by Sir Thomas Browne. It seems Justinian built a strong tower in a prominent position in Byzantium, and there incarcerated for life his most detested victims. Once thrust within the gates they were never more heard of; whether they died or lived no man knew. Their wives, children, relations, were compelled to renounce their names, which were also expunged or effaced from every written memorial. Everything they had possessed was destroyed. It was death to utter their names. Truly, when we picture such a punishment and imagine the feelings with which loving eyes may have gazed over the glittering Bosphorus and splendid Golden Horn, over the gardens and the cypresses, the imperial palaces and the domes of churches, to that dread Tower of Oblivion frowning over bright Byzantium, we seem to see a torture more exquisite than that of which knives or fagots could be the instruments. The land in which such a tower was built might well be the land also in which men desired above all things the perpetual record of their names, the perpetual affectionate remembrance of their genius or their patriotism.

Turning from the current popular notions of the Greeks concerning a future life to those held by the philosophers, we seem to come on traces that even here also there was less interest felt in the subject than amongst us. It has often been remarked how singularly Socrates seems to have postponed all instructions on the subject to his disciples till the last hours of his life, after he had discussed with them such a multitude of topics of minor interest. Unless it be the art of Plato, falsifying the facts for rhetorical purposes, the whole band were uninformed of their master's views on the matter, and only drew them out by their questions in the final scene detailed with such matchless perfection in the *Phaidon*.*

Among the Roman philosophers also the subject, though not entirely neglected, does not seem to have excited the interest it possesses for us. It was not often disbelieved. Cicero speaks of those "who had lately begun to assert that the soul also dies with the body."† And there seems to have been only the Epicurean school who summed up human hopes and fears in the solemn lines of Lucretius—

> The worst which can befall thee—judged aright,
> Is a sound slumber and a long good night.

But the discussion of the subject seems hardly to have borne the stamp of their usual free and fearless inquiry and bold suggestions of hypotheses. It

* May I venture to suggest that the famous argument in this dialogue (that as we can only think of a dead body and not of a dead soul, therefore the soul cannot die) has been unjustly treated too often by modern critics as a mere verbal quibble, and neglected as a real argument in favour of immortality? According to Kantian philosophy, a fact of which we cannot even imagine the reversal, is a necessary truth, and known to us by the transcendental source of knowledge. We say that grass is green and Rome a great city. These are contingent truths, which we may imagine changed. But when we say that a triangle contains two right angles, or that the superficies of a sphere is equal to four great circles of the sphere, we announce necessary truths which (once we have apprehended them) we cannot ever imagine altered by any power whatever. If the idea of a soul cannot admit the notion of death, then immortality is a necessary truth, and known to us intuitively. Plato would doubtless have assumed the veracity of such intuitions as an accepted principle.

† *De Amicit.* iii.

was rather a continual attempt to proffer topics of support and consolation, or rather to prove that death under any aspect could be no real evil. Seneca, Epictetus, and Antoninus are full of such reflections, but not of inquiries into the probable or possible forms of a future existence. A fact still more remarkable is that when we descend to Christian times, and find the pious and magnanimous Torquatus Boethius waiting in his dungeon for the cord wherewith the cruel Theodoric crushed the brain which contained the last wisdom of the Roman world—even then we find his Consolations of Philosophy entirely derived from considerations foreign to that of an approaching entrance into the kingdom of heaven. There is no allusion to Christian hopes in the whole book of the martyr-philosopher.

Perhaps no better result of the thoughts of the ancients concerning death can be found than in the beautiful words of Marcus Aurelius: "Death is a cessation of the impression through the senses, and of the pulling of the strings which move the appetites, and of the discursive movements of the thoughts, and of the service to the flesh" (vi. 28). "Do not act as if thou wert going to live ten thousand years. Death hangs over thee. While thou livest—while it is in thy power—be good! Man! thou hast been a citizen of this great state—the world. What difference does it make to thee whether it has been for five years or for three?

Where is the hardship, if no tyrant or unjust judge sends thee away from the state, but nature which brought thee into it? It is the same as if a prætor who has employed an actor dismisses him from the stage. 'But I have not finished the five acts, but only three of them.' Thou sayest well, but in life the three acts are the whole drama; for what shall be a complete drama is determined by him who was once the cause of its composition, and now of its termination. Depart then, satisfied; for He also who releases thee is satisfied."

In passing from the ideas of the Greeks and Romans concerning the future life to those of the Egyptians, we seem to have changed our whole atmosphere of thought. For some reason unknown to us, the spirit of the Egyptian seems to have been as grave as that of the Greek was bright and joyous. All the memorials of his art that have descended to us bear the same stamp of ponderous solemnity; and to him it is clear that instead of life being vivid, and the under-world a dream, this existence on earth was merely a shadowy passage to the tremendous realities of the judgment-seat of Osiris. The work of the greatest kings through the whole of their reigns was the erection of their tombs. From the wealthy priest and noble down to the mechanic, whatever luxury could be spared was devoted to the sepulchre and the coffin. At all feasts, and apparently at all times in the houses, the mummies yet unburied were present; and for a description of all the elaborate processes and ceremonies of embalming and entombing a volume is required.

The privilege of being embalmed in the most perfect manner was not, however, a mere empty honour, but exceeding important for the welfare of the individual. It is, I believe, the opinion of the best Egyptologers that the object of preserving the body in its mummied condition was to keep it ready for the return of the soul after three thousand years of such purgation or beatitude as Osiris might have decreed. The doctrine of the "Resurrection of the flesh" seems to have been either the origin of the practice of embalming, or perhaps suggested by the constant sight of the mummies which the tender care of the survivors had found the means to preserve. In any case it was the great aim of the embalmers to render the corpse inaccessible for an enormous period of time to the causes of decay. And well did they perform their marvellous work. It is not a little affecting to consider that for the great mass of the mummies now lying in the tombs of Egypt a period very remarkably tallying with their three thousand years has actually elapsed. Their hope and aim has been fulfilled—their corpses are existing still, after that vast interval wherein lies the whole cycle of human history. Where may the souls be now whose hope it was to reassume those poor, withered, and shrunken bodies? Do they smile now, in the glorious forms of the radiant denizens of a larger and a grander world, at their once humble ambition? Is it not thus with us all, that we are for ever desiring and labouring to return to the dry bones of a withered past, while God, more merciful than our wishes, bears us on to a nobler and a holier future?

It is a piteous sight, travelling in Egypt, to see how the remains of the dead are habitually violated, and that not so much by barbarous Fellah Arabs as by educated Europeans. It would seem as if the respect for a human corpse which an Englishman or a Frenchman, with any shadow of good feeling, could not be tempted to neglect elsewhere, is completely annihilated when the dead body in question happens to be a mummy. Ideas of the ludicrous seem to replace all other considerations. The very care which the surviving relations bestowed on the remains of their lost parent, brother, husband, wife, or child, has exposed them to our stupid contempt; and after the lapse of thirty centuries we drag them from their beautiful tombs and tear them in pieces as ruthlessly as if no human soul had ever dwelt in and hallowed for ever that tenement of clay. Every one who has visited Egypt must have seen, as I have done, the most frightful instances of such desecration. In the sepulchres crowded round the Sphinx I have entered grave after grave and found each one had been not only rifled but wantonly profaned—cere-cloths, bones, and actual human limbs and flesh lying scattered about the floors. It was not the Arabs who had done this, nor the wild beasts of the desert, the hyæna I saw climbing the giant steps of the third pyramid, nor the vulture I found preying on the carcase of an ass in the ruined Cyclopian temple. It was the work of polished European gentlemen pursuing their scientific researches. Truly science needs to be the noble thing it is to answer to so many responsibilities as it is made to stand for just now. Better let it pull dead mummies to pieces, however, in Egypt, than dissect live horses and dogs in the schools of Paris.

One idea of the Egyptians concerning a future state is so remarkably beautiful that we cannot omit referring to it. Among the various deities who all (the best Egyptologers seem to agree) were but personifications of the different attributes of the One Supreme God—the God whom they supposed to be the Judge of the Dead was Osiris. Osiris was the representative, not of the Divine Justice, Power, or Wisdom—but of the GOODNESS of God. The soul then went after death to be judged by Infinite Goodness; it passed into a realm wherein presided the very impersonation of Mercy! No marvel was it that this same Osiris was the deity worshipped most universally through the land, and that his images are found by hundreds in the sepulchres of the dead, and that the favourite amulet of the living should have been the representations of his all-seeing Eye! With such a doctrine as this prominent in its theology, we can have little space for supposing that the religion of ancient Egypt was a mere gross polytheism and idolatry, even if we had not the testimony in Iamblichus' book on the Mysteries to the devout fervour of the higher minds of the nation. Not many modern treatises contain deeper words concerning prayer for spiritual benefits than this book written by the high-priest of Egypt.

The doctrine of Metempsychosis, so prominent in the Egyptian ideas of a future life, links together in a singular manner the theologies of very different nations. The Pythagorean sect in Magna Græcia doubtless derived the idea from Egypt; but the Brahmins, we must needs suppose, held it in coeval antiquity. The extent to which the latter carried out the idea of retribution as inflicted in animal forms, is a curious instance of the childlike minuteness of the Eastern mind. In the Institutes of Menu at least thirty different creatures are named in whose bodies malefactors are imprisoned, according to their crimes; the scale descending down to such particulars as that he who stole perfumes should be changed into a musk rat. Having already touched on the subject of transmigration in another article, I shall here only repeat the observation that our contempt for the doctrine may possibly be a little excessive, and that foolish and unphilosophical as it must be held in a physiological point of view, in a moral one it may bear comparison with many of higher pretension. It is very absurd and even ridiculous to think of a human soul being changed (as in the bas-relief on the Theban tomb) into a hog; but the idea was not a low one, that the punishment for sensual sins in another life was the loss of that human dignity which we had voluntarily relinquished in this existence, and that a man who had chosen to grovel in swinish vices here should be compelled to wallow in them hereafter, conscious of his degradation and yet compelled to endure it, till by shame and repentance he has expiated his offence, and is fitted once more to assume a human shape. The minds to which such a notion of punishment could have occurred were assuredly not far down in the moral scale, however monstrous and childish we must admit the doctrine to be when gravely stated as a theory of the future existence. In countries where the doctrine prevails, animals are usually treated with some tenderness, and their lives must be estimated as on the whole sufficiently happy. Thus the punishment of transmigration involved no threat of physical suffering, only of moral and intellectual degradation. It is not a very low people to whom such a threat holds out any salutary terror. "Tortures vile" appeal to the fears of the basest; but to dread degradation without suffering, we must have a good deal of human nobility left in us.

The Brahmin theology, beside the transmigration of souls, holds out also the punishment of Padalon, the tremendous hell, with its eight gates and brazen beds of torture, so splendidly described by

Southey. This seems to be the abode of the Asuras, or evil spirits, and also (like Tartarus) of the most extraordinary criminals. It would, alas! however, we fear, be sufficiently well filled (if we may judge by the testimony of our Civil Service residents), supposing the denunciation in the Institutes of Menu to be carried into effect—"Headlong in utter darkness shall the impious wretch tumble into hell, who being interrogated on oath, in a court of justice, shall answer one question falsely!"

There was a termination, however, eventually—in the Brahmin system, as in all others of the heathen world—to the future punishment of the wicked. The length and degree of debasement, of transmigrations or tortures, were apportioned to the guilt of the offenders, but not infinitely prolonged. "When the vital soul," say the Institutes of Menu, "has gathered the fruit of sins, and when its taint has been removed, it approaches again those two most effulgent essences, the Intellectual Soul and the Divine Spirit." (12—18).

Mount Meru—the abode of Indra, God of Heaven—is the antipart of Padalon. Its geographical position is singularly mundane, since in the Mahabharata, the hero, with his brothers and the wife and dog of the family, set off to walk from this weary world straight up to Mount Meru. Apparently the place was, according to the usual Eastern idea of an original "paradise"—simply a park of trees and waters, fruits and flowers, such as that of Kubla-Khan, glorified in Coleridge's "Opium Dream"

> In Xanadu did Kubla-Khan
> A stately pleasure-dome decree,
> Where Alf, the sacred river, ran,
> In caverns measureless to man,
> Down to a sunless sea.
> So twice five miles of fertile ground
> With walls and towers were fenced round.
> And there were fountains bright, with sinuous rills,
> Where blossomed many an incense-bearing tree.
> And there were forests ancient as the hills,
> Enclosing sunny spots of greenery.

Such a paradise, or "park," as the word signifies, was in fact the original type of all blessed places past or future, or placed in imaginary Utopias, like the garden of Hesperides, till the time when, as Gibbon remarks, "a pastoral paradise was no longer suited to the condition of men's minds in the artificial civilization of the Roman Empire, and cities with gold and jewels took their place." At the end of all, it may be doubted whether, as men can imagine nothing absolutely, but only put together and modify the objects they have actually beheld, Martin was wrong to give us Milton's Eden for the future heaven. Art can but represent the scene of celestial joys, the soul must indicate their spiritual character. A garden of green pastures and still waters would be as good a place to enjoy the supreme blessedness as any other we on earth can know of. Conceived of without such blessedness of divine communion, the paradise of Hindoo or Moslem is a poor thing indeed. The vast Brahmin faith however, with all its miserable errors, was by no means able for so many millenniums to feed the souls of hundreds of millions of men without some salt of noblest principles partially to redeem it. There were spiritual ideas of a future life taught in the sacred books, which some of us would be none the worse for occasionally calling to mind.

"A religious act proceeding from selfish views, in this world or the next," say the Institutes of Menu, "is declared to be concrete and interested; but an act performed with the knowledge of God, and without self-love, is called abstract and disinterested. He who frequently performs disinterested acts of religion, he sacrifices his own spirit by fixing it on the Spirit of God, and approaches the nature of that sole Divinity who shines by his own effulgence" (B. 12, v. 89). "He who purifies himself in the river of a subdued spirit," says Vishnu Shurma, "will be liberated; but liberation cannot be attained by any outward observance." (*Punchu Tuntru.*)

The Brahmin ideas of a future state, whatever we may be inclined to think of them, have manifestly exercised an immense influence over the lives of men, and over the care to perform for the dead such ceremonies (like incremation and the casting into the Ganges) as are believed to benefit the condition of their souls. There are no more amazing chapters in human history than the voluntary tortures whereby the Hindoo devotee seeks to obtain special beatitude, by remaining for years in the same painful attitude till his limbs wither—by hanging from iron hooks through his flesh—throwing himself under the cars of idols, and similar torments. That our nature should be capable of such sacrifices for lowest conceptions of God and duty, and yet should so perpetually fail to meet the demands of a true faith and rational morality, is one of the standing miracles of the world. The way in which the Hindoo law assumes the readiness of great offenders to inflict their own punishment, and lays down the method by which they shall starve and torment themselves to death in the solitude of the woods, is something which transports us into another state of things from any we can conceive in Europe. It is said that these extraordinary regulations in the book of the Institutes of Menu, treating "Of Expiations," are actually observed in India; but even the assumption that they would ever be so, is sufficiently surprising.

In any case, the prevalence of the Suttee system, the willingness of the victims to continue it, even when British influence would have protected them against priestly tyranny, is proof of the vividness with which the idea of future reward was seized by the Hindoo. That the hope of being reunited to their despotic husbands could have been so effective is not the least singular part of the business from our point of view. However, as the law decreed, "a woman must be subject always during her life to her male relations—first to her father, then to her husband, and after his death to her brother, or, if her brother be dead, to her son,"—it is possible that the prospect of being "subject" to her own child was not a pleasant alternative to the rule of the husband! Colonel Sleeman gives an instance from his own experience of the pertinacity with which a widow persisted in undergoing suttee, which seems one of the most curious facts of psychology ever recorded. I quote the story from memory; but the reader can refer to Colonel Sleeman's very interesting volumes.

On one occasion, when he held some command in the country, a Brahmin gentleman died in the neighbourhood, and a poor Soodra woman immediately afterwards sought an audience of Colonel Sleeman. Her object was to obtain his official consent, which was needful, for her performance of the suttee on the pyre of the deceased gentleman. Colonel Sleeman, naturally much surprised, remonstrated with the woman, that she was not the wife of the gentleman, and had a living husband of her own caste. "That is true," she replied; "but the gentleman was my husband in three previous lives, and if I am now burnt with him I shall be his wife in the next life." "You must be mistaken," answered the bewildered Colonel, "for you are a Soodra, and a Soodra cannot have been the wife of a Brahmin." "I was a Brahmin woman," she retorted; "but I was degraded in this life because of an offence I committed in my last existence. I was standing in my husband's house one day, when a holy man came to me and asked alms, and he asked for sugar, but I gave him salt, and he cursed me that I should be born a Soodra; and so, for this life I have been degraded; but if you will permit me to perform suttee on the Brahmin gentleman's pyre, then I shall be born again a Brahmin, and shall marry him again." In vain Colonel Sleeman expended his rhetoric and his logic in trying to persuade the woman to give up her delusion. Finding all argument useless, he ended by forbidding peremptorily that the ceremony of suttee should be performed in his jurisdiction. But the woman was too resolute to be defeated in her intention. She made her sons build for her a pyre in a lonely corner of the jungle, and there, on the day of her imaginary husband's incremation, she was privately burned by her real husband and children, without any of the pomp, or noise, or intoxicating drinks which usually serve to madden the poor victims of this hideous superstition. Whether we consider the extraordinary and precise nature of the delusion which seized on this hapless creature, or the firmness of faith and resolute courage which induced her to endure martyrdom on its behalf, the tale is equally worthy of remembrance.

The *Adee Grunt'h*, the sacred book of the Sikhs, has a beautiful passage condemning such immolations:—

They are not Suttees who perish in the flames, O Nanuk!
Suttees are they who die of a broken heart.

Turning from the Brahmin to the Buddhist religion, we come upon the doctrine which, above all others, strikes the European mind as unaccountable —the doctrine of *Niwane,* or Absorption into the Deity. The ultimate summit of Buddhist hopes is this final termination of personality. For all manner of sins the future life contains conditions of expiation, long and terrible, but yet finite. "He who has gone to the place of misery," say the Buddhist authorities, "after he has suffered enough for his miserable sins, it appears that he can become free."* But when all expiations and changes of happiness and suffering have been gone through, if the man reaches the highest pitch of virtue, his reward is this mysterious Niwane. It will be fresh in every one's mind that the precise nature of this state was disputed two or three years ago in the public papers in England by the best Buddhist scholars, and that at the end of the controversy it appeared that various views of it might be entertained, according to passages in different books, all of equal authority. Niwane means simply "no thirst," and it may be understood to signify the fulfilment of all "hungering and thirsting after righteousness," in full spiritual union with God; or else the absolute and entire sinking of the whole nature in the abyss of

* Buddhist tract, appended to the copy of the *Mahawanse,* in the British Museum, p. 11.

Deity, whereby no separate consciousness of the individual would remain. The latter view, though the most surprising to us, seems at least to hold good so far as that the hope of Niwane always implies a hope of the merging of personal existence, more or lèss completely, in the One great All.

We have here reached our moral antipodes. To our Anglo-Saxon feelings, personality is the thing we crave should be saved from the wreck of the grave. That inward and profound self-consciousness to which I have already referred, as distinguishing us from the sensuous dwellers in brighter climes, comes out in its intensity when we figure to ourselves the life hereafter. We cannot be satisfied with the idea of parting with any portion of it, but rather insist that it should be strengthened and sharpened :—

> 'Tis life, not death, for which we pant;
> More life, and fuller that we want.

We are impatient if any tell us that even memory may be lost or clouded of earthly things, and that, for all the moral purposes of existence, it may be left behind—that "a saddler remembers not every stitch he took when he was an apprentice, but every stitch helped to make him a saddler." The result of our earthly labour seems not to satisfy us, unless we are to be allowed to recollect the labours themselves. Still less can we endure the notion of losing our self-consciousness even in the higher consciousness of the most blessed of Beings. Of course the whole idea is above our grasp; but we do more than ignore, we shrink from it with all the vehemence of our natures—quite as much perhaps as from absolute annihilation. But the Buddhist state of mind is the reverse of all this. Some four hundred millions of our fellow-creatures are at this moment apparently perfectly indifferent to the idea of retaining their self-consciousness hereafter; nay, the highest aspiration of the noblest souls in those lands for some three thousand years seems to have been to lose themselves in the infinite ocean of the Supreme Spirit. They wish for immortality. We are not to confound this doctrine of Niwane (close as it seems to it) with the idea of the extinction of being. It is the immersion of the drop in the sea—the loss of self-consciousness in one stupendous life-consciousness, filling eternity. Truly the differences of nature leading to acquiescence in such a prospect are worthy of our study. This life, which to the Englishman is so earnest as to force him to project his personality into eternity, and which to the ancient Greek was so joyous as to make him look on his best Elysium in comparison as a world of shadows—this same present life on earth must be to the Buddhist a languid dream, wherein bodily wants and even spiritual desires are wearisome impediments, and whose noblest outcome and termination would be a condition wherein "no thirst" would ever more be felt, no intrusion of personal sentiments of any kind, but a great final Peace—

holy, and still, and motionless for ever. We cannot judge these things. Only Him

> . . . before whom ever lie bare
> The abysmal depths of Personality,

can know of these feelings and their source in the profoundest caverns of our nature. It seems but a necessary sequel to a theology whose Deity, once incarnate, has long ago ascended beyond human call, that the future life of man should also be thus impersonal. The wonder perhaps remains that the Buddhist creed, with so little to attract the hearts or warm the hopes of its followers, should yet demand and obtain such sacrifices of devoted lives in its vast monastic system, and maintain ethics often of such extreme beauty. We know of few precepts of ancient or modern times more admirable than the Buddhist one mentioned by Sir Emerson Tennent,—that each man should every night wish well in his heart to all mankind. If he find there is any individual whom he cannot regard with this benevolence, he must then resolve to perform some act of kindness to that person, and then he will find it easy to wish him well!

The doctrines of a future life attributed to Zoroaster, and at all events to be found in the Zend-Avesta, and now believed by the Parsees, are exceedingly elevated. There is a hell, *Douzakh,* the abode of Ahrimanes and the Daroudj—of course a realm of darkness; but this hell only exists till the great day of resurrection. On that last day "death and hell give up their dead;—the good, who have been happy, and the wicked, who have borne their punishment, all meet together. Then follow three tremendous days of expiation, during which sinners must bear the final penalty of their offences in the presence of the virtuous. But these latter (very far from some notions of beatified spirits we have heard of in Europe), at the sight of the sufferings of their sinful fellow-creatures, weep for pity, and spend three days in grief and prayer on their behalf. Then comes the end. The fervent heat melts the solid mountains of the world, and down their sides roll rivers of molten gold, through which the evil and the good alike must pass: that is the final purification. All souls are redeemed. Even Ahrimanes himself, the great "Evil Glory," source of all woe and sin, repents, and is forgiven. All created beings join in one vast pæan of praise to Ormusd, the Lord of Good, and are happy for evermore in his paradise of Gorôtman, the World of Light.

That a nation should have framed such ideas as this of the future world, it must needs have attained a very high degree of ethical progress. Suffering is contemplated directly as purifying and corrective, and happiness is understood to consist in reconciliation with Ormusd, and eternal abode in a heaven of which no other element is mentioned than light and glory. The pity of the good for the sufferings of the wicked, is a touch of Christian-like beauty, which it were much to be wished could be conveyed into the theology of those who tell us that in that future life the blessed will find no drawbacks to their felicity in the knowledge that their nearest and dearest earthly friends are enduring the torments of eternal perdition. But the superlative excellence of the whole conception rests in the faith that good will eventually triumph over all—even over Ahrimanes himself—and evil be entirely vanquished and annihilated. It is no wonder that in another part of the Zend-Avesta among the beautiful morning prayers commanded for the use of the Parsee—after his resolutions of duty and prayers for help to Ormusd, he is directed every day to repeat this all-inspiring announcement, "Hell shall be destroyed at the resurrection." It is not easy to doubt that such a doctrine would aid the man to fight valiantly here in that battle against evil whose end he foresaw would be in final triumph. Is it a mistake to suppose that the heartiness with which the Zoroastrian undertook that great battle, the clearness with which he distinguished between good and evil, and the earnestness with which he ranged himself on the side of good, helped him to this faith in its eventual victory. His was no dreamy, inactive, ascetic religion. It called on him to his utmost to promote life and happiness on earth. He was bound to work, to marry, to plant and sow, to give in charity—even in the splendid manner the actual Parsees do in India. As he was sententiously informed in his sacred book, "There are those who do not love to give. The abode which awaits them is below." Fasting was forbidden to him as "a culpable weakening of the powers entrusted to him for good use." Perhaps it was only a natural consequence of such ethics that he should deem Good the dominant power in the universe. It is those who worked hardest to make it so, who never see evil or suffering but they strive to amend it; who seem to gain most confidence in that truth—the last word of our philosophy, the first of a really filial religion,

> That somehow good
> Shall be the final goal of ill.

The ideas of the ancient Jews concerning a future life, we shall not discuss in this place, as touching too closely on the controversies of divines. Whether "Sheol," the Pit, was or was not believed before the Babylonish captivity, to be equivalent to annihilation, is one of the vexed questions which necessarily arise when dogmatic conclusions are thought to be involved in points of criticism, otherwise sufficiently obvious. These "Bermoothes" of divinity fortunately concern us not now. It is certainly a striking fact, however, that the deep-hearted literature of the Hebrews contains expressions of what, at least *seems*, hopelessness of immortality not to be paralleled in any heathen writer in the world; even as Christian creeds have embodied doctrines of the eternal perdition of the wicked, which no pagan system ever announced. We look in vain elsewhere for such words as those of David, Job, and Solomon: "In death no man remembereth thee, and who shall give thee thanks in the pit?" "If a man die, shall he live again?" "I go whence I shall not return, even to the land of darkness and the shadow of death; a land of darkness as darkness itself, and of the shadow of death without any order and where the light is as darkness." "For him that is joined to all the living there is hope, for a living dog is better than a dead lion. But the dead know not anything. There is no work, nor knowledge, nor device, nor wisdom, in the grave."

On any possible hypothesis it must be admitted that the Jews had infinitely less hope regarding the future world than the surrounding nations—and notably than their old Egyptian masters. What was the cause of this phenomenon it is hard to conjecture. We are almost driven to the conclusion that the extraordinary vividness of their belief in a present over-ruling Providence; the "theocratic pragmatism," as the German divines call it, which referred everything immediately to God, and made this world a complete drama of rewards and punishments—left them without many of the motives for strong faith and hope in the future which determine our anticipations. Certainly, every-day experience proves that so far from very vivid religious feelings, and very fervent future hopes, being invariable correlatives, they often exist almost in inverse ratios in different minds. To some of the best and most spiritual of men it happens, that "their heaven and hell are in this world, where their God is present to smile or frown."

Another explanation may be suggested in the variety of the force of hopefulness in different individuals, and consequently, probably, in different races. As phrenologists would say, the organ of Hope is predominant in some mental constitutions, and very feebly developed in others. It is not only its direct antithesis, Fear, but a certain disregard of all future good or evil, which distinguishes them. Either from the want of imagination or from very vivid present interests, the distance of a few years places a veil before all objects, and they are incapable of being seriously earnest on the subject. I know not how far this would apply generally to the Jewish race. It has been said that to the present day, although a future life has so long been a recognized article of their creed, they do not appear to dwell upon the hopes so held out with any special comfort. At least for their own nation, however, such prospect of immortality should be one of unmixed happiness. Calmet says that the Talmud (Gemara Arabin) promises that all Jews should be shortly released from their sufferings, at the intercession of Abraham. The paradise to which they were exalted was denominated generally "Abraham's Bosom," separated (as the parable of Dives and Lazarus recalls) by a "great gulf" from the world of torment.

Whether the Jews since their dispersion have, however, cared much or little for their prospects of personal immortality; or whether the hopes of national restoration have superseded such aspirations —they have at least displayed extraordinary interest in the burial of their bodies so as to insure (as they suppose) their speediest participation in the great final consummation of Jewish glory. The efforts they have made and the sufferings, losses, and humiliations they have borne for the purpose of obtaining sepulture in the Valley of Jehoshaphat, form a singular feature in human history. No other nation has ever thus struggled, not to *live* in their own land; but to be suffered to lay their dust therein. Many descriptions have been made of this marvellous place; but I confess none of them ever afforded me a notion of its actual appearance. Wandering alone past the fountain of Siloam and by the arid bed of Kedron, it suddenly opened on me a perfect mountain of graves—a hill-side paved with sepulchral slabs. Each stone is small, so small as to lead to the conclusion that the bodies must be buried perpendicularly. At all events, if the multitudes there interred were simultaneously to arise, they would form a crowd as dense and compact as it would be enormous. Short Hebrew inscriptions (some evidently of great age) are on all the stones; and these are laid together with intervals only of a few inches, as in our oldest city churchyards. The slabs are almost on the level of the ground, and of equal height, so that it is literally one large pavement of Death. An appalling, almost an overwhelming sight.

Perhaps the least interesting of all ideas of immortality ever held in the world are those of Islam. Doubtless the more spiritual among Mahometans have striven to see in the descriptions of paradise, parables of exalted moral pleasures, as the Song of Solomon has been transformed into the most sublime religious poem. But the fact apparent to any plain reader of the Koran, is that Mahomet employed his thoroughly Eastern imagination in devising as many circumstances of pleasure for his heaven, and of pain for his hell, as he had space to describe. The houris, the lake, the Tooba-tree, the flowers, the miraculous vine, are very little better than the subterranean treasures of Alla-ed-deen. The bridge of silk thread which passes over the abyss and whereon only the good can tread, while the wicked fall off, may be construed possibly in higher sense. Hell itself, where "the skulls of the wicked shall boil like a pot," is an idea possessing no sort of recommendation—not even novelty. Probably Mahomet found some consolation in consigning thereto all his enemies, including troublesome insects! The exasperation of those small "plagues of Egypt" on a hot summer's day, is surely recorded in his fierce denunciation, "All flies shall be destroyed in hell fire except the bee!"

Besides heaven and hell, Mahometanism has a purgatory, El-Araf, for the benefit of true believers only. Therein they are tormented for nine hundred or for seven thousand years, according to their guilt; or else for the period called Barzak—the interval between death and the resurrection. Besides this purgatory there is a hideous ceremony called Ad-habal-cabor, or the Penalty of the Sepulchre. Soon after burial, the corpse is called up by two terrific examiners, called Monkir and Nekir, who make it sit up and answer all their questions concerning its former faith and practice. When these replies prove unsatisfactory, Monkir and Nekir beat the corpse with sticks till its howls of pain may be heard all over the country. Terrible idea! One had almost as well believe we might after death be obliged to answer a medium, and rap out answers to impertinent questions with the leg of a table! Islam was a Reformation, not an original product of the religious sentiment. Its theology was like the columns of the early mosques of Cairo, a mere patchwork of the ruins of other churches. We have no right to expect from it any original ideas on such a matter as the immortal life.

A very powerful engine, however, has the Moslem paradise proved as an incentive to military devotion. The early history of Islam testifies amply to its influence. For such a purpose, indeed, it is vain to imagine a more spiritual hope proving very efficacious over wild hordes of warriors. The paradise of houris, and perfumes, and luxurious food, promised to the dead, precisely afforded sufficient counterpart to the pleasures remaining for the living on the conquest of a wealthy city. Kaliph Omar declined to enter Damascus lest the sight of it should destroy his relish for the joys of paradise. The idea of Mahomet in proposing such a reward for his followers after death, seems to have been carried out with additional ingenuity by the singular character who comes like a *Deus ex machinâ* into the stories of the Crusaders. The "Old Man of the Mountain," by supplying his soldiers with haschish, and thereby causing them to dream the ecstatic visions proper to the use of that drug, gave them something more than a mere hope of a sensual paradise. Each man who had partaken of the haschish, conceived that he had actually seen, felt, tasted the joys of heaven, and was only impatient till the hour should arrive for him to take final possession of his inheritance. Thus the haschish-eater was either ready to go forth as an "assassin" on the murderous errands of his master, or (as we are told was actually done) to leap at his word of command from the battlements of his castle in Lebanon into the abyss below. Whether Mahomet's hell has exercised as potent an influence as his paradise, we have no means of knowing.

On the whole, Islam, by its doctrine of the absolute unity and sovereignty of God, has always been a solemn creed, impressing its disciples with that profound reverence for spiritual things which strikes so forcibly the traveller who passes from the Churches of southern Christendom, with their gabbling priests and distraught worshippers, to the stillness of the mosques of the East, and the solemn prayers of their prostrate crowds. How far the doctrine of punishment after death may add to such religious awe, will probably be differently decided according to our views of the force of such doctrines generally on human nature. Curzon gives us a curious instance of the small effect which equally dreadful denunciations have, in comparison, upon Greek Christians. He says that happening to remark to his Greek servant that throughout his travels in Asia Minor and Armenia, he had never once been deceived or robbed by a Moslem; the Greek replied, "Oh no, wretched infidels! They are afraid to lie or steal. Their religion forbids it to them, the dogs!"

The most awful case of religious fear, which we cannot regard as the result of any dogmas, but of the natural terrors of an outraged conscience, is to be found in the history of the Mogul Emperor Aurengzebe. At the termination of his long reign of triumphant crime and splendour, he was seized with horror at the prospect of approaching retribution. As he lay dying in his palace he fell into the most abject state of terror, and continually repeated: "Whenever I wake, I only see God! I cannot escape from God, I am falling into the hands of God!" The Lord of the East brought thus low by the mere force of self-condemnation, must have been a tremendous spectacle of moral realities asserting themselves in the face of all pomp and power.

From the luxurious Orient to the wild fierce North of old, what a change! And what a corresponding change in the hopes of men concerning the unseen world! Valhalla, the reward of the mighty warriors of Scandinavia, truly offers the most perfect contrast conceivable with the Moslem paradise of houris and flowers. Here, where only heroes killed in battle could be admitted, the dead went forth to battle every day, till the horn sounded for the feast, and they returned to the Hall of Odin, healed of the wounds of the fray, and ready to pledge each other in celestial mead till close of night. This was Heaven, the highest heaven conceived of by the Goth. Those who had died peacefully—women, and all less glorious souls—were debarred from Odin's palace, and compelled to seek refuge in Freya's domain or in "Hela's iced abode," the original of our hell. We have seen that the warriors of Islam fought bravely in view of a paradise of repose and luxury. The Goth fought no less fiercely in prospect of a world of eternal strife. The inference seems obvious that to the former sensual gratification was the aim of his labours, while the latter loved war for war's sake, and could conceive of no happiness in which it was not to find a prominent place. There was apparently nothing to be gained by the daily battles of the heroes; they merely went forth to hack and hew one another in no courteous tournament, but with sharp swords and blows altogether in earnest; and then the pleasure for that day was over. Perhaps it is not very wonderful that the descendants of the race which fought for the Moslem's paradise, when they have come across the descendants of the race who fought for Valhalla, should invariably go to the ground. Assuredly the process of converting the wild worshippers of Odin to peaceful Christians sighing for an apocalyptic New Jerusalem, with gates of pearl, must have been one of no ordinary difficulty. We are not surprised to hear of Olaf the Saint endeavouring to accomplish it by the rough and ready method of placing all the bards and priests of the ancient faith on whom he could lay hand upon those rocky islets round the coast of Norway, which to this day are called "Skerries of Shrieks," in memory of the victims left there to be slowly engulfed by the tide.

The worst penalty of wickedness threatened by the Odinist religion is one as widely diverse from the always recurring fiery cave of the southern imagination, as Valhalla is diverse from Paradise. The description of it, as well as I can remember, was quoted from the *Prose Edda* not long ago, and runs as follows:—

"On Na Strand (the shore of the dead) there is a great hall and a bad! It is all built of adders' backs, wattled together. And the adders' venom runs on the floor of the hall to the height of a man's breast; and in this venom the souls of the perfidious and of murderers must wade for ever and ever!"

We must now draw these superficial observations of a most curious subject to a close without noticing more particularly the ideas of the remaining nations. Many of these deserve, however, careful attention, as for example, the Druid with his doctrine of eternal progress from Abred, the state of darkness and ignorance, to Gwynwyd, the state of knowledge and felicity; the Sabæan, with his four thousand years of purgatory; the Peruvian, with his long ages of wearisome labour (most dire of penalties to his indolent nature); the Aztec, with his hell ruled by the terrific devil Tlateacolocotl, *the Rational Owl;* and the Red-man, with his "Happy Hunting Grounds," where

> United in that equal sky,
> His faithful dog shall bear him company.

Perhaps of all the simple notions of futurity held by uncivilized tribes, and revealing their humble hopes and fears, the most noticeable is that of the Greenlanders. If it happens, they say, that on the day of a man's death the weather be stormy, it will be very dangerous for his soul, which is pale and soft, and devoid of bones, to perform the difficult journey through the rocks and chasms leading to the under world. Should he be able, however, to pass in safety, he will arrive at last at the paradise which is under the sea. There he will never be cold any more, for there will be fires all the year round, as much as he could desire. Neither will he ever be hungry again, for there is salt fish laid up in that place which will supply him to all eternity!

Is this review of so many varied dreams of worlds of joy and agony a melancholy one? Shall we leave it with a sigh for hopes so contradictory, and fears so vain? Surely it need not be so. The necessary limitations of human nature make the imagination of all details of another existence, *on the hypothesis*, absurd. Because it *is* another and a different world from this, our ideas of it are inevitably false; for we can but re-combine and modify the conditions we know of here, and *there* all things must be changed. The one thing we can predicate of Heaven is that it must be like nothing on earth. But the universality of the belief that such a world exists, the conviction common to all races that the soul of a man never dies—that is not a melancholy subject of reflection, but a blessed one. From the opposite ends of the earth, from remotest time till now, from the Brahmin to the Greenlander, from the contemporary of the mammoth to the civilized man of to-day—all have borne the same testimony. The faith in Immortality is written on the heart of humanity. There is but One Hand which could have engraved it there, and that Hand writes no falsehoods.

THE END.

JOHN CHILDS AND SON, PRINTERS.

www.ingramcontent.com/pod-product-compliance
Lightning Source LLC
LaVergne TN
LVHW021131110826
845150LV00005B/997

9781425549725